The SPIRIT *of* VOLTAIRE

Voltaire

The SPIRIT *of* VOLTAIRE

Norman L. Torrey

PROFESSOR OF FRENCH IN
COLUMBIA UNIVERSITY

New York: Morningside Heights

COLUMBIA UNIVERSITY PRESS

1938

TO

MORRIS R. COHEN

AUTHOR OF

Reason and Nature

Foreword

EXCEPT for minor revisions this book was completed before I was able to read the admirable work on Voltaire by Alfred E. Noyes. His masterful and painstaking defense of Voltaire's moral integrity amply confirms my own conclusions, as does his method of returning to primary documents, especially to Voltaire's voluminous correspondence. In writing of Voltaire as he has so often been portrayed, I omitted a reference to Dr. Jekyll and Mr. Hyde, because Mr. Noyes had already found the same comparison and expressed it more succinctly as follows: "To turn from the vague 'charges' to the solid ground of the known facts and the ascertainable character of Voltaire's own mind as it is consistently expressed, not once or twice, but thousands of times, in the written and irrevocable word, is to turn to a world and an atmosphere so utterly different that the charges almost cease to have any meaning. It is true, perhaps, that in his writings a man may be a Jekyll, and that for the untraceable anecdotist, with a sectarian axe to grind, he may be a Hyde; but in the case of Voltaire there is a consistency between the works and the immense correspondence that precludes any possi-

[vii]

bility of mere duplicity. The man himself is revealed for good and for evil in his own writings. His merits and his faults are all there.''

While agreeing heartily with the general argument of this paragraph, I have taken pains to point out that a certain form of duplicity was the necessary condition of Voltaire's life and works. It is on this point that my interpretation of Voltaire's religion differs so radically from the view presented by Mr. Noyes. Voltaire's spirit, too, has always exerted its civilizing force, but never so cogently as in periods of increasing religious and civil fanaticism. For these reasons I am encouraged to believe that it is worth while to publish one more book on Voltaire.

A fellowship from the Guggenheim Foundation made it possible for me to consult a vast amount of primary material in Voltaire's private library at Leningrad and in Paris. For this aid I am extremely grateful. I have attempted to indicate as fully as possible in the pages of the book as well as in the notes my indebtedness to scholars in the field. For helpful and sympathetic criticisms in the preparation of the manuscript it is a great pleasure to express here my deep gratitude to Mrs. Harriet M. Andersson of Washington, D. C., Professors Andrew R. Morehouse and Joseph F. Jackson, of Yale University, Professor Harold M. March, of Swarthmore College, and Professor Horatio Smith, of Columbia University. For my final, quite personal, conclusions I must take the sole responsibility.

FOREWORD

My justificatory notes have been placed unobtrusively at the end of the volume. The information that they impart is secondary and of interest only to the Voltaire specialist.

NORMAN L. TORREY

Columbia University
June 14, 1938

Contents

[xi]

Illustrations

Introduction

THE Chevalier de Boufflers, visiting the seventy-year-old Voltaire at Ferney, described his host to his mother as follows: "He is the king and father of the country where he dwells; he brings happiness to all about him and is as good a paterfamilias as he is a poet. . . . His printers will work in vain, for he will always be the best edition of his books. . . . You can't imagine how lovable the man is in the privacy of his home; he would be the last old man in the world if he were not the first of all men, his only fault is that he is too often shut in; but without that, he couldn't spread himself so much abroad. . . . He is too great to be contained within the limits of his country; he is a present that nature has given to the whole world."

It is not true that Voltaire's works were one thing and his personality another; and it cannot be too often repeated that his life is his greatest masterpiece. "Voltaire," said M. Lanson, "is a procedure, a method of education, a philosophy of life." After the long years of wandering and unrest in Paris, Holland, England, Belgium, Prussia, and the Rhineland, ever in search, not of a philosophic system, but of a philosophy of life, he found it at last in a little kingdom of his own within the boundaries of France, on the outskirts of Geneva. There the Patriarch of Ferney was indeed the father of his country, loved by all about him and "so happy that he was ashamed of it."

Many of Voltaire's suggested reforms have happily been adopted, many of his crusades and battles won, many of man's more ridiculous postures successfully laughed into oblivion. But until the essential identity of our human organism changes, and as long as the more fundamental human needs call for the same fundamental satisfactions, his way of life will lose none of its freshness. Man's inner nature is much less subject to changes of fashion and opinion than are its outward manifestations.

The search for Voltaire's inner nature prompted the present treatise. Through a study of the man we hope to arrive at a more accurate interpretation of his ideas and beliefs. This approach is indicated by the very humanistic nature of his philosophy and by its dependence on the results of experience rather than on systematic or logical principles. Instead of making a systematic analysis of his accumulated thought, it would seem much more interesting, in a review of some of the more important relationships and events of his life, to try to discover what he thought while he was living them. It is in the man that we shall discover the philosopher.

The title "philosopher" is one to which Voltaire

does honor and yet one which many modern "philosophers" have refused him by the simple process of enclosing the word in quotation marks. The historically and empirically-minded nineteenth century has included in its histories of philosophy only the builders of philosophical systems. It is not at all clear, however, that the systematizers have contributed any more to true philosophy than have skeptical lovers of wisdom such as Fontenelle and Voltaire. The latter maintained the Cartesian principle that doubt is the beginning of wisdom and perhaps its end. They thought that knowledge increases in direct proportion to the absence of intellectual inhibitions, of which the most repressive are dogmatically accepted metaphysical systems. Education, Voltaire believed, if it has any intellectual validity whatsoever, should first break down these barriers to thought, a process much decried by parents, guardians, and trustees. Voltaire retained to the end of his long life the normal adolescent revolt against conventional ideas, revealed or absolute truths, and opinions enforced by authority. His *Candide* was written when he was sixty-four, and nine years later he published his most authoritative philosophical confession of faith under the modest title, *Le Philosophe ignorant*. Candide was inclined to judge values naïvely on the basis of his personal experiences—and Voltaire gave him experiences in abundance. But Dr. Pangloss was so obsessed with the systematic optimism of his "All is for the best in the best of all possible worlds" that he was blinded to the most simple realities. As the wounded and thirsty Candide was lying at his side amid the ruins of the earthquake at Lisbon, the doctor was embarking upon a philosophical explanation of the disaster. "Nothing is more probable," said Candide, "but in God's name give me a little oil and a little wine." —"What do you mean, probable?" replied the philosopher; "I maintain that it is demonstrated." At that point of the argument Candide lost consciousness, while Pangloss finally came to earth and brought him some water from a neighboring fountain.

Here, also, lies one of the most remarkable contrasts between Voltaire and the anti-intellectualistic Rousseau. The latter, ill and unhappy, disturbed by his own doubts and by those he heard expressed around him, sought consolation as the end of truth through the acceptance of principles which he wanted to be fixed and final. Voltaire clung tenaciously to his idea that doubt was the beginning of wisdom; praised Locke because he had dared to doubt; pricked all metaphysical bubbles within his reach; condemned even his friend Diderot, whose materialistic atheism seemed too narrowly systematic; and in fact made impossible the development in France of any such ferment of absolutes and dialectics as has been witnessed in Germany since his day. Rousseau himself was forced back by the skepticism of his age into an acceptance, on non-rational grounds, of a modified and emotionalized form of revealed religion.

If Voltaire was not a philosopher in the present

narrow acceptation of the term, in what sense, then, can he be called a philosopher? The answer may in part be found in one of the most successful of the *Dialogues des morts*, or *Elysian Discourses*, by his predecessor Fontenelle. The "wise" Anacreon was reproving the philosopher Aristotle for the nights he had passed futilely over thorny questions of dialectic and also for certain disorders in his personal life, of a nature similar to those charged later against Francis Bacon. He dared put himself on a par with Aristotle, who in turn mocked his claim of having achieved more fame with a lute and a bottle than the greatest of men had achieved with vigils and labor spent in the solution of nature's enigmas.

Philosophy [said Anacreon] is in itself an admirable thing and might be very useful to men, but because she would incommode them if they employed her in their daily affairs, or if she dwelt near them to keep some check on their passions, they have sent her to heaven to arrange the planets and measure their movements; or they walk her all over this globe to make her examine what they see there. They always keep her busy as far away from their intimate lives as possible.

Anacreon insisted that philosophy should concern herself with men, that philosophers should be philosophers, not physicists or astronomers. "For myself," he added, "I was by no means inclined to speculation, but I am sure that there is less philosophy in a great many books which pretend to treat of it than in some of my little songs which you so greatly despise."

[5]

For Voltaire this picture will do only on the negative side; yet it is of great importance in understanding him. In his time, as today, a philosophy which approached the nearest to heavenly bodies or heavenly values, which avoided the "mundane," "terrestrial," "earthly," "lowly" concerns of man, not only was safer for the philosopher's reputation (and material comfort) but also was encouraged and subsidized by those in authority. Voltaire's insistence on man as the measure of all things and as the focal point of philosophical observation together with his skeptical method of dealing with human problems made him many enemies who were in turn aided and protected by the representatives of authority, the court at Versailles, the Jansenist parliament, and the clergy. The great majority of contemporary documents on Voltaire's life are therefore hostile. To draw a black picture of his character, a biographer needs only a little incomprehension of his subject, a temperamental inability to understand the skeptical method, and an ever-so-slight application of ill will.

Voltaire's reputation has suffered also from the uncritical enthusiasm of many biographers of Rousseau. It is a vicious, but hardly escapable, method to accept the implications of determinism and the responsibility of heredity and environment in treating one's hero while at the same time considering his enemies as acting with perfect freedom of will or ill will and holding them personally responsible for their shortcomings. Knowledge brings sympathy and understanding, and biographers naturally understand the springs of their subject's acts and thoughts much more profoundly than those of his enemies.

Yet if it be admitted that Voltaire's greatest recreation, the writing of verses, may properly be compared with Anacreon's lute, and that he used the bottle in great moderation, and "for his stomach's sake," it is evident, nevertheless, that he differed widely from the Greek sage on the subject of speculation. Rarely has a man as firmly convinced as he that all theological and metaphysical systems so far devised or to be devised were simply escape mechanisms or substituted fictions on a par with novels spent anything like the same amount of time and energy on theological and metaphysical speculations. The reason is clear. If philosophers insisted on carrying their systems into the realms of the angels, Voltaire, to use his own metaphor, had to follow them there to refer them back to man on this terrestrial plantation. These speculative flights left him, as we shall see, with a certain mystical adoration for the creator of mysteries—but the important thing is that he always came back to his reference point.

The word "skeptical" as applied to Voltaire's way of life perhaps needs some explanation. How can the term be properly applied to a man who had faith such as his in the age of reason and whose life was so tremendously full of action? First let us forget the old sophistry of the absolute skeptic who succumbs, like Buridan's ass, because he becomes skeptical of his own skepticism. In the first place, skepticism is extremely wary of absolutes, and in the second place, it is a method, not a system. The end is, in the last analysis, individual happiness; and to Voltaire, as well as to many others before and since his day, skepticism has proved the most satisfactory approach. For he was sincere when he wrote to one of his friends, "I am so happy, I am ashamed of it," at a time when old age and infirmities would have thoroughly depressed any ordinary mortal. An extraordinary zest for living and joy in the struggles of life, together with remarkable recuperative powers after defeats and disappointments, are outstanding characteristics of the man. Skepticism and actions in behalf of humanity are by no means mutually exclusive, nor are they even proportionately related. The searcher for absolutes too often refuses to act, on the ground that he has not yet discovered his principles, or the student defers taking part in social affairs until he has had that last advanced course in economics or sociology; but the skeptic assumes that all the evidence will never be in and that there are limits to the advisability of deferring action. Voltaire's life gives the lie to the charge that either skepticism or the acceptance of the theory of determinism leads to hopelessness, inaction, and stagnation. Such a way of life requires great moral strength and courage; and yet there are reputable critics who have refused to credit to Voltaire these qualities.

It is Voltaire's philosophy of life, again, which

has aroused the enthusiasm and admiration of many
generations of readers—his method, perhaps, even
more than the direct results. These latter need not be
minimized: *Le Siècle de Louis XIV* and the *Essai sur
les mœurs* are still of primary importance to historians; *Candide* killed once and forever in France the
philosophical optimism of Pope and Leibnitz as a
metaphysical system, and many of the occasional
poems and miscellaneous satires, personal and otherwise, are unsurpassed in their *genre*. In spite of the
results, however, the modern student is interested
particularly in the methods, in the first genuine
application of the modern critical method to history,
in the feeling that the way a thing is said can be
of as much importance, even to the author, as the
thing that is said, and in the felicity of statement
that so often successfully defied the handicaps of
rules and the paucity of vocabulary. Yet the student
is not satisfied. He wishes to know the real Voltaire.
Turning from his works to the biographies, he is
lost in a welter of seemingly contradictory detail.
Voltaire was an angel yesterday and an antichrist
the day before, and we never quite know what he is
today. No man such as many biographies picture
Voltaire to have been could possibly have lived
since the two-faced Janus. His works often faced in
two directions—and therein lies their charm—but
not the man himself. We feel as we do when confronted with a difficult scientific experiment; to
arrive at satisfactory results, we need either a greater
number and a larger variety of instances or a better

control of the data. It is true that a fairly consistent picture emerges from the accumulations of the eight-volume biography by Gustave Desnoiresterres. Better still, a reading of Voltaire's own voluminous correspondence is both refreshing and convincing. For there we shall most nearly find the man whose existence we have so long suspected and sought. We shall find it necessary, however, continually to check back to biographies, histories, and memoirs. The letters were intensely personal, and we must know to whom they were written, under what circumstances, and for what purpose. For instance, when Voltaire wrote to his former teacher, Père de la Tour, and confessed his desire to live and die in the bosom of the Holy Catholic Church, we need to know that he was at that time a candidate for admission to the French Academy and was meeting strong clerical opposition. And again, when he wrote to the Duc de Noailles that he would never think of sacrificing a noble family's reputation to historic truth, it is useful to know that Voltaire was trying to extract from this nobleman a bit of information he could get in no other way, and that his courage and accuracy in writing history were generally remarkable.

Another difficulty in seizing the essential Voltaire arises from his lack of what are commonly accepted as principles. We are at first tempted to agree with Mme d'Épinay, who wrote, in a letter to her perhaps jealous and certainly uncharitable lover, Grimm, that the man was without principles. In a sense this observation is very true and helps to explain the contradictions which pervade so many biographies and criticisms. It is far, however, from the whole story. Just as Voltaire is bound to be considered blasphemous when he writes mockingly of what other people consider sacred, so he appears unprincipled to critics who see him time and again defying the tenets that they themselves have accepted as truths. This does not in any way mean that to Voltaire nothing was "sacred" (we do need quotation marks) or that he had no principles.

The two great and opposing tendencies of the nineteenth century were the reversion to the consoling and somewhat romanticized dogmas of authoritative religion and the evolution of an empirical historical philosophy along the general lines of positivism and pragmatism. Voltaire's enemies were the authoritarians, his friends the empiricists; and it is still doubtful which group of interpreters has done him the most wrong. Philosophically speaking, he was the greatest and the most complete of the French classicists. That he could not write plays as well as Racine or that he left no "Art of Poetry" to be compared with Boileau's is no invalidation of this statement, for classicism was much more than a literary movement, it was a consistent and well-rounded conception of nature. His *Poème sur le désastre de Lisbonne* and *Candide* were protests against the increasing romantic tendency of his age to identify the good life with the full life, protests aimed directly at the philosophical optimism of Pope and

Leibnitz and the philosophical romanticism of Rousseau.

Conduct, science, and art [writes Professor Cohen] depend on rational discrimination. Rational philosophy tries to meet this need by defining the good, the true, and the beautiful. The essence of the romantic use of the terms *life*, *experience*, and *reality* is that it avoids this necessary task, and is therefore flattering to those to whom the use of reason is irksome. But the way to serenity and happiness through wisdom is more arduous and requires a purified vision into our hearts as well as courage to face the abysmal mystery of existence.

In science as well as in philosophy Voltaire upheld the classical conception of nature, according to which the variation of phenomena is to be referred to some unitary law. In literature his tastes ever led him back to the great classical age of Louis XIV, which he celebrated in prose and in verse. His violent opposition to Shakespeare can thus be explained as the normal reaction of the classicist to the increasing efforts of the romanticists to appropriate Shakespeare as hero and prototype of the new philosophies. In this struggle for principles he was ably seconded by D'Alembert and encouraged by Mme du Deffand. Yet we must disagree with the pragmatists who would say that Voltaire was wrong because he lost the battle. Two centuries are as nothing in the eyes of the Lord of Hosts, and the battle is not yet over.

On essential problems such as the nature of knowledge and of reality Voltaire's conceptions were also classic. Reality was to him a very definite physical universe which is governed by fixed laws, which is "out there" to be known and to be known by slow and painful processes through the too-often deceptive sense perceptions, through imagination, reflection, and reason—all controlled where possible by scientific experimentation. The stars moved in the heavens along certain regulated orbits long before there was any human eye to perceive them, and masses were subjected to the laws of gravitation long before Newton evolved their principles. In how many ages has science made such vast discoveries as were made during Voltaire's beloved century of Louis XIV? To Voltaire, then, reality was not created by the human mind; it was a physical antecedent, even to the mind itself; it was the great mystery; it was matter set in motion according to fixed laws by a supreme, intelligent being. Here he disagreed with Lucretius and Diderot; but all three agreed that the question was outside the pale of scientific investigation and could be met only by hypotheses.

It was through knowledge, intelligence, and reason, then, that Voltaire would make somewhat more tolerable man's brief sojourn on "this atom of mud." The driving force was love of humanity in the particular as well as in the abstract. The idea that Voltaire was a purely rational and emotionally cold creature is a ghost which, in spite of its frequent and widespread appearances, will be found extraordinarily easy to lay. We may be obliged still to call him at times unprincipled because his principles were different and irreligious because his religion was different. This is purely a question of terminology. It is difficult to decide whether we should confine the term "religious" to the super-natural and revealed explanations of the mysteries of life or allow it to embrace all forms of human attitudes and adaptations to the unknowable. According to our choice, Voltaire was intensely irre-ligious or intensely religious. The intensity remains in any case an important and essential characteristic.

Therefore Voltaire's philosophy may prove to be less inconsequential and inconsistent than it has often been thought if its underlying principle can be discovered and properly applied. This prin-ciple is in a measure more difficult to define than to describe. It springs from his classical conception of man, founded in reason and nature, manifesting it-self as a durable type of humanism, and associating itself intimately with the acts of his daily life. We will attempt, therefore, to seek the philosopher through the man, but will select only the more re-vealing biographical details. Without being too much the slave to chronology we will indicate his emotional sets and characteristic attitudes in the general order of their development. While some overlapping is, of course, inevitable, it is hoped that this unsystematic approach to his philosophy will yield compensating gains in clarity and com-prehension.

CHAPTER II

Libertinism

"NATURE made a great mistake," Voltaire wrote to his royal friend, Frederick, "in having me born a bourgeois of Paris." His frequent and often long absences from that city show that he rectified in large measure Nature's error. He was, nevertheless, essentially Parisian. It was in Paris that he was educated, and there that his tastes were developed; and it was for Parisians that he began and continued to write plays, epic poems, and philosophical tales and treatises. Paris, with its noise and bustle, was too much for him in the flesh, but the spirit of Paris pervaded his houses of voluntary or involuntary exile, providing relief from the studious seriousness of reforming activities. He was homesick in England, very homesick in Berlin and Potsdam, and homesick, but resigned, during the final twenty-five years when he was forced to live on the Swiss frontier, far from the scenes of his youth. The underlying paganism of Parisian society during the declining years of Louis XIV and the open licentiousness of the Regency account for much of his libertinism, in both its freethinking and its free-living manifestations.

It is customary to note that Voltaire was educated
by Jesuit masters, at Louis-le-Grand, a school as
important to French culture as Eton is to English.
His real education, however, in the broader French
sense of the term, was in the salons of his mother's
society and under the tutelage of her more intimate
friends, the Abbés Gédoyn and Châteauneuf. Mme
Arouet came from the lesser provincial nobility of
Poitou to grace the house and society of Voltaire's
bourgeois father, whose official connections with
the Court introduced her into the gay, worldly
society of the Parisian nobility. Voltaire's god-
father was the Abbé de Châteauneuf, younger son
of a noble family, whose living constituted his sole
ecclesiastical preoccupation. He was a worldly fellow who passed on to Voltaire the culture and
paganism of Ninon de Lenclos's famous salon. He
was irreverent as well as gay, and he carefully protected his young godson from those early emotional
religious experiences from which the best-inten-
tioned freethinkers emerge with difficulty.

Through Châteauneuf and his mother, too, Voltaire became acquainted with the Abbé de Chaulieu,
one of the more distinguished poets of the pagan
tradition who flourished in a very unofficial way
during the declining years of Louis XIV. Chaulieu
found an ardent and talented disciple in the young
man, whose facility in versification was already
remarkable and many of whose best early poems
reflect clearly the deistic pagan philosophy of his
teacher. With two such fervent admirers of the

classical writers as Châteauneuf and Gédoyn in his home and with such a poetic master as Chaulieu, it seems apparent that the abbés as well as the fathers at Louis-le-Grand are to be credited with Voltaire's classical education and enthusiasms. Unlike the Jesuit teachers, the abbés had accepted not only the literary forms and stylistic excellencies of their favorite Latin authors but also the very spirit of pre-Christian Roman culture. The Renaissance was slowly extending its influence to fields other than the literary field. The easygoing Epicureanism and Stoicism of Montaigne had never died but had been revived in the salon of Ninon de Lenclos and had made tremendous inroads on the externally Christian France of Louis XIV. Voltaire's *libertinage* was thus in no sense a revolt against the teachings of his Jesuit masters. Under them he merely went to school; his education was a somewhat different matter.

Voltaire was sixteen when his formal education was completed. During his last months in school he wrote friendly letters to an absent schoolmate, M. Fyot, Marquis de la Marche. These two young men already called themselves philosophers and Epicureans, the former term used undoubtedly for freethinkers and lovers of the wisdom of the ancients, and the latter with the necessary distinctions. "If you are an Epicurean," wrote Voltaire, "you find your pleasure in wisdom and virtue"; and as a graceful compliment he added that he knew no pleasure himself except that of writing to his friend.

There are also some knowing remarks on the folly of the monastic life for intelligent people and criticisms of comrades who accepted it in ignorance as the path of least resistance; also gentle mockery of the fact that when Father Porée prayed for rain he got it immediately and in abundance.

A tempered Epicureanism, or a rational hedonism, was always a part of Voltaire's way of life. "The great business of life, the only real business, is to live happily," he wrote, as a youth, to his friend Mme de Bernières. In fact, happiness as the highest goal, supreme value, and sole criterion of the success of human life was such a popular idea in the France of Voltaire's time that many orthodox churchmen accepted it as a principle secondary only to salvation in the life to come. Pascal himself had written: "All men desire to be happy; there is no exception to this rule. Whatever different means they employ, they all tend toward this goal. . . . The will never makes the slightest move except in this direction. It is the motive of every act of all men, even of those who go and hang themselves." Voltaire subscribed wholly to this deterministic hedonism. He differed from Pascal in believing that the goal could in some measure be reached in this life, that there was no other life in which the term happiness had meaning. It is perfectly true, however, that each man sought and found happiness in his own way—Pascal in the abrogation of pleasure and denial of life and Voltaire in the full acceptance of life's realities and society's responsibilities.

This form of Epicureanism is only the personal and philosophical side of what may be called Voltaire's *libertinage*. His physical constitution would not allow physical indulgence; but when, after the Duc de Vendôme returned from exile, in 1715, the dinners and orgies at the Society of the Temple were again in full swing, Voltaire enjoyed them in the body vicariously, but with the spirit in full participation. Here, as well as in the châteaux of his aristocratic friends, his presence was desired because of his ready wit and readier facility for incorporating it in neat verse. The earlier sections of his notebook, or *Sottisier*, bear witness to the taste of this society for bawdy poetry, on subjects often especially designed to please the physical and mental corruption of the syphilitic, homosexual Grand Prior. Voltaire was himself too strong a partisan of reason and nature to be himself corrupted. Yet, like Plato in the *Symposium*, he was a tolerant onlooker. He says flatly that medicines are not equally efficacious for various people, so he was perfectly willing to let people seek their pleasure in their own way, provided that no harm was done to others in the process. Yet, with a decided preference for the normal, he was glad when La Trimouille was dismissed from court for attempting to turn Louis XV to homosexuality and glad again when the young king chose a mistress, citing a verse from La Fontaine to the effect that "Chimon fell in love, and became thereby ennobled."

The moralists maintain, of course, that freethinking necessarily leads to free living, and they prove the assertion by referring to the change in meaning of the word "libertine." The lives of certain free-thinkers and atheists, such as Spinoza, Gassendi, and Luther Burbank, are proof that there is not necessarily any connection. The truth of course is that the abandonment of authoritarian principles and a belief in the relativity of moral values may well lead to conduct which is no longer moral according to the abandoned standards. Voltaire had his own standards, which he believed to be grounded in reason and nature; and yet he was inclined, because of his weak constitution and his spirit of caution, to avoid shocking his contemporaries. "No one has ever attacked my morals," he wrote, late in life. Upon reflection, one can take little exception to the statement; judged by the standards of his time, he was more wholesome in his personal habits and more keenly aware of his responsibilities to society than the great majority of his pious and Christian contemporaries.

By 1716, when Voltaire had attained his majority, he had nearly succeeded in persuading his father, after countless conflicts, that he was destined for the poorly rewarded and much despised career of man of letters. A satire in answer to the unjust awarding of a prize for which he had competed brought out all his native maliciousness, as injustice always did, and got him exiled from Paris. The frivolity of château life was again his escape, but the brilliant "white nights" at the home of the

Duc de Sully were complemented by serious preparation for the epoch-making history of the age of Louis XIV. Voltaire paid for his meals with his witty conversation and verses. He described himself at that time as "thin, long, and fleshless, without buttocks, less malicious than he is reported to be, perhaps cursed of God because he is in love and because he versifies." He was homesick for Paris and remembered fondly the banquets at the Temple, "where little suppers and handsome feasts gave birth to a thousand malicious skits which Cupids, inclined to laughter, collected in their chapbooks." "Ah," he wrote, "how I love those mocking lines, those naïve nothings full of grace, such as the ingenious Horace would have made the soul of a repast when he sat at table between Augustus and Maecenas." Having "no desire to assassinate partridges" with the gentlemen of the company, thus preferring, as the eighteenth century would have it, Apollo to Diana, he wrote his evenings' entertainments while the others were devoting themselves to the hunt.

In 1720 Voltaire's master, the Abbé de Chaulieu, died, "unknown," as Voltaire remarked, "to the theologians." From him he had culled many a thought and many a verse in praise of pleasure, many a stoical attitude on death, and many a pagan precept to fling in the face of theology. Chaulieu's verses were unpolished; his disciple surpassed him beyond question. But Chaulieu was nevertheless instrumental in giving his pupil and admirer a philosophical background for the libertine influences that surrounded his youth, a classical conception of the oneness of human nature, a deism which insisted on a universal, impartial, nonsectarian God, of whom Voltaire could say "I am not a Christian that I may love thee more." All these things he expressed in his *Epître à Uranie*, or *Le Pour et le contre*, a poem which he endeavored in vain to keep hidden, and which admirably revealed the early philosophical turn of his mind.

When Voltaire returned to Paris, in 1729, after nearly three years of exile in England, he was, at nearly thirty-five, in the very middle of the normal span of life. His youth was now over, but not all its sins and follies. For Voltaire was an eternal adolescent. If he had reasons to repent of his youth, his repentance was on a different score: his philosophy of hedonism was merely confirmed with age, and his later works are as full of the mischievous, the naughty, and the racy as those of his youth.

His love affairs hardly match Casanova's, nor do sexual passions play anything like the rôle in his life and temperament that they did in Rousseau's. No one, I think, has been rash enough to apply Freudian methods in the effort to interpret his inner spirit. Yet he had no great respect for virginity and in all probability was himself no virgin. In some witty lines which certain readers have misinterpreted he stated that he was not even the son of a virgin, judging that the bearing of five children was sufficient evidence of his mother's fall from grace. The piety that one misses here is not filial piety. His first recorded love was perhaps the most passionate, and the only one in which marriage was seriously considered and proposed. In his nineteenth year, Father Arouet sent his rebellious son to The Hague as attaché to the French ambassador, the Marquis de Châteauneuf. The young man had the misfortune to fall violently in love with the daughter of a French woman, a Protestant refugee, who was editing one of the well-known scandal sheets of the day. The plan, very seriously elaborated, was that Voltaire should flee to France with his beloved Pimpette, turn her over to Father Tournemine for reconversion to Catholicism, and then marry her and live happily ever after. Pimpette decided, probably wisely, that lack of parental blessings, flight in disguise, and rapid conversion were not the smoothest roads to marital serenity. When, after several escapades, the plot was discovered and "her lover and true friend" was sent back to his irate father, she preferred under pressure to remain at The Hague. Later she married a man who had "the interesting foible" of never being able to forgive Voltaire's primacy.

In 1716, at Sully, Voltaire was again in love. He was abandoned by his mistress in 1717, just before his first imprisonment in the Bastille. He learned early that lack of amorous attentions to certain actresses was a handicap to budding young authors who had plays in their portfolios, a lesson which led to a long and honorable attachment with the famous tragedian, Adrienne Lecouvreur. He fell in love, too, with the pious Duchesse de Villars, who admired him somewhat in return; but Voltaire was the poet, not the Don Juan of the many ladies who gave him shelter and entertained him. To his hostess Mme de Bernières he wrote: "One couldn't love his mistress as much as I love you." In 1722, when he was being honored at Brussels, he was taken, according to custom, to the best brothel in town, where he wrote a poem, in which one of the girls declares that "here love is the child of nature, elsewhere she is the child of art." Rousseau, on a similar visit in Venice, was advised to go back to his mathematics; Voltaire seems to have resorted to verse.

He needed the feminine touch in his dwelling and feminine companionship more than he needed ardent love. He preferred simple women, too, to the wives of the grandees of the realm. After his devotion to Mme de Mimeure, he attached himself to Mme de Bernières and then to Mme de Fontaine-Martel. It was because, in 1732, he had no mistress that the last-mentioned good lady consented to harbor him. On her death, in 1733, Voltaire contracted with the learned but ardent Emilie, Mme du Châtelet, his most durable and celebrated liaison. The lady had had other lovers, among them Voltaire's friend and hero, the Duc de Richelieu. Her ardor is attested by the fact that at the end of one of her more serious affairs she was with difficulty prevented from taking her life with poison.

Voltaire lived with her for the next sixteen years, now in Paris, now in her country home at Cirey, now in Belgium, where a protracted lawsuit often called her, and finally at the court of Stanislas, former king of Poland, then duke of Lorraine and father-in-law of Louis XV. According to the customs of the times, the Marquis du Châtelet, often away at his military post, gave the couple a very generous freedom and was grateful to Voltaire for remodeling his country estate. In return, appearances were saved, and the liaison was heralded, with no very serious injury to truth, as the spiritual communion of two philosophic minds.

For Voltaire's physical constitution was now rapidly showing the effects of age. At the very beginning of his friendship with Mme du Châtelet he explained to his friend Cideville that it was a matter of coquetry, not of passionate love, and in light verse asked the gods to spare him "a cruel ardor which would corrupt my friendship." Such protestations were something more than mere convention. His early notebooks show that he took a premature interest in Horace's celebrated ode of farewell to love—there may be found there two English versions as well as parts of the original—and in 1741, Voltaire wrote and addressed to Mme du Châtelet, in a little poem that ranks among literature's most delicate and felicitous, his own swan song:

> If you wish me still to love
> Give me back love's youthful days;

Join to twilight's fading rays
Dawn's resplendent heavens above.

Man dies twice, 'tis very clear;
Cease to love, be no one's swain,
That's a death that brings great pain;
Cease to live, that's no man's fear.

Si vous voulez que j'aime encore
Rendez-moi l'âge des amours;
Au crépuscule de mes jours
Rejoignez, s'il se peut, l'aurore.

On meurt deux fois, je le vois bien;
Cesser d'aimer, et d'être aimable,
C'est une mort insupportable;
Cesser de vivre, ce n'est rien.

The philosopher's love troubles were not over,
however, nor was he fated to attain immediately
that serenity and detachment that the various odes
seemed to invoke. For Mme du Châtelet was not
content to follow his way of life—was perhaps not
capable of doing so. Frederick, in answer to one of
Voltaire's apologies for his liaison, replied in a
mocking vein: "How fine it is that Mme du Châtelet has preferred the love of truth to the illusion
of the senses, and has abandoned the false and
fleeting pleasures of this world in order to give herself over entirely to the search of most sublime
philosophy." Some eleven years later, however,
Voltaire discovered that impassioned nature had
won the battle and that the young Marquis de
Saint-Lambert was making up for his own deficien-
cies. A first flare of jealousy quickly subsided into
philosophic calm, only too rudely disturbed when

it was discovered that Mme du Châtelet, who had long been absent from her husband, was pregnant. Voltaire met the situation in his most characteristic manner, feeling intensely its seriousness and at the same time treating it as lightly as could only one for whom the category "sacred," applied to marriage, was meaningless. A reunion was quickly arranged at Cirey, and a pretext found for recalling the absent landlord. In the course of the festivities the unsuspecting husband was teased and put to bed with his wife, a privilege that he had not claimed for many years; the legitimacy of the future child was thus assured. Voltaire is reported to have said that the child would have to be classed among Mme du Châtelet's *Miscellaneous Works*. This attitude of apparent levity was reflected in many of his literary works. He laid a revolutionary basis for moral conduct in general, but many of the customs and manners of the age in regard to sex and marriage he accepted with tolerant indulgence.

"I was not born to celebrate the saints," he wrote in the opening lines of *La Pucelle*. This burlesque poem on Joan of Arc, maid of Orleans, has rarely been judged on its literary merits; the devout believe that Voltaire's punishment began at the time of its unwelcome publication and that he has ever since been tortured, during the rest of his sojourn on this earth and subsequently in hell, in atonement for his heinous authorship. French patriots are only a little less indignant than the devout at the sacrilege against nationalism in the person of the nation's favorite heroine. The very nature of burlesque is, however, to make heroes, saints, and gods descend to the earthly human plane, and the greater the descent, the greater the incongruity and subsequent comic results. For those who believe with Voltaire that a little mockery, even of very serious human problems and attitudes, perhaps especially of such, is a necessary purging of the mind in behalf of sanity, *La Pucelle* is still one of his more distinguished masterpieces. People who have lived in intimacy with clergymen realize that their levity in off moments is applied to just those values which they esteem the most weighty.

Voltaire's earliest reference to the poem is in a letter to his friend Formont, written probably in the year 1734. He was nearly forty then, and it seems unlikely that the poem was begun much earlier. Objecting to the name "epic" that Formont had given it, he explained his reasons for writing it:

I have worked rather in the vein of Ariosto than in that of Tasso. I wanted to see what my imagination would produce when I gave it free rein, and when fear of that narrow critical spirit now reigning in France did not restrain me. I am ashamed of having progressed so far on such a frivolous work, which is not designed for publication; but after all, time might be employed to worse advantage. I want this work to give my friends amusement from time to time; but I do not want my enemies to know a thing about it.

Mme du Châtelet rightly distrusted Voltaire's desires in the matter. She carefully guarded the manuscripts under lock and key. After her death,

copies were multiplied, and by 1755, at a very in-
auspicious and uncertain moment in Voltaire's career, it was impossible to prevent publication.

We may minimize many of his defensive and dep-
recatory statements at this time, but not his fears
that his enemies, crusading under the banner of
the divinely inspired maid, would succeed in dis-
lodging him from his newly found retreats at Lausanne and Geneva. He protested in his letters that
it was a sin of youth and that "never had a maid so
maddened an old man." He was worried for fear
that his enemies would publish a copy vitiated with
interpolated lines of their own devising—which did
not fail to happen—and also that some of his own
broader versions would be rediscovered and published, especially a "Donkey Canto" that had "escaped from the oven with the first batch."

You cannot imagine how afflicted I am [he wrote to
his Paris correspondent, D'Argental]. The work as I wrote
it more than twenty years ago is today in very disagreeable contrast with my position and my age; and in its
present current condition it is a horror for any age. The
bits that have been sent me are full of folly and impu-
dence; they are enough to give the tremors to good taste
and decency; it is the height of opprobrium to see my
name on the title page of such a work.

Voltaire had very persuasive reasons for fighting
to suppress this poem. He spread abroad as many
different versions as possible, grosser than the orig-
inals, until it is almost impossible, even today
after years of research, to know exactly what he
wrote and intended. The general authorship could

never be questioned, however; everyone knew that no other living man could possibly have written *La Pucelle*.

Yet it would be a mistake to believe that he was genuinely repentant or that the poem was merely a youthful folly. Canto after canto were added for the amusement of his friends and hosts, such as Frederick the Great, Wilhelmina, Margrave de Bei-reuth, Frederick's sister, and the Duchesse de Saxe-Gotha. To the latter, shortly after his departure from her court—he was in his sixtieth year at the time—he wrote that he wished he were back at work in her library " giving the morning to kings who have brought confusion into the world, and the evening to Joan and tender Agnes, who have made men more gentle." It was these same princes and princesses whom he had so delighted with his lighter works, who came later to his aid in his great fight against the Inquisition. They were not alone in discouraging Voltaire's penitence. The Swiss pastors were not nearly as shocked as Voltaire had expected. His friend Pastor Bertrand wanted a copy. In reply to his request Voltaire wrote: "As for *La Pucelle*, I assure you I am in deep penitence for this sin of my youth. I would send you my sin if I had a copy. I have none; but I'll send to Paris for one right away and just for you. You will read at your leisure and with philosophic friends." For self-protection against interpolations, Voltaire had invited the French resident at Geneva and a magistrate to read his authorized version. "They were so

interested they burst out laughing," he wrote, "and
they said that only a fool could be scandalized."
Publicly he still insisted that the publication of the
poem had poisoned his life. "Let me weep," he
wrote to D'Argental, "over *Joan*, who has nevertheless brought laughter to a great many honest souls."
The burlesque was in fact not at all too strong for
the great majority of eighteenth-century readers;
its reputation suffered much more during the following age of nascent nationalism and Victorian
prudery.

"The calm joy and security of conversation,"
Voltaire wrote to his aging friend Mme du Deffand,
"is a pleasure as real as that of a lover's tryst in
youth." As he grew older, his pleasures of the flesh
consisted almost exclusively of relatively rare moments of freedom from pain. As a compensation, he
never lost the gaiety of the burlesque spirit nor the
enjoyment of broad language. Classical restraint,
however, prevented him from putting coarse words
in print. If we except certain passages of *La Pucelle*
and of his private notebooks posthumously published as *Le Sottisier*, it is remarkable how free from
obscenities are the works of this follower of
Rabelais.

A distinction has frequently been made between
Rabelais's frank and open obscenity and Voltaire's
literary libertinism. The critic Saintsbury, who was
a Pantagruelist, had such a very decided preference
for the former that he constantly applied the word
"sniggerer" to Voltaire, apparently in a pejorative

sense. A sniggerer is, however, a snickerer, and a snicker is a half-suppressed laugh. The hearty unrepressed laughter that Rabelais indulged in and invokes—the French, since the World War, call it an American laugh—would not have been tolerated in the Parisian salons for which Voltaire wrote. The difference is not in the men and has nothing whatsoever to do with the relative purity of their minds. French society was simply much more polished in Voltaire's day than in that of Rabelais. Saintsbury's distinction, it may be greatly suspected, was due to a confusion between the treatment accorded religion by the two writers and the nature of their wit. The point is often made, too, that Voltaire is more suggestive than Rabelais. Here again, the difference can be best explained by the passing of the centuries. From Rabelais's time to the present there has been an increasing literary interest in the suggestive power of words, until the extreme seems to have been reached in much of our modern poetry.

Until rather late in life Voltaire had no stomach for Rabelais's obscenities and criticized them severely. He finally repented and could admit to Mme du Deffand that "except for the low expressions with which his book was overloaded, a good part of it gave him extreme pleasure." Yet he feared his very Parisian correspondent was too delicate and too little learned to appreciate it.

Comparative judgments concerning the two men should be closely related, then, to the centuries in which they lived. It will be useful, too, to consider

La Fontaine, especially his rhymed tales, as examples of libertine literature in the intervening seventeenth century. It is a matter of record, for instance, that Ariosto, Rabelais, La Fontaine, Voltaire, and Anatole France were all amused by the scabrous story of Hans Carvel's ring. The story was related by the first three. Of these three versions, Voltaire preferred the first: "We must not believe," he wrote, "that La Fontaine embellished all that he imitated. He took Hans Carvel's ring from Rabelais, Rabelais took it from Ariosto, and Ariosto admitted that it was a very old tale; but neither La Fontaine nor Rabelais made this story as probable or as amusing as it is in Ariosto." Now La Fontaine's version is less crude, more polished, more suggestive than Rabelais's, as we should expect; but even he was condemned by Voltaire for his too frequent use of common, vulgar, and proverbial expressions; whereas Ariosto represented, in Voltaire's opinion, the finest flower of the very refined literature of the Italian Renaissance. Coming down to more modern times, a mere allusion to Hans Carvel's ring, instigated by Anatole France, was enough to break up a meeting of the French Academy. The story has not changed, but merely the manner of telling it. The manners of the present age are not nearly so polished as were those of Voltaire's era, and a Saintsbury may still prefer Rabelais's less subtle and certainly coarser laughter to the half-smile, half-repressed laugh induced by *Candide*. It is a matter of literary taste, not of morality.

In no sense, however, did Voltaire close his eyes to physical realities or to those pleasures which are most fundamental in human nature but not for that reason to be valued as morally "lower." Like the wise men of antiquity, he still found pleasure the sole excuse for living, and life far too short, pleasure being a kind of dream between the states of non-existence and annihilation. Many of the more carnal pleasures he enjoyed vicariously. He thought he could write an impartial article on "Fornication" for the *Encyclopédie*, "because of his personal disinterestedness." He supported a certain Genevan, Robert Covelle, convicted of fornication, in his fight against the ceremony of genuflexion before the members of the City Council; but in the process, he introduced his protégé regularly as "Covelle, the Fornicator," a title which the latter seems to have accepted proudly on the strength of its high-sounding combination of vowels and consonants. With no more regard than was common in his century for the sanctity of marriage, he nevertheless took great interest and pleasure in marrying off, usually with marked success, the young people who made his old age a bit more gay at Ferney. "Young people," said his secretary, Wagnière, "came every Sunday to dance at his château. They found there every variety of refreshment; he went to see them dance, urged them on, and shared the joy of these settlers, whom he called his children." His influence in this community was on the side of convention; but he considered it ever a wicked act to embroil a lover and his mistress. With an indulgence rare in people of his age toward youthful vagaries, he wrote to his friend D'Argental, "I have already told you that I was like the Chevalier de Condom, who got a great reputation for contributing to the pleasures of youth when he himself was past the age of enjoying them."

An attitude of generous philosophical tolerance to the ills of the flesh and to human weaknesses was a characteristic trait of this man who was so deeply sensitive to human sufferings and who resented so keenly any unnecessary intensification of human trials. When a Swiss seamstress had lived in too great intimacy with one of his servants, he made arrangements with friends in Lyons for her lying-in and also for her conversion, since a disparity in their religions made marriage impossible. But he had to have his little word about "the Swiss Huguenot who took it into her head quietly to make half-breeds with a papist." On another occasion he wrote to a neighbor at Lausanne: "Just because men are barbarous enough to punish with death the fault of a girl who spares a little bundle of flesh the miseries of life, opprobrium and punishment should not have been attached to the making of this bundle of flesh. I recommend this unfortunate girl to your generous philosophy." The spirit of gentle humaneness runs through his letters as it did through his life: a love for humanity, unprincipled if you like to call it such, because he saw human values that transcended all abstract notions and moral absolutes. Formalists are insupportable, he thought, and formalism should be forgotten when human lives are at stake. "Some people," he wrote at another time, "could go gaily to the Opera and to their houses of vice over the bodies of those killed on St. Bartholomew's day. . . . There are others who look seriously on all such happenings and who groan over them. I like to laugh as much as anyone else, and I have laughed perhaps too much; but I like also to weep over Jerusalem." His temperament could not have withstood such bitter weeping over Jerusalem if he had not been able "to laugh it off" afterward. A bright little poem called *Jean qui pleure et Jean qui rit*, written in his seventy-eighth year, expresses this twofold aspect of his temperament. In the morning John weeps over the ravages of nature and the even greater sufferings brought to mankind by tyrants; in the evening, with "libertines" and many a good-looking woman, over a supper of partridges and good Burgundy—all this is vicarious—and far from rogues and fools, he seeks gaiety, songs, and witty conversations, sings of the new loves of Cleon and his mistress, while friendship, his last remaining passion, makes him forget his old age; or he rereads *Ariosto* or *La Pucelle*, and then he laughs. It is a question of temperament; the most one can say is that such was Voltaire's way, leaving judgment, as in in the past, to the moralists, even if they do not always make clear what is meant when they call him a "libertine."

CHAPTER III

An Emotional Temperament

IRRITABILITY AND SENSITIVITY

THE preceding sketch of Voltaire's libertinism has introduced us to a distinctive and rather unusual temperament, to a man whose moods changed, not literally, as he would have it, from morning to night, but sometimes with alarming rapidity. It would not do to borrow a technical term and call him manic-depressive; yet he does without doubt seem to have been affected by a mild form of this mental condition. The classic restraint of his writings and the observance of decorum and nicety, because of which he has so unjustly been deemed cold, were ever warring with an extremely emotional and often irritable temperament. "His brusqueness had displeased me," wrote his secretary, Longchamp, at the beginning of the period of his service with Voltaire and Mme du Châtelet; "I took it at first for brutality; but it did not take me long to see that with him it was nothing but an extreme vivaciousness of character, which exploded at times, only to become calm at almost the same instant. I came to see later that just as his vivacities were momentary and, so to speak, superficial, so were his indulgence and kindness solid and durable qualities."

There is abundant evidence of Voltaire's intensely emotional nature. Unusual depth of feeling and a high degree of sensitivity were the cause and source of his best works in verse and in prose. For instance, the news of the terrible Lisbon earthquake of 1755, in which thirty to forty thousand people lost their lives, produced in his highly nervous organization a prolonged state of dejection and despair, followed by a period of intense emotional exaltation. The inspiration of *Candide* clearly dates from this period. His first reactions were directed against Pope's dictum that "Whatever is, is right." To M. Tronchin, at Lyons, he wrote:

There, sir, is some cruel physics for you. It will cause people no little embarrassment to divine how the laws of nature bring about such frightful disasters *in the best of all possible worlds;* a hundred thousand ants, our neighbors, crushed at one blow in our ant-heap, and half of them perishing doubtless in inexpressible anguish, in the midst of debris from which they could not be rescued; families ruined to the ends of Europe, the wealth of a hundred merchants from your country swallowed up in Lisbon's ruins. What a sad game of chance it is, the game of human life! What will the preachers say, especially if the palace of the Inquisition was spared? I dare say that at least the Reverend Fathers, the Inquisitors, were crushed like the others. That should teach men not to persecute one another. For while a few holy rogues burn a few fanatics, the earth swallows them all up together.

And Voltaire proceeded immediately to write his best philosophical poem, charged with deep human

VOLTAIRE GETS UP IN THE MORNING

emotion, the *Poème sur le désastre de Lisbonne*. This contained the entire emotional tone and philosophical substratum of *Candide*, which he rapidly composed two years later during a period of separation from his books. It is not to be wondered at that a masterpiece owes its inspiration to the intensity of its author's emotional state. Voltaire was, however, more than ordinarily susceptible.

Wagnière, a secretary who lived in close intimacy with Voltaire for more than twenty years, gives still more convincing testimony with regard to the emotional, high-strung organization of his master:

> He was in the habit of sleeping very little, and got me up several times every night. When he was composing a play, he was in a fever. His imagination tormented him and gave him no rest. He would say on these occasions: "I have the devil within me; but of course one should have, to write verse."

Of one of his plays he himself wrote, "I like the pomp of the spectacle, but I prefer an impassioned line." Wagnière was the witness again of such emotional scenes as the following:

> When he had his plays rehearsed in his presence he was beside himself, so entirely was he seized by the different emotions. . . . At a showing of *Zaïre*, in which he played the part of Lusignan, at the moment of recognition of his children, he melted so completely into tears that he forgot what he was to say; the prompter, who was weeping too, could not give him the cue.

Of this same play, Voltaire said:

> *Zaïre* is the first play in which I have dared give myself

over to all the feelings of my heart; it is the only tender love tragedy that I have produced.

There was nothing cold or dispassionate about this man and no mere pretense of feeling in this play; if many of his plays appeared cold to the critics of the romantic age, it was on account of the restraint morally imposed on all authors of the classical school.

THE PASSION FOR JUSTICE

Voltaire's passion for justice was no cold, calculating, reasoned acceptance of a principle; it had its roots in his innermost physical and emotional nature. Neither the personal reaction to domineering injustice nor the altruistic impulses occasioned thereby are created by reason; reason is merely their governor and director. Since this passion is one of the characteristics which most thoroughly explain the man, it will not be amiss to seek, for the moment, its more physiological manifestations. To Voltaire himself the phenomenon was perfectly clear. He insisted that his philosophy was emotional, that he was a man of feeling more than he was a philosopher, and that he had more feeling than his rationalistic predecessor, the coldly analytical Fontenelle. "I always have a fever around the 24th of August," he wrote to Count de Schomberg, "as well as the 14th of May." The former date was the anniversary of the massacre of St. Bartholomew, the latter, that of the assassination by Ravaillac of the tolerant Henry IV, sponsor of the Edict of Nantes.

Enthusiasm, in its older sense of zeal, was a trait usually too closely connected with religious persecutions and fanaticisms to find favor with Voltaire. "I'm not subject to enthusiasm," he explained, "at least not in prose. You know that in writing the *Histoire de Charles XII* I found only a man where others saw a hero." But a month later he wrote to his friend D'Argental: "I just can't write in prose when I am not animated by some dispute, some fact to clear up, or some criticism to make." His enthusiasm for justice was boundless. "I am still a bit enthusiastic," he wrote in 1753, "in spite of my age. Oppressed innocence melts my heart; persecution makes me wild and indignant." Cheated by a moneylender at Frederick's court, he brought the case to court even when it was clear that his own conduct in the case was not impeccable. "I was piqued," he wrote to Frederick; "I was mad enough to want to prove that I had been deceived." When he once thoroughly realized that Maupertuis, President of the Academy of Berlin, had had Koenig condemned as a forger by the force of authority and that the merits of the case seemed to be entirely on Koenig's side, his demon would not let him alone until he had crushed the domineering Maupertuis and had yielded only to the superior force of Frederick the Great. "You know, sir," he wrote to Koenig, "that I am a bit enthusiastic over what I consider to be the truth. You have been witness to the fact that I sacrifice my opinions to no one." He knew full well that the king was on the side of authority and that the result could only mean a final break between them. The very day after he had learned the details of the case and long before the storm broke, he wrote to his niece: "There is still something new under the sun; it is the first time criminal procedure has been seen in an Academy of Sciences." He knew, too, when he was possessed by this demon and accurately foresaw the consequences of its exorcism.

To the journalist Formey, who sent him news of the affair, he replied:

> I will say to you, incidentally, that sometimes those whom we believe to be eagles [Maupertuis] are nothing but turkey cocks; that a despotic pride, with a bit of science and much of the ridiculous, is soon detected and detested by the learned men of Europe ... I am very glad that you show me marks of friendship; and if you are more philosopher than priest, I will be your friend all my life. I am of an unyielding character, unshakable in friendship and in my opinions, fearing nothing in this world nor in the world to come. If you want me under these conditions, I am yours boldly, and perhaps more effectively than you think.

Voltaire's delicate and high-strung nervous system was in fact the best detector of injustice that Europe had ever known.

The torture and death of the young Chevalier de la Barre produced in Voltaire genuine and prolonged physical suffering.

> The atrocity of this deed [he wrote] seizes me with horror and anger. I am sorry that I have ruined myself in buildings and improvements on the border of a country

where, in cold blood, and on the way to dine, barbarities are committed which would make drunken savages tremble with horror. And that's what you call a gentle, light, and gay people! Cannabalistic harlequins! may I never hear of you again! Run from the stake to the ball, from the execution grounds to the Comic Opera; put Calas on the wheel, hang Sirven, burn these five unhappy youths, who deserved, as you say, six months in the prison of St. Lazare; may we never breathe again the same air!

This is pure indignation. It expresses the first written reaction to the news. The mood continued for months, and Voltaire in all earnestness tried to found a colony of philosophers, to be composed of Diderot, Helvétius, D'Alembert, and others, at Clèves, under the protection of Frederick the Great, where their combined efforts and a hardworking printing press could make such atrocities impossible in the future. To his favorite actor and protégé, Lekain, he wrote a week later: "The tragedy at Abbeville excites such indignation within me that it is impossible for me to reread the tragedies that you are performing: they are rose-water, in comparison with that one." Nearly a year later, to his faithful correspondent, D'Argental, he expressed again the depth of his emotions: "The Abbeville affair still commands my heart, and I forget nothing; St. Bartholomew's Day makes me suffer as much as if it happened yesterday." Defending his activities in this affair to Richelieu, whose lifelong friendship he had risked losing, he said five years later: "I listened only to my heart; and it was intimately persuaded that the former Parliament of Paris was as wrong as during the Fronde; nor can it ever love the murderers of Calas, nor those of poor Lally, nor those of the Chevalier de la Barre." Later, to Mme du Deffand, he wrote that the affair was forgotten in Paris: "French levity dances on the tombs of the unfortunate. For my part, I have never let my levity make me forget things which make nature tremble with horror." For five long years the ordinarily patriotic Voltaire had been ashamed of the barbarity of his fellow countrymen, while his physical reaction to the atrocity of this persecution seems to have diminished very little in intensity.

The crisis over the Chevalier de la Barre affair whipped Voltaire into ceaseless activity. He did not succeed in persuading his group of philosophers to retire with him to Clèves, but he found printing presses nearer at hand which for the next seven years he kept busy, not only with the publication of his own tracts, but also with the republication of every book or manuscript he could find which he thought would contribute to the cause of religious toleration or break the back of the persecuting spirit of the Church. Meslier, Fréret, Boulanger, Boulainvilliers, Dumarsais, Bolingbroke, even Jean Jacques Rousseau, and many other philosophers of the enlightenment, unwittingly contributed either their works or their names to this feverish propaganda. Eight years later, in 1774, he was still making efforts toward concerted action.

Good people should be better united [he wrote to the Chevalier de Chastellux]; the flock is dispersed. We have, moreover, on our side only reason and men of honor. That's very little to pit against the dignities, the riches, and the rage of domination. We are not yet exposed to martyrdom, but that will come, unless you and your friends work with all your might to pour water on the fagots that this monster would always like to keep burning.

Even nine years after the event all the details of the death of De la Barre are vividly present in the imagination of this eighty-year-old war-horse. After describing the horrors of the scene to his friend Condorcet, he added: "Tears come to my eyes, and rage into my heart, when I think that a single bigot of Abbeville produced all these horrors, a hundred times more hellish than the Calas assassinations."

No greater injustice has been done Voltaire, no greater misapprehension of his temperament has been revealed than by those critics, all too common, who have denied him any warmth of heart and who have attributed his fight for justice to a coldly calculated desire for personal glory and his attack on religion to a mean desire to destroy. His passion for justice may have led him to excesses, but it led him time and again into exile, into disfavor at the French court, and finally into virtual banishment for life from the kingdom.

We are chiefly concerned here, however, with the intensity of his passions rather than with their direction, and we shall adopt, as Voltaire did in the face of an ever-increasing romantic rehabilitation of the passions, the classical notion that they are the driving force, but dependent on intelligence and reason, not so much to keep them in restraint as to guide and direct them. Voltaire has given us his theory in *Zadig*. Zadig and the hermit visited the house of a philosopher, and the conversation turned to this much-debated subject of the passions:

"Ah! how baneful they are!" said Zadig.—"They are the winds which fill the sails of the vessel," replied the hermit; "they sometimes sink it, but without them, it could make no progress. Bile brings anger and illness; but without bile man could not live. Everything is dangerous in this world of ours, and everything is necessary."

It follows that the stronger the winds, the greater the danger; but Voltaire was no enemy to dangerous living. Diderot proclaimed himself the champion of strong passions; Voltaire, on the basis of his own bitter experience, was more inclined to deplore them. But Diderot would have liked to believe that the passions could find their own control through some inner principle of balance and harmony, while Voltaire continually asserted the governing power of reason.

It might be considered dangerous to assume that Voltaire knew better than we what passions most beset him and to what excesses they led him. Close communion with the most intimate documents concerning him show, however, that he did know himself thoroughly. Shortly after his break with Frederick, adrift between the two havens of Paris and Berlin and with no welcoming port in sight, he searched very deeply into his soul. He asked himself why he had been unable to live with kings and why so many men whom he had greatly and generously befriended, especially the Abbé Desfontaines and D'Arnaud, had turned against him. Others, such as Linant, Lamare, and Lefebvre, had given him no cause for complaint, but that was perhaps, he surmised, because they had died before the full development of their talents and self-pride.

If you are dealing with self-love and self-interest [he observed] you may have rendered the greatest services, but you have only warmed vipers in your breast. That was my first misfortune [through Desfontaines, Voltaire had been utterly discredited in Paris], and the second has been that I have been too deeply moved by the injustice of men, too proudly philosophical to respect ingratitude on the throne, and too susceptible to that ingratitude; irritated that the sole reward for all my labors has been bitterness and persecution; seeing on one side only detestable fanatics, and on the other, men of letters unworthy of the name; aspiring no longer to anything but a refuge, the only course possible for a completely disillusioned man.

On many other occasions he made the same analysis and confessed that he ran the danger of becoming misanthropic when the injustices of men brought him too grievous affliction. It is clear that he was faced with two difficult problems; the first was to prevent his enthusiasms from soaring too high and the second was to devise some means of breaking their fall. It was especially after the soul searchings of this bitter period of his life that he was able to enlarge and depersonalize his hatred of injustice and that he found efficient enough consolations and attitudes of resignation to make life bearable before a new enthusiasm sent him off again crusading against human ignorance and stupidity. But never again was he to say that the dream of his life had been an almost continual nightmare or that this world of ours was nothing but a vast shipwreck.

Voltaire always found himself far in advance of his troops [writes Paul Chaponnière] and was always rather poorly rewarded for all his activities. He changed his cause after each disillusionment. He maintained in his work a faith which recalls, with all due reverence, that of the first Christians—a soaring of all his faculties toward the goal proposed.

COUNTERIRRITANTS AND CONSOLATIONS

The development of counterirritants for his irritable and deeply emotional temperament was of capital importance. Otherwise he would have become misanthropic with Swift and Rousseau or cynical along with Fontenelle, Frederick the Great, and D'Alembert. The last two mentioned tried to persuade him in their letters that men were stupid and ignorant and that nothing could be done about it; while on a more philosophical plane, the optimism of Pope and Leibnitz maintained that all degrees of stupidity and ignorance entered necessarily into God's plan for this best of all possible worlds —that monkeys should not try to be men, nor men, angels, lest a necessary link in the chain of degrees between imperfection and perfection be broken—a most hopeless and desolate doctrine, thought Voltaire, in spite of its consoling name. So he wrote his racy *Candide, ou l'Optimisme*, which completely demolished a philosophical system that ponderously asserted that all was for the best and that man's efforts to make it better were not only useless but sacrilegious. It was not *Candide*, in spite of its form, that was frivolous, it was the devitalizing optimism of Leibnitz. There is, too, the more popular form of optimism which refuses to see the physical and moral evils of this world. As an answer to this the naïve Candide is conducted on a tour of misery over the whole western world and hardly misses a spot where the wounds of humanity are particularly festering or where nature is at her worst. The only land where men are wise and happy is Eldorado, which does not exist. After having lost one illusion after another Candide receives the final stunning blow when he discovers that his beloved Cunégonde, whom he has spent so much time and effort seeking, has lost all her beauty and is now an old hag with red-lidded eyes and yellow, sagging skin. What is left, then, in life for the completely disillusioned man? Nothing but to cultivate his garden.

Candide being one of the better known of Voltaire's works, the conclusion—"Cultivate your garden!" —has been widely discussed. Some have interpreted it as an expression of pessimism, a counsel of inaction and of withdrawal from all efforts to better the lot of mankind. This conclusion is so obviously in contrast with Voltaire's own way of life that others have sought an allegorical interpretation and have seen in the words an exhortation to enter the fight for humanity. Voltaire's tales have a way, however, of summing up certain periods of his existence and certain problems with which he was then faced. *Zadig* has a definite and unmistakable bearing on his struggles to enter the French Academy and on his ideas concerning destiny, or Providence. *Candide* sums up the period of personal discouragement after his departure from Berlin until his settlement near Geneva, where he found peace and repose and, above all, a beautiful garden overlooking the lake in which were reflected the mountains beyond. He had suffered many a personal rebuff, many a heartache over the Lisbon earthquake, and, while reading in preparation for his general history, many a desolate moment over the stories of human stupidity. After every emotional crisis came the period of calm and, during these last years, of quiet cultivation of his garden. The following verse, borrowed by Waller from Tasso, which Voltaire picked up in England, to which he often referred and which he incorporated as the only genuinely lyric passage in his tragedy *Mahomet*, appealed to him very evidently because it touched so closely his own experience with life:

> Our passions gone, and reason on her throne,
> Amaz'd we see the mischief we have done.
> After a tempest, when the winds are laid,
> The calm sea wonders at the wrecks it made.

His letters from this period on show very definitely
that the exhortation at the end of *Candide* meant
literally what it said, but that it was meant only
for those periods when he had reached the bottom
of his emotional curve.

Before *Candide*, Voltaire had sought consolation
for suffering and disillusionment in many ways. In
1728 he suggested to a friend as a remedy the serious
application of the mind to other things. Ten years
later and in *Zadig*, twenty years later, he was consoled to think that in the face of the marvelous
newly-discovered universe men were nothing but
crawling atoms or insects on this almost imperceptible ball of mud. There are here and in other
passages very definite indications that he sought
consolation in a well-developed form of mysticism
—but this is apparently such an unusual interpretation that the discussion must be left for a later chapter. Resignation to the decrees of destiny is the
theme of *Zadig*. "My fate for forty years has been
to suffer ills patiently," he wrote to his agent, in a
time of financial reverses, "and a man, without
being devout, can still submit to Providence."
There is a suspicion of fatalism during these moments of depression. Unhappy and disillusioned at
the court of Versailles, he wrote to his boyhood
friend Cideville: "What man is master of his fate?
We are in this life marionettes whom Brioché moves
and manipulates without their suspecting it." During his first months at Berlin he was still smarting
under the accumulated injustices of his past life,

persecutions, indignities, and atrocities which were still bleeding wounds. He attempted to justify to his friend D'Argental his departure for Berlin and added: "I yield to my destiny, and throw myself, head first, into the abyss of that fatality which governs us all." He fought off disillusionment at Berlin, first with an extraordinary application to his *Siècle de Louis XIV:* "The more I advance in life," he wrote, "the more I find work necessary. It becomes, in the long run, the greatest of pleasures, and makes up for all the illusions one has lost." Later, when his philosophical abode came tumbling down during the Maupertuis - Koenig quarrel, he found his consolation in laughter. "Fight first and laugh afterwards" was an often repeated motto. "When I am attacked," he admitted, "I defend myself like a devil, and yield to no one; but I am a good devil, and in the end I laugh." His secretary, Wagnière, confirms again this purging through laughter, in the interests of sanity: "When my master was depressed or ill, he would say to me: 'Go get a volume of Ariosto, or else my *Joan.*' "

With the later years came the consolation of gardening. Voltaire had at last found a place to dig himself in. Unable to purchase land directly in Genevan territory, because of his Catholic faith, he acquired, through his friends the Cramers and the celebrated Tronchin family a property which he called *les Délices*, and another near Lausanne, which was to be his winter palace. With great gaiety of heart, he proceeded to put both of these houses in order.

I have become mason, carpenter, gardener [he wrote to Thieriot, giving him at the same time a pressing invitation for a year's visit]: You will be fed, watered, shaved, carried from Prangins to *les Délices*, from *les Délices* to Geneva . . . to Monrion, which is my house near Lausanne; you will find good wine and good countenance everywhere; and if I die during the year, you will write my epitaph.

To the Comtesse de Lutzelbourg, he wrote:

We forget, in our hermitage, kings, courts, and the follies of mankind; we think only of our gardens and our friends. I end my career at last by leading a patriarchal life: it is a gift of God which he makes us only when our beards are gray; it is old age's plaything.

And to the Duchesse de Saxe-Gotha, who long tried to attach him to her court, he replied:

It is very unlikely that I shall leave a charming house and delightful gardens where I am master, and a country where I am free, to go to live with a king, were he the king of Cocagne. I shall leave *les Délices* only for greater delights, to pay court once again to your Serene Highness. I shall not go to Berlin to undergo cruel caprices, nor to Paris to expose myself to confessional notes ["billets de confession"]: I fear monarchs and bishops. I shall live and die in peace, if it please destiny, the sovereign queen of this world: for I revert ever to that idea; it is she who does everything, and we are only her marionettes.

He was inordinately happy in his newly-found liberty and tranquillity, in the beauties of Switzerland and Savoy, and in his gardens. "I date my life from the day that I buried myself," he wrote, five years later. After the most stormy period of his life, he could now peacefully cultivate his garden; at least, so he seems half to have believed. But in his very letter of triumph to his friend Thieriot there are clear indications of battles to come: disfigured fragments of his *Pucelle* were already current in Paris; and the celebrated tragedian, Lekain, was coming for a visit: "He will declaim his lines to the children of Calvin. Their ways of life have noticeably softened; they would not burn Servetus today, and they exact no confessional notes." The "War of Geneva" is here in the germ, and the Protestant wrath of citizen Jean Jacques Rousseau will have none of Voltaire's theater.

His life continued, then, to consist of periodic crusades, undertaken with tremendous enthusiasm, unequal battles in which he was ever forced to compromise, to quiet his ardor, to accept partial defeat, and to find consolation as best he could until the next cause set him again on fire. In 1764 he wrote to the aging Comtesse de Lutzelbourg: "You should have had a pretty garden made at Jard; that is very enjoyable, and we have to enjoy life; the fountains, flowers, and shrubbery console, and men do not always console." During the same year he was discouraged by civil war in the ranks of the philosophers; his literary friend Palissot had wantonly attacked his philosophical friend Diderot, and he was sorry to say that Hobbes was right in claiming that man was born in a state of war. He ended a note to Palissot in the following manner: "I have been shown some poem or other by the Abbé Trithème, entitled *La Pucelle;* there is a canto in which everybody is mad; each actor gives and receives a hundred punches. That is the image of this world. I conclude with Candide that we should cultivate our gardens. But I've written too much already for a poor sick man." Here again the garden and the Maid are associated as agents of consolation.

In October, 1767, Voltaire was again enjoying a spell of ill health and thanking his stars that he lived far from the noisomeness of society. "The poor Parisians," he wrote to his niece, "do not know what a pleasure it is to cultivate one's garden; only Candide and we are right." In September and November of the same year, however, he was all for the fight; during the latter month he wanted D'Alembert to write a pamphlet: "The time of the fine arts is past," he wrote, "and philosophy, which was honoring this century, is persecuted. . . . You have no desire to be a martyr, but be a confessor: your words will have more effect than a stake. My dear philosopher, keep up the hue and cry like a devil." The following year, in a letter addressed probably to M. Bordes, he noted that Rousseau was herborizing and added: "Let the rest of us keep on quietly cultivating the Lord's vineyards." This is, of course, in direct contrast to the cultivating of one's own garden and expressed an entirely different mood.

In 1771, again, the Paris Parliament condemned La Harpe's *Eloge de Fénelon*, and the forces of repression were keeping philosophical books out of Paris.

"Paris is a besieged city," Voltaire wrote to D'Alembert, "where any nourishment for the soul may not enter. Like Candide, I end my life in the cultivation of my garden; that's the only path left to follow." His pessimistic moments of resignation became more and more brief, however, and there was no real lessening of activity or loss of faculties until his very death. He soon launched a scathing attack on the persecuting Parliament, nearly losing thereby the good graces of the Duc de Choiseul, who had protected his Ferney colony. Another case of the persecuting folly of mankind arose the following year, and Voltaire again wrote to D'Alembert: "I always come back to the conclusion that one should cultivate one's garden, and that Candide discovered the truth only toward the end of his life." After the same wise counsel a year later, he added: "This world is a chaos of absurdities, and I can prove it"; and again, when the mails to Paris were strictly supervised, he decided that the cultivation of pure literature and of one's garden was the only course left. In midwinter, 1773, he wrote to D'Argental of the difficulties of cultivating gardens in winter: "I can now only cultivate my garden, after having toured the world; but unfortunately one cannot do it in winter, and this winter is furiously long between the Alps and Mt. Jura. I'll have to die, then, without seeing you, without embracing you again."

The conclusion of Candide's philosophy was thus a recurrent theme, with which Voltaire soothed the troubled waters of his stormy life. Like his passion for justice, his passion for gardening also spread beyond the limits of his own immediate presence. It was a very real thing, however, and not a mere figure of speech. The colony which he founded and directed from Ferney in his old age was agricultural as well as industrial. He drained swamps, reclaimed land, assisted in the harvest, and took great pride "in raising two ears of corn where only one had grown before."

CHAPTER IV

Pride and Prejudice

SELF-LOVE AND LOVE OF HUMANITY

"Modes of self-love the passions we may call."
—Pope, *Essay on Man.*

IN A letter previously quoted, in which Voltaire, at the age of fifty-eight, analyzed his passions in an attempt to account for the misfortunes and disappointments of his life up to that point, he had much to say about self-love and personal pride and of the vicissitudes of friendship, as well as of his passion for justice. That he had his full share of personal pride is very apparent; whether or not he was overweening and inordinately jealous is a question which must be examined. He had at least an abundance of friends, old, loyal, and true friends, and considered disloyalty in friendship the clearest sign of a vicious nature. Finally, because of his fine sensibilities and his keen imagination, he was a rare lover of humanity. The phrase "love for humanity" is, of course, a relatively meaningless abstraction, unless it means, as in Voltaire's case, that one is gifted with altruistic impulses and that one rejoices in the joy of other human beings and suffers for their sorrows. It took, indeed, a rarely sensitized organization to suffer for weeks with the victims of the Lisbon earthquake and for years thereafter to feel as keenly as one feels a fresh wound the atrocious killing of the young Chevalier de la Barre.

Justice and altruism would seem, then, to be two clearly dominating principles in the character of this "unprincipled" man. "From the political point of view," wrote Philip Wheelwright in the *Symposium*, "justice is the highest moral ideal. Politics should realistically accept the fact of human selfishness. From the individual point of view, unselfishness is the highest moral ideal promoting social disinterestedness and a love of social justice." In another sense, however, there is no such thing as unselfishness from the individual point of view; and only a social evaluation of a man's conduct, leaving piety aside as a form of sanctimonious egotism, can give rise to the terms "selfish" and "altruistic." For Voltaire, too, the terms "virtue" and "vice" had no meaning apart from the relations of the individual to society. This explains why he considered justice superior to love and why the pattern of his cardinal virtues did not strictly follow the Christian category.

Self-love is nevertheless the emotional basis of all human virtues. When La Mettrie, the "mad" doctor at Frederick's court and one of the wisest men of his century, had reduced "natural law" to the principle of self-love and had persuaded Frederick and his sister of the truth of his philosophy, the deistic Voltaire reacted definitely in favor of considering justice and conscience qualities just as basic in human nature. He admitted defeat in the argument, however, and at the age of seventy-five acknowledged, with reservations, the logical force of Frederick's manuscript treatise on the principles of morality. On reading the treatise he carried on the discussion in a letter:

You certainly have a great deal of genius to be able to show at last in your treatise the true way to be virtuous without being a fool or an enthusiast. You are right, you hit the mark. It is well-directed self-love that makes men of good sense truly virtuous. So the only problem left is how to have good sense; and everyone doubtless has enough to understand you, since your treatise is, like all good works, within everyone's reach.

Yes, self-love is the wind which fills the sails, and which conducts the vessel to port. If the wind is too violent, it sinks us; if self-love is disordered, it becomes a frenzy. Now, with good sense it cannot become a frenzy. Therefore, we have reason married to self-love; their children are virtue and happiness. It is true that reason has had many miscarriages before putting these two children into the world. People still claim that they are not entirely healthy, and that they are still attended with childish ailments; but they manage to struggle along on a diet.

I admire you, my dear Lorrain, when I read these words: "What is more beautiful and more admirable than to draw from a principle which may lead to vice the source of all good and of public felicity?"

Leaving aside for the moment that little problem of how we may have good sense, let us follow Voltaire's argument that self-love is the basis of all virtues. He had himself written that it was like the instrument of our perpetuation, in that it was necessary, cherished, and pleasurable, and yet it had to be concealed. As early as 1733 he clashed with the strict Jansenist views of Pascal, who would destroy all passion. "Man is neither angel nor brute," wrote Pascal; "and unfortunately he who would act like an angel merely reveals his brutish stupidity." Voltaire's comment is a concise criticism of the central doctrine of Pascal's way of life: "He who would destroy the passions, instead of governing them, attempts to act like an angel." In his fifth *Discours en vers sur l'homme* (1738) he began again with an attack on Pascal and upheld the classical theory of control against the more ascetic Christian theory of suppression of the passions. "Nature . . ." he wrote, "calls us to God by the voice of the passions," and "the salutary goodness of a merciful God everywhere attaches a necessary pleasure to human needs." Among the somber devout, self-love is damned; it is the enemy of man and was born in hell; but

All love comes from heaven . . . and self-love is manifested in ourselves, in our goods, in our children, in our fellow citizens, and especially in our friends. . . . Yes, to lift us to the level of great deeds, God, through his goodness, gave us passions. Dangerous though it be, it is a celestial gift; the use of it is happy, even though abuse is fatal.

In a note, Voltaire showed his resentment toward the already narrowing signification of the word "passions." The desire to succeed in one's art, conjugal love, paternal love, a love of the sciences, all these were passions which were certainly not criminal.

He was thus willing, on occasion, to admit the necessity and usefulness of the basic passion of self-love, and he agreed with his century in the effort to rehabilitate the passions in general. Mme du Deffand, to whom he had sent some of his more recent publications, wrote to him, in a letter dated 1765: "I cannot get over my surprise at all I find out about you; you upset all my opinions concerning philosophy. I had believed, up to the present, that it consisted in destroying all the passions; you make me believe today that one must have them all, and that the only problem is in properly choosing their ends." This is as far, however, as he would follow the rising romantic theory that strong passions were essential to genius, that they could be controlled by an internal adjustment or harmonizing within themselves, or that they perhaps did not need as much control as people had generally supposed. To Voltaire that little problem of how to have the necessary controlling good sense was an intellectual, not an emotional, matter and a matter of perhaps greater importance than was Frederick's skillfully academic theorizing concerning self-love as the source of all human virtues. In describing the four ages in the educational development of man, Rousseau had reversed the classical order and had made the age of feeling follow, as more mature, the age of reason. Such doctrine was anathema to Voltaire, to whose more pagan conceptions both the formerly ascetic Christians, on the one side, and the unbridled romantics on the other, seem in the present age to have reverted. This difference in theory is almost enough to explain how, during the romantic age, the legend arose that Voltaire was cold and dispassionate—a rather strange charge against a man who was in that same age considered inordinately proud and jealous, hypersensitive to adverse criticism and unconscionably irascible.

THE ACQUISITION OF PERSONAL DIGNITY

By the time he had reached adolescence and even before, Voltaire was known as a precocious child, with a brilliant mind, an extraordinary facility in writing verse, and a concise and pleasing style. His early brilliance led the aged Ninon de Lenclos to bequeath him a sum of money for books and inspired the Abbés Châteauneuf and Chaulieu to show off their pupil in the literary salons. It was due to his obvious talents that he was welcome at the Society of the Temple, where he rubbed elbows with members of France's most noble families. At school and later he numbered among his intimate friends and admirers many dukes, marquises, and counts—the Ducs de Richelieu and de Villars, the Marquis de la Marche and d'Argenson, and so forth, not to mention the many brief and casual contacts with such persons as the Ducs de Caumont and de Sully, the Prince de Vendôme, and countless others. It was in all probability from personal contact with this society that he very early developed a set of values

[63]

more favorable, indeed, to his own position, which placed intellectual prowess and artistic taste above ranks, titles, and dignities. His earliest works reveal a spirit of revolt against the high esteem bestowed indiscriminately on such accidental considerations as birth and title. He had an intensely humanistic scale of values, according to which even kings and popes were to be judged, not in the light of divine or traditional authority, but according to actual and essentially human standards. Knowing full well this characteristic, Frederick, when he became king, asked Voltaire to forget his royal titles and to see in him only a zealous citizen, a somewhat skeptical philosopher, and a truly faithful friend; and Voltaire replied that the order to treat Frederick as a man rather than as a king was according to his own heart and asked permission to address his royal friend as "Your Humanity," rather than as "Your Majesty."

It was this respect for essential human values that made the lesser scions of greater families, such as the Chevalier de Rohan, look upon Voltaire as a conceited commoner whose shoulders evidently itched for a drubbing. At the age of twenty-three the already well-known poet and author of *Œdipe*, now only recently released from the Bastille, had added to the lowly name of Arouet the more aristocratic nom de plume, De Voltaire. Pride in his own worth, contested in his day only by a jealous few, as well as poetic considerations of euphony, were responsible for this change. Never in the long course of his life, however, did he try to deceive anyone about his bourgeois birth, nor did he change his ideas concerning the emptiness of titles. It was a quarrel over names that led to the beating he received from Rohan's lackeys. Yet so carefully guarded were the prerogatives of birth that few of his former friends among the nobility protested against this injustice; eminent among those who sided with him were the Duc de Villars, a truly intimate friend, and Montesquieu, a baron by birth who, like Voltaire, had little esteem for the fawning courtiers of the age and great esteem for human justice.

Montesquieu reports that Lord Bolingbroke, activated by the same haughty motives that prevented the Duc de Sully from coming to Voltaire's defense, refused to shelter him at London. Voltaire's own story that it was he himself who refused the invitations of English lords and accepted the hospitality of Sir Everard Falkener, a simple country gentleman, is much more plausible. Much earlier in his life he had tired of the frivolity and restraints of château life and had expressed his desires for a simpler life with simple people, where he could find time to work by day, sleep by night, and carefully guard his freedom. A gay portrait of his attitude is found in verse, written two years after his return to Paris from England, in the heading of an otherwise very serious letter to Thieriot. The translation will succeed of course only in rendering the thoughts expressed in the original lines.

A fever makes my writing painful,
Yet firm of mind, of death disdainful,
Unprejudiced, unpatriotic,
I mock the great, and fate despotic:
Patient in suffering, in gayety rollicking,
   At foolish pride forever laughing,
   With one foot ever in the coffin,
   And with the other blithely frolicking.

Je t'écris d'une main par la fièvre affaiblie,
D'un esprit toujours ferme, et dédaignant la mort,
Libre de préjugés, sans liens, sans patrie,
Sans respect pour les grands, et sans crainte du sort:
Patient dans mes maux, et gai dans mes boutades,
   Me moquant de tout sot orgueil,
   Toujours un pied dans le cercueil,
   De l'autre faisant des gambades.

This native repulsion for dignitaries and dislike for empty titles, whether used by courtiers, patriots, philosophers, literary men or scientists, developed in Voltaire an attitude that could not fail to do him harm. He found it difficult indeed, with one foot ever in the grave and with the other gamboling, to stand on his own dignity; and he thus laid himself open to frequent misunderstandings and attacks on the part of the lesser spirits of his day and to calumnies which finally so infested the Parisian area that he found life there intolerable.

Disrespect for empty titles, for great names which conceal human weaknesses, stupidity, and greed, irreverence for all religious shams, hatred for frauds, pious or otherwise, these were the dominant characteristics of the Voltairean attitude. There were

times, to be sure, when he could use titles in the
main business of his life, and when these times came,
he played the game with cynical abandon. The
ends, which were justice, truth, tolerance, and
humanity, seemed ever in his eyes to justify some
compromise in the means. "One should always have
a few crowned heads up one's sleeve," he wrote.
And when he needed help in reversing the judgment
of the intolerant and fanatical judges of Toulouse
against Calas, he pulled his crowned heads out of
his sleeve and took all the tricks.

The Duc de Richelieu was not only the intimate
friend of his youth but also the patron of the
Théâtre Français and a very useful hero for an
intriguing and militant playwright. Cardinal de
Bernis represented the more literary, tolerant wing
of the Church, and Voltaire had many reasons for
cultivating his friendship; Italian cardinals and even
the pope, Benedict XIV, rendered service in time of
need, when his orthodoxy had been too frankly
questioned. The dedication of his tragedy, *Mahomet,
ou le Fanatisme*, to this pope in exchange for the
papal blessing was a masterstroke of strategy in his
successful campaign for admittance into the French
Academy. Yet he never sold his personal integrity
nor his intellectual freedom. He realized perfectly
well that he could have continued to write light
verse and serious plays to please the powers and
principalities of eighteenth-century Europe—no one
could have done it better; that he could have played
the court buffoon, if he had been willing to suppress

his finer feelings; and he knew that this would have been the easier way—easier, if only he could have exorcized from within him that demon which called for justice, tolerance, and humanity. Looking back over this period with all the rich philosophy of his eighty-one years, he wrote to the Abbé Duvernet, his future biographer:

Those who have told you, sir, that in 1744 and 1745 I was a courtier, have advanced a sad truth. I was; I amended my ways in 1746, and repented in 1747. Of all the time I have lost in my life, it is that time that I regret the most. It was not a period of glory, if I ever had any. I erected, however, a *Temple de la Gloire*. It was written on order, such as the Maréchal de Richelieu and the Duc de la Vallière could read. The public did not relish the architecture of this temple; and I did not like it any too well myself.

It was at this time that he fought for worldly honors and obtained them. Besides becoming a member of the French Academy, he acquired the empty titles of Historiographer—which he tried in all seriousness to fill—and Gentleman Ordinary of the King's Chamber. If he was proud of his titles, it is significant that he used them without false pride and only when addressing people to whom titles might mean something and who might be thus persuaded into giving him support for cherished projects. At Frederick's court he accepted certain charges and a pension in order to enable his niece, Mme Denis, to keep house for him at Berlin; but the spoiled lady could not be persuaded to leave her civilized Paris, and the uncle bitterly regretted later

the ensuing obligations to Frederick. It was clearly
a fight for the principle of intellectual and moral
freedom against the arbitrary decisions of authority
that caused his break with the Prussian king; he
saw the eventuality and the difficulties long in
advance and accepted them courageously and freely.
The circumstances of his quitting the French court
are not so fully known. It is apparent, at least, that
he was emotionally and intellectually unfitted to
play the rôle of buffoon or sycophant at the courts
of kings. He has most unjustly been called "the
playboy of the aristocracy." That he could most
easily have been, if he had not been too proud; but
for self-love, for his own personal pride and dignity,
he fought an arduous and unusually prolonged battle,
and it was only after his settlement near Geneva at
the age of sixty that he felt the battle had been
won. From that date, he said, his life truly began.

The last twenty years of his life, spent in and
about his estate at Ferney, were indeed years of
personal triumph, during which he was courted and
praised throughout Europe, excepting always Paris,
that stronghold of re-echoing slander and resentment
which was always so near to his heart and which
he finally captured only on his return in 1778.
Rarely has a man of letters had such temptation to
lose his head completely in a sweeping current of
adulation. His newly-found dignity withstood the
strain; there is a very definite tone of humility in his
letters during those final years. His mysticism gave
him the attitude of the psalmist who wrote: "What

is man that thou art mindful of him?" And his sense
of the ridiculous preserved him from false pride and
kept him sane. He had acquired various new titles
such as Lord of Ferney and Count of Tournay and
the more humble and cherished Temporal Father of
the local order of Capuchin monks. It is not certain,
but probable, that he very wisely discouraged an
effort to make him cardinal: he himself was not the
only strange aspect of a strange century. Much later,
when, after the death of the hostile Louis XV, there
was a movement on foot in Paris to give him the
title of Marquis in appreciation of his services to
the neighboring county of Gex, he refused with the
good humor and dignity of a representative man of
letters: "Marquis Crébillon, Marquis Marmontel,
Marquis Voltaire," he replied, "would be good
only to be shown at fairs with Nicolet's monkeys.
The gentlemen from Paris apparently wanted to
make me ridiculous, and I do not accept the honor."
Such titles as he had, he used with great moderation
and in order to advance his crusades; his letters were
much more frequently signed: "The little Swiss,"
"the Swiss owl," "the cacouac of Lausanne," "the
sad old owl of Ferney," "the old man of the mountain," "the old woodchuck of the Alps," "chie-en-
pot-en-perruque," or "Friar Voltaire, unworthy
Capuchin."

For a man of his emotional temperament and
especially with his passion for justice and his sense
of the ridiculous, it was difficult to arrive at that
goal of classical restraint and moderation which

was ever his ideal. Far too many times, when he had been stung by injustice and insidiously willful misunderstanding, his pride had rushed over the barriers. And when he had finally conquered himself, he showed himself still the fighter rightfully proud of his achievements and yet an essentially humble man.

For his pride, as well as for his need for justice, he soon discovered fields of activity wider and more fertile than those of his immediate personal concerns. Many dignities he cared little about, but the necessity of establishing and maintaining the professional dignity of writers and actors never failed to incite his ardor. These two ambitions were closely associated in his own experience, and his crusades in their behalf, which were to last his lifetime, explain many apparent contradictions in his character.

For many years before his exile to England he had been the warm friend of the celebrated actress, Adrienne Lecouvreur, a woman of generous instincts and noble sentiments. It was in her box at the theater that there occurred the verbal clash between Rohan and Voltaire which led to the latter's banishment. His friendship with the lady continued as warmly as ever after his return. Strange as it may seem, it appears that a common passion for her strengthened his friendship with D'Argental. She was endowed with a nervous emotional temperament, a soul of fire, which made of her an excellent tragedian, but soon wore out her frail body. Many years before, she had bravely nursed Voltaire when he was ill with the smallpox, and he now had an occasion to repay her services. Like Molière, she persisted in playing out her rôle while she was being consumed within by a fatal malady. Four days after her swan song on the stage, she died in Voltaire's arms. Actors and actresses were not allowed Christian burial, and the priest of the parish took steps immediately to prevent any infraction of the rule. The corpse of Paris's most charming and idolized actress was carried at night under police escort and buried in an open field—"thrown on the dump," as Voltaire expressed it, with only slight exaggeration. Indignation was general among the more philosophically minded; but Voltaire was cut to the quick. Again from the depths of an emotional crisis there came forth some of his most impassioned and eloquent verse. "You know," he wrote to Thieriot, "that I sent you, about a month ago, some lines on *La Mort de Mademoiselle Lecouvreur*, filled with the just grief that I still feel at her loss and with indignation, perhaps too bitter, over her burial, but indignation pardonable in a man who was her admirer, friend, and lover, and who is also a poet." By this last phrase he meant that he was a man of feeling; he often envied the conciseness of Pope's philosophical verses, but he considered himself the better poet because he was capable of deep emotions, whereas Pope was cold.

What will you say, posterity, [asked Voltaire in his ode] when you hear of the withering insult that cruel men have inflicted on the stricken arts? They deprive of burial her to whom the Greeks would have erected altars. While she was alive, they sighed after her; I have seen them pressing about her, enthralled: when she has breathed her last, has she then become a criminal?

> Que direz-vous, race future,
> Lorsque vous apprendrez la flétrissante injure
> Qu'à ces arts désolés font des hommes cruels?
> Ils privent de la sépulture
> Celle qui dans la Grèce aurait eu des autels.
> Quand elle était au monde, ils soupiraient pour elle;
> Je les ai vus soumis autour d'elle empressés:
> Sitôt qu'elle n'est plus, elle est donc criminelle?

Is it only in England, Voltaire continued to ask, that men dare think and that such celebrated actresses as Mrs. Oldfield are honored with burial, along with Dryden, Addison, and Newton, in such memorial temples as Westminster Abbey? And he expressed his regrets that in his own country honor and glory were not the rewards of genius. He therefore encouraged Thieriot to let his ode become public, and accepted the possibility of persecution and exile with the following statement:

And were the troupe of the devout, always inflamed with pure zeal, to surround my body with fagots, and all for the good of my soul, I cannot help letting out these verses, which were dictated by indignation, tenderness, and pity. . . . I add my voice to all the voices of England to make the difference felt between their liberty and our enslavement, between their bold wisdom and our foolish superstition, between the encouragement that the arts receive in London, and the shameful oppression under which they languish in Paris.

Here, frankly expressed, is the theme and the

method of his *Lettres philosophiques*, or *Letters concerning the English Nation*, a collection upon which he was working at that time and which was (on its publication in France in 1734) one of the great literary events of the century. The themes were aspects of England's religious, political, social, and literary life; the method was to choose mainly those aspects which would serve as object lessons to his fellow countrymen; the result was a pleasant, unpretentious, witty little book, which criticized every fundamental assumption of French life under the Old Régime.

Voltaire's exile to England was not caused by his unjust beating by Rohan's lackeys, but by his obstinate rage in seeking redress. Besides the smarting injustice resulting from personal violence, there was also the question of the dignity of his profession. Not so very many years before, even in "enlightened" England, Dryden had been beaten, for a satire, by the Earl of Rochester's negro. And during the preceding century in France the most noted authors were dependent upon the good graces and the table of their patrons. Voltaire wished above all else to be no servile parasite. His appeal for the just treatment of men of literary and artistic talents became less and less a personal matter; more and more an altruistic crusade. In a letter addressed, in 1732, to an aspiring young author he listed the difficulties and disappointments that would beset his path: "The career of letters, and especially that of genius, is more thorny than the road to wealth. If you are unfortunate enough to be mediocre (which I do not believe you are), you will be remorseful for life; if you succeed, you will have enemies: you will walk on the edge of an abyss, between contempt and hatred." The censor, Voltaire explained, may not be of the author's school of thought, or he may be his rival's friend, or he may even be his rival himself. He had already experienced or was to experience most of the difficulties which he here set forth. The censor was long his most serious dramatic rival, Crébillon, who was supported by the self-righteous court; and it can hardly be forgotten that when Crébillon *fils* succeeded his father, he was persuaded with difficulty to pass on Montesquieu's *De l'esprit des lois*, because of its "unworthy style." When an author had once succeeded in courting writers, protectors, abbés, doctors, and book-agents, it was often only to fall prey to one of the several literary gazettes, which were purposefully satirical in order to satisfy the malice of the reading public and so increase their sales. It seems a sad historical fact, indeed, that critical malice yielded, a century later, only out of consideration for the greater profits of advertising.

If your work be a play, [continued Voltaire] you are faced with the ill will of the comedians or unjustly flayed by the public, by the organized efforts of a rival cabal, by a malicious pleasantry from the pit which can often ruin a good play, by libels and parodies, and by the contempt of pedants. If you carry your play to a lady at the court, you are insulted by her lackey, whose rich livery contrasts strikingly with your poet's rags. You must choose one school of writing, or all will be at your heels. There are a great many small literary societies in Paris, always presided over by some woman who, as her beauty wanes, exhibits the brilliant dawning of her intellect. One or two men of letters are prime ministers of this little kingdom. If you neglect to place yourself in the ranks of her courtiers, you are considered to be in the ranks of the enemy and are crushed. Positions destined for men of letters are given to intriguers, not to talented writers.

Here again Voltaire speaks from experience or with prophetic insight. He steadfastly refused to ally himself with the group around the intriguing Mme de Tencin, and to that fact alone could be attributed his major difficulties for thirty-five years to come, including the unkind, often unjust, criticisms of his character and his works. For in her salon, such frank enemies as the Abbé Desfontaines undoubtedly influenced the opinions of Montesquieu, Marivaux, the Abbé Prévost, and Piron and even brought about Voltaire's betrayal by the unstable and parasitical Thieriot, who would accept a good dinner from no matter what source. On the fringes of this group the insulting *Voltairomanie* and *Voltariana* were hatched, and the Parisian area was so infected thereby that the victim was forced out of the country, for twenty-eight long years of exile. In this atmosphere it took the good-hearted Diderot many years and much good will to overcome his early prejudices against his greater contemporary. Mme de Tencin kept Voltaire for many years from admission to the French Academy, and her brother, the Cardinal, whom Voltaire called "that terrible miscreant," never forgot the family slight.

"If you try to reply to libels and calumny," Voltaire continued in his letter, "the public eggs on both parties and condemns both to ridicule." Here again he was referring to his quarrels with the Abbé Desfontaines and J. B. Rousseau, while lying in wait for him were similar proofs of the accuracy of his insight, in his verbal combats with Fréron, J. J. Rousseau, and many others, with results as prophesied. The ills that attended the business of writing, both personal and general, were very real. It has been too easy to judge, from the vantage point of time, that he would have enhanced his reputation if he had refused to fight back. From another point of view, it appears that he has long been half buried in calumny and that only by the most heroic and desperate efforts was he able to justify himself in some measure to his fellow citizens and to posterity.

At the end of this long and friendly letter to the young author Lefebvre, who died that same year, thus avoiding, as Voltaire pessimistically observed many years later, the sin of ingratitude to his benefactor, the veteran poet said it was not his intention to turn his friend away from literary pursuits—he would not thus oppose destiny—but rather to exhort him to patience. Many repetitions of the same theme were to follow in his later works and letters. He could hardly accept Rousseau's arguments that the pursuit of the arts and sciences in general tended to corrupt morals. Such endeavors acted rather as civilizing agents that soothed in man what was left of the savage beast, and it was his firm belief that a theater in Geneva would increase the tolerance and gentility of his Calvinist neighbors. In his witty reply to Rousseau's discourse, however, he avoided the main issue and complained again of the evils that had beset him personally. The humanizing rôle of the philosopher-poet was too much a part of his classical philosophy, an ideal which ''common sense'' approved, even if it contained an essential paradox. To Mme du Deffand he wrote during the later years of his life: ''There is perhaps one rather agreeable station in this world, that of the imbecile; but it is no use proposing that manner of existence to you: you are too far removed from that kind of felicity. It's rather amusing that no intelligent man would desire a state of happiness based on folly; it is clear, however, that it would be a very fair bargain.'' This paradox, expressed more fully in the *Histoire d'un bon bramin*, is as far as this classical humanist would let himself be drawn into the anti-intellectualistic argument.

To the end of his long life he fought unsuccessfully for the decent burial of the members of the theatrical profession. He was much more successful, however, in ennobling the status of the man of letters. His example was no less effective than his precept, for as patriarch of Ferney, he ruled over intellectual Europe. Never since has such a humane cosmopolitan society flourished in that politically divided territory, and never since have the influence and reputation of one man of letters succeeded more effectively in subduing narrow patriotism and in uniting into one human family the reading public of that continent. The lines of demarcation between political and religious groups were growing fainter and fainter, while the more broadly human principles of justice and tolerance were rapidly spreading. Certainly, it was not Voltaire's fault that the Revolution indulged in excesses and parodied his goddess or that the romantic reaction undid the greater accomplishments of his life. It may be true that most of his minor crusades were for reforms which have since been effected; but the great ambition of a tolerant, just, and cosmopolitan humanity is perhaps farther than ever from fulfillment. The modern world has just as great a need for the dignified and influential man of letters or, more particularly, for the poet-philosopher. Poetry may well become dehumanized as a result of losing itself in philosophical abstraction or of wandering off into the blind alleys of *surréalisme* while philosophy, never less poetic, is again all too often the plaything of systematizing academicians.

VOLTAIRE THE FIGHTER: FRIEND OR ENEMY?

Friendship, for a man who lives dangerously and who is forever battling in the thick of the fray, has much more than ordinary significance—it is at once more precarious and more precious. Voltaire's relations with an unusual number of friends and enemies can hardly be understood apart from the seriousness of his embattled career. Current hostile opinions that he was the "playboy of the aristocracy," that he was in no way the leader of a great intellectual and rationalistic movement, and that he had no capacity for friendship are so far from the truth that they could not withstand, even in the most prejudiced mind, a reading of any one volume of his correspondence or a hundred pages of any factual biography. Even if he were judged by aesthetic standards alone, "playboy" is hardly the word for a man whose literary genius even his bitterest contemporary enemies were forced to recognize. But he never himself separated artistic beauty from truth or the poem from its human interest. *Œdipe*, among his earliest successes, contained energetic lines against oppression, political and religious, and the *Henriade* was in praise of a tolerant king; *Zaïre* was an attempt to show the universality of moral values as against the narrowing influences of religious sects; *Alzire* condemned ruthless imperialism in Spanish America; and *Mahomet* was an explanation and condemnation of fanaticism. He could be much more justly charged with overseriousness, with didactic and reformist intrusions into the realms of artistic beauty, than with frivolity. His gayest and most apparently frivolous works he considered to be weapons in the war of humanity: even *La Pucelle*, he thought, would help to make the Swiss more civilized and more tolerant.

His greatest satisfaction he found in work; his keenest pleasure, in intellectual warfare. It has been noted that early in life he sickened of the regular château life of his aristocratic friends, because it could not satisfy the two great necessities of his life —work by day and sleep by night. Parisian life was too noisy and too busy; he tried to find quarters away from its main streams, but complained often that he could accomplish little work. In England, in 1726, he retired to Wandsworth to avoid the distractions of London; there he worked on the new edition of the *Henriade*, wrote his *Essai sur la poésie épique*, and prepared for the *Histoire de Charles XII* and the *Lettres philosophiques*. There, too, he learned the English language and thus enlarged his intellectual horizons; on trips to London he sat in the front row of the theater and listened to Shakespeare's plays, following the text by the light of the candles. In 1732 he wrote to Thieriot in English: "I have nothing at heart but the pleasure of study and the desire of your return. I never go out of doors. I see nobody but at home; I hope to employ such a studious leisure with *Eriphile*, the *English Letters*, and the *Age of Lewis XIV*." And to Cideville, in the same period, he wrote: "My dear Cideville, what a delightful life it would be to live together with three or four men of letters, with talent and without jealousy! To love one another, to live tranquilly, to cultivate our arts, to talk about them, and to instruct one another!" The Mme du Châtelet period of his life, from 1733 to 1749, was spent, for all its diversions, in much such mutual instruction. Together the two scholars read aloud Latin verses and English treatises and translated Mandeville's *Fable of the Bees* into French; together they set up apparatus and worked in their physics laboratory at Cirey, examined together the courses of the stars and the works of Descartes, Newton, and Leibnitz. In all seriousness Voltaire "abandoned Ovid for Locke," as he expressed it, and learned to appreciate the sciences and the scientific method, the discovery of "truths founded on experiments." He suffered cruelly when forced to remain so long with Mme du Châtelet in Belgium. "Just imagine," he wrote to the Marquis d'Argens, "that for two weeks, my philosophy has been playing comedy in the daytime, and 'brelan' at night. But I'll have to get back to work, for time lost in pleasure leaves the mind empty, and hours spent in study leave the soul replete."

The letters from Berlin and Potsdam show again very clearly that he sought at Frederick's court not personal glory, but friendship, and freedom to work hard and tranquilly, without fear of persecution or of distractions caused by literary quarrels. His main desire, the completion and publication of the *Siècle de Louis XIV*, he accomplished. When he realized that he must sacrifice Frederick's friendship, he still found contentment and peace in his own work at Sans-Souci. Hard work, in fact, became both a necessity and a consolation. The few years that he spent in Berlin were unusually fruitful. Besides publishing the *Siècle de Louis XIV*, he found time to write the *Défense de Milord Bolingbroke*, *Micromégas*, the *Poème sur la loi naturelle*, the *Diatribe du docteur Akakia*, several plays, probably an early version of the *Sermon des cinquante*, and many articles for his *Dictionnaire philosophique*; in the meantime he corrected his collected works and had them published at Dresden. These were the accomplishments that mattered and that took his time and energy, and yet they have been the most readily slighted in the welter of biographical anecdotes.

During the very days when he was leaving Germany, he undertook to write, for the Duchesse de Saxe-Gotha, the *Annales de l'Empire*, an ungrateful task which nevertheless kept him very hard at work during a trying period of homelessness. His acquisitions of property at Geneva and Lausanne he hailed with joy; for now he could enjoy true peace and independence. But if ever a man "was, in repose, to work condemned," that man was Voltaire. Twice he wrote to his Benedictine friend, Dom Calmet, asking for a cell in the Abbey of Senones: "Sir, I prefer retreat to the court," he said, in 1748, "and great men to kings. I should be very glad to pass several weeks with you and your books. I should need a warm cell, and if I could have a thick soup, a little mutton, and some eggs, I should prefer that happy, healthy, frugality to royal fare." Ten years later, he passed some weeks at the Abbey. "It is good military strategy," he explained, "to seek in the camp of the enemy the weapons with which to attack him." But that was not all. From the sum-mer resort at Plombières a letter expressed his regret at being obliged to leave Dom Calmet's "respectable and charming solitude." "Life here is a bit tumul-tuous," he added, "which makes me cherish all the more that happy tranquillity that I enjoyed with you." Voltaire needed too much the feminine touch in his home and the society of women to make a good monk, but the hard scholarly labors, the frugality and calmness of monastic life would not have troubled him.

The latter-day peace of *les Délices* and of Ferney was to be disturbed by countless battles. The clash between Voltaire and the Swiss clergy over D'Alem-bert's article "Geneva," the struggle against Rous-seau and his fellow Genevans who supported Calvin's interdiction of the theater, the "Battle of Geneva" which he waged against the privileged and domi-neering aristocracy of Rousseau's dream republic, the establishment in and about Ferney of a manu-facturing and agricultural colony, personal sallies against Lefranc de Pompignan, Fréron, and Chau-meix, filled up his restless life; but underlying all these activities was the war against "infamous superstition." His correspondence shows very defi-nitely that he was the accepted leader in this struggle. As early as 1757 he was trying to patch up the differences between Diderot and D'Alembert over the proposed abandonment of the *Encyclopédie*, at first siding with D'Alembert, but later giving Diderot his wholehearted support in the continuation of that vast project. He was ever exhorting his fellow philosophers to deal greater and lustier blows at "infamy," to unite as their persecutors were united, to stand by each other through thick and thin, to work their printing presses in Germany if France got too hot, and to lose no occasion to spread the gospel of tolerance, justice, and humanity. Open attacks on the Church and on theological and historical Christianity were extremely rare in his publications before 1762. From that time on, that is, from his sixty-eighth year to the end of his life, he worked feverishly against them.

It seemed that work was necessary for his very existence [wrote Wagnière, the secretary of these final twenty years]; most of the time we worked from eighteen to twenty hours a day. He slept very little and made me get up several times during the night. . . . Work was his only excess. . . . When he worked, we were often obliged to warn him that he had taken no nourishment. He had no fixed hours for his meals nor for sleep. In general, he passed the greater part of his life in bed, working.

His books surrounded him, stuffed with notes and markers, which his prodigious memory kept always at his command. The most learned volumes were no barrier to his curiosity if he thought they might be useful. His own collected publications are alarmingly voluminous, and his correspondence, if it could all be assembled, would match the rest in volume. "One does not pass on to posterity with so much baggage," he complained. But these works and these letters were not written for posterity;

there was hardly one that was not struck off hurriedly, sometimes just to please a friend, but usually in the heat of conflict and for a definite strategic purpose. His subordination of literary beauty to political considerations was a conscious choice; for example, to Pastor Vernes he wrote in 1767: "My dear philosophic priest and citizen, I send you two memoirs on the Sirven family. This little pamphlet will inform you of their case. Count on it that they will be justified like the Calas family. I am naturally a bit obstinate. Jean Jacques writes only for the sake of writing, while I write in the interests of action." When a man labors like a demon, fights hard, and lives long, he can hardly help it if his literary baggage piles up. As a result, Voltaire's works are usually collected in unwieldy volumes. A French concern recently announced a new edition of his complete works and published the Tales and Novels in four volumes of convenient size. If the project had been continued and all the published letters had been collected, the edition might have run to considerably more than two hundred volumes.

The bulk of Voltaire's work alone would be proof that he was no playboy even if other proofs were lacking; the tone of the works and letters of the last twenty years of his life reveals nothing more clearly than that he was the spiritual leader and most active worker of the philosophic group. It was he who was ever encouraging them to greater endeavors, begging them to forget personal quarrels and to unite in the war against intolerance and persecution, urging them to join him at Clèves (where they could print what they believed without fear of the stake), finding publishers for their works outside the limits of France, and aiding in every possible way the clandestine trade in their forbidden productions.

The conflict with the enemy centered at first in the *Encyclopédie*. The completion of that engine of war was due principally to the tireless efforts of Denis Diderot; but Voltaire was ever in the background contributing and soliciting articles, defending the philosophers against his friend Palissot, attacking their enemies (Fréron, Rousseau, Chaumeix, Pompignan), and striving to obtain the sympathy and protection of his influential friends, such as Mme du Deffand, the Abbé Bernis, Richelieu, and Choiseul. The position of party whip was often delicate: it would not do to enrage too thoroughly the "monster," because brothers Diderot and D'Alembert were in Paris "under its claw." His devotion and tact in this cause are unquestionably revealed in the correspondence. "As long as I have a breath of life," he wrote to D'Alembert in 1755, "I am at the service of the illustrious authors of the *Encyclopédie*. I consider myself greatly honored to be able to contribute, even feebly, to the greatest and handsomest monument of the nation and of literature. I pay my very sincere compliments to all who are working on it. I am very much alarmed about M. Rousseau's health, and should like to know more about it." In the same letter he offered articles on Taste, Genius, History, Facility, Falsity, Fire, Finesse, Feebleness, Force, Frenchmen, and Fornication. Moreover, he enlisted the services of his friends among the Swiss pastors, whose articles on theology were often too liberal to face the censorship.

He had his literary friends as well as his philosophic friends and thereby was thrown into many a cruel dilemma. Mme du Deffand represented the group that would have liked to keep Voltaire for pure literature. She endeavored to embroil him with his fellow fighters and protected Palissot in his attack on Diderot and the Paris group. Palissot had been Voltaire's friend, too, and a disciple in the fight for the maintenance of literary taste. On the other hand, Diderot's expansive nature and revolutionary literary theories were not according to Voltaire's taste. In this dilemma he clung to philosophy, attempted energetically to persuade Mme du Deffand and Palissot of the merits of the *Encyclopédie* and of the esteem due to its authors, supported and avenged Diderot for the insults of Palissot's play *Les Philosophes*, and long urged as a master stroke against fanaticism Diderot's admission to the French Academy. There was no trace of "art for art's sake" in his literary theories, and except in a very few of his plays Dame Literature bent the knee to Dame Philosophy.

The philosophers [he wrote to Palissot] are a small flock who must be kept from the slaughter. They have their failings like other men; they do not always write excellent works; but if they could all write against the common enemy it would be a fine thing for the human race. The monsters called Jansenists and Molinists, after biting each other, are now joined in barking at the poor partisans of reason and humanity. These should at least protect one another from their fangs.

The five weeks spent by D'Alembert in 1756 at *les Délices* as Voltaire's guest had momentous repercussions in Voltaire's life. D'Alembert was given a royal welcome by the Genevans as hero of the *Encyclopédie* and as a mathematician of unusual merit. Informal talks with the Swiss pastors led him to believe that they were fundamentally deists who would sacrifice the doctrine of the divinity of Jesus Christ to more human considerations. When the article "Genève" appeared the following year in the seventh volume of the *Encyclopédie*, there was consternation among the Genevan clergy, who were greatly displeased to see that through D'Alembert's praise of their liberalism and humanity they were openly convicted of the Socinian heresy. He had attacked neither their frankness nor their sincerity but had betrayed, so they felt, their hospitality by his imprudent publication of their more intimate opinions. Voltaire was of course immediately blamed, was indignant at the charge, but secretly enjoyed this public airing of deism and urged D'Alembert not to retract. Moreover, Voltaire was held responsible for the insertion in the article of a paragraph in behalf of the establishment of a theater at Geneva. It cannot be proved that he was guilty on either count. Yet he and D'Alembert were the closest of friends and held the same general views on religious and literary questions. What is important, however, is the fact that the pastors believed Voltaire guilty and discovered his real support of D'Alembert's position in the ensuing quarrel; and Rousseau believed with all his might that Voltaire was trying to corrupt with a theater the primitive moral purity of his fellow citizens. Thus after two years Voltaire lost the support and friendship of many of those pastors who had so warmly welcomed him and who had hoped to convert him to Calvinism, and he also incurred the openly-expressed hatred of Geneva's potentially greatest citizen, Jean Jacques Rousseau. Other events served to add to his troubles.

In a letter from Voltaire to Thieriot, inadvertently published in the *Mercure de France*, the adjective "atrocious" was used to characterize Calvin's execution of Servetus. Voltaire denied his use of the word, but like Galileo in the cathedral he secretly maintained that the action was none the less atrocious. Strangely enough, his former friend Jacob Vernet, who now turned against him, agreed with him at heart but did not believe in expressing his opinion in the same terms. At first intimidated and genuinely grieved by the loss of Vernet's friendship, Voltaire yielded finally to his destiny, accepted the fight, and waged it as usual with such vigor that he was believed, again without proof, to have resorted to unscrupulous methods. The quarrel with the Swiss clergy gradually subsided. There was, after all, too much in common between them and this crusader who was soon to rehabilitate the Calas and Sirven families, persecuted because of their Protestantism, and to make of the Ferney colony a living example of his theories of tolerance and humanity. Their admiration, early mixed with anger, was finally purified, and it was one of their number who wrote to him: "I only wish you were as good a Christian as you deserve to be." Many of the best Christians in Geneva expressed their wonder whether in the presence of the Sovereign Judge their faith would balance the works of this impious man.

VOLTAIRE AND ROUSSEAU

The struggle with Rousseau over the theater was a long and complicated affair. "It's against me that he bears a grudge," wrote Voltaire, "that's as clear as day. Possessed of extravagant pride, he would like to be the only one spoken of in his native country." This opinion was justified by Rousseau's letter of June 17, 1760, in which he wrote to Voltaire:

I don't like you, sir; you have hurt me, your disciple and enthusiast, in things which were the nearest to my heart. You have ruined Geneva in payment for the retreat that you accepted there; you have alienated from me the affections of fellow citizens in payment for the applause that I have lavishly given you among them. You are the one who will force me to die in a foreign land, deprived of the consolations of the dying, and to be thrown, not otherwise honored, on the dump, while all the honors that a man can expect will attend you in my native land. I hate you, then, since you have so desired; but I hate you as a man still more worthy of loving you if you had so desired.

It is difficult to find a logical interpretation of Rousseau's rage on any other grounds than those alleged by Voltaire. In 1755, in a letter to the author, Voltaire had half-mockingly, half-seriously replied to Rousseau's two discourses: on the corruption of morals brought about by progress in the arts and sciences and on the social and economic origins of inequality. He did not attempt to answer the general question of the effects of intellectual progress on morals and happiness; he had himself proposed the question, admitted the paradox, and accepted as a fact borne out by experience the superiority of the intellectual life and its pleasures. His belief in the benefits of human progress contrasted with Rousseau's nostalgia for a more primitive state of society is no more effectively stated than in the first paragraph of this letter:

I have received, sir, your new book against the human race; I thank you for it. You will please men, to whom you frankly tell their faults, but you will not correct them. It is impossible to paint in bolder colors the horrors of human society, from which our ignorance and weakness lead us to expect so much consolation. Never has anyone employed so much wit in trying to make us witless; the reading of your book makes us want to creep on all fours. However, as it is now more than sixty years since I lost that habit, I feel unfortunately that it is impossible for me to take it up again, and I leave that natural attitude to those who are more worthy of it than you and I. Neither can I embark to go and live with the savages of Canada: first, because the ailments with which I am afflicted retain me by the side of the greatest doctor of Europe and I could not find the same attentions among the Missouri Indians; secondly, because war has been carried into those countries, and the example of our civilized peoples has made the savages almost as wicked as we. I content myself with being a peaceful savage in the solitude that I have chosen near your native land, where you ought to be.

At the end of the letter, Voltaire added:

M. Chappuis informs me that your health is very bad; you should come and recover it here under your native skies, enjoy liberty, drink with me the milk of our cows, and browse our grasses. I am very philosophically, and with the greatest esteem. . . .

Rousseau was notoriously lacking in a sense of humor; he took himself and his world with all the seriousness of an adolescent acolyte. But most temperaments require comic relaxation for the preservation of sanity. The classic principle of balance again clashes with romantic excess. It is to be wondered whether Rousseau completely grasped at first the mordant irony of Voltaire's letter. In 1755 he consented to its publication; in 1756 he showed himself piqued, for in a letter to Voltaire he said he would not, of course, say that his Lisbon poem was written against Providence, as Voltaire had charged that his own discourse was written against the human race. Four years later he was stung to the quick by the remembrance of Voltaire's taunts to the effect that as apostle of the simple life and opponent of the literary arts he should not be seeking in the salons of Paris a literary reputation but rather should be regaining his health and enjoying the bucolic pleasures of his native land. Yet, partially accepting the challenge, he had meanwhile abandoned Paris and had sought refuge in the Hermitage and in the not-too-solitary fastnesses of the forest of Montmorency. There he had written his most substantial works, of which he was justly proud; already by 1760 he was well-established as an author and a philosopher and could meet Voltaire on more even terms—could even enjoy the luxury of telling this man that he hated him, because he was poisoning his native land for him.

Much more had happened during these five years, however, than Rousseau's acquisition and control of his literary genius. For this was not merely a personal quarrel between two distinguished authors; it involved some of the most important distinctions in eighteenth-century thought; it was an intellectual and a party quarrel, intimately connected on the one hand with the struggle of the philosophic group against the oppressions of authority and tradition, and on the other, with the battle between the growing romantic and the declining classical conceptions of literature and life. These were critical years in intellectual and political France, and a review of their principal events, in so far as they concern Voltaire, will serve as an excellent case history in the study of his philosophical position as well as of his theory of friendship and his abundant capacity for making both friends and enemies.

Of foremost importance is the intensity of the battle of the Church and State against the *Encyclo-pédie*, the spirit of authority against the scientific method of trial and error through experimentation. Voltaire early saw that the philosophers must band together for mutual protection. Montesquieu remarked that Voltaire, like any other monk, worked for his monastery. The remark is profoundly just, except for its connotations: "monk" is hardly the word to use in describing a fighter whose principles are founded in reason and nature, nor does monastery fittingly describe the cosmopolitan field of his activities. In 1757 Rousseau broke with the Encyclopedists, with Grimm, Mme d'Épinay, D'Holbach, and especially with his formerly close friend Diderot. The more personal causes of the break are as usual the least known. On the intellectual side Rousseau revolted against his friends' materialism and revolted chiefly because their arguments did not satisfy him emotionally. Sick in body and in soul, he found in them none of the consolations of which he was so desperately in need. He could find no answer to their arguments against the goodness and providence of God and against His very existence; these things, however, he felt with all his heart, and so he abandoned the rational method and its defenders. "I feel that God exists," he exclaimed in one of the salons of the period, "and will leave the room if you say another word against Him."

This emotional act of faith and its subsequent explanation in his addition to *Emile*, *La Profession de foi du vicaire savoyard*, was one of the most significant events in French religious history. The rationalism of St. Thomas Aquinas was very different from Voltaire's rationalism; the one appealed to the reason only after the acceptance on authority of traditional axioms and absolutes; the other appealed to reason itself as a final, if relative and often uncertain, authority. Rousseau's revolt was more radical, for he attempted to appeal from reason to the emotions. Christian apologists in the nineteenth century, from Chateaubriand on, eagerly welcomed this escape from reason's oppression.

Now Voltaire was not himself a thoroughgoing materialist. There was also a good bit of intuition, of "common sense," in his conception of reason. In his more doctrinal works, such as the *Poème sur la loi naturelle*, he had spoken of conscience, of instinctive remorse and sense of justice, in ways that Frederick II and his sister Wilhelmina, schooled in La Mettrie's philosophy, had been unable to follow. Certain parts, too, of *La Profession de foi du vicaire savoyard* Voltaire liked very much, and he published them time and again. Rousseau's attack on scriptural authority was more daring and more complete than anything that Voltaire himself had been bold enough to print, until he published his *Extrait des sentiments de Jean Meslier*, earlier in the same year. For purposes of propaganda such works as Rousseau's *Profession de foi* were very useful in freeing mankind from the oppression of theological and political authority; whereas, as he himself often repeated, Diderot's atheism could never render any service to humanity. But that after such a rationalistic attack on authority it was necessary, as Rousseau maintained, to accept traditional Christianity on emotional grounds or as a civic duty Voltaire would not of course admit. One is nevertheless obliged to look elsewhere to discover why he so vituperated Rousseau and so cherished Diderot. The answer is that Diderot was an indefatigable worker in the cause of enlightenment and thereby gained, in the face of many a trial, Voltaire's undying loyalty; while Rousseau abandoned and split the party and refused to play the game according to the rules.

Voltaire's epithets against Rousseau have often been collected and repeated, but it has not so often been pointed out that they were inspired much less by differences in thought than by questions of party loyalty. "Oh, how we should have cherished this madman," wrote Voltaire to his Parisian agent, Damilaville, "if he had not been a false brother"; and when Rousseau was persecuted for attacks on religious authority, Voltaire wrote: "He has ever been persecuted for opinions that are my own." But later, after renewed unpleasantness, he stated that "the infamous Jean Jacques is the Judas of the brotherhood."

Any man should, of course, be able to change his mind and his party. This change of Rousseau's was not sudden, for as early as 1750, in his first *Discourse*, he had spoken disparagingly of the philosophers. His reaction was caused by such "personal enemies of God" as D'Holbach, whose principles Voltaire himself could hardly condone, rather than by Diderot. Nevertheless, Diderot must have long been aware of his approaching apostasy. There is evidently more here than a mere change of mind; Diderot and Voltaire believed, whether justly or not, that there had been a real betrayal of friendship—possibly they knew of some act which has not been divulged to posterity. Several of Voltaire's special grievances are, however, well enough known. In a letter to the Abbé Morellet, he stated one of the principles that governed the group of philosophers: "The philosophers must always maintain that every philosopher who is still living is a good Christian and a good Catholic": "like Ninon de Lenclos," he added in a similar letter of warning to Palissot, "who did not think that any woman should be called a whore." As late as 1766, when the Chevalier de la Barre execution proved that the Inquisition was not dead, it was still dangerous to charge a fellow countryman with heresy. It was especially deplorable when a once-intimate member of the group revealed secrets which endangered the very life of one of his former friends. It was a betrayal of this nature that finally exasperated Voltaire.

In reply to the *Poème sur le désastre de Lisbonne*, which Voltaire had sent, through Thieriot, to Rousseau as one of his philosophic friends, the latter wrote a long letter in which he took exception to the main arguments of the poem. Voltaire, in a state of despondency over the terrible disaster, had painted in vivid colors the sufferings of its victims and had questioned not only the philosophical optimism of Leibnitz and Pope but also the general view that the universe is benevolent. Rousseau, then, who preferred to sacrifice God's omnipotence to his goodness, accused Voltaire of writing against Providence. The charge was true, and Voltaire admitted as much in the sprightly dialogue of his dictionary article on Providence. Sister Fessue might have prayed for her sparrow, and the sparrow, by a happy coincidence, might have regained its health; but since his school days Voltaire had denied both particular revelation and the value of intercessory prayer. "I believe," said the imaginary metaphysician whom Sister Fessue had charged with heresy, "in a general Providence, my dear sister, from which has emanated through all eternity the law that governs everything, just as light springs forth from the sun; but I do not believe that a particular Providence changes the economy of the world for your sparrow or your cat."

Voltaire's best works, as the late Frances Newman remarked, faced two ways. The Lisbon poem is no exception. In one way he was defending the orthodox doctrine of original sin and redemption against a philosophical system which regarded evil as necessary from the beginning and in the nature of things and beyond man's power, as it should be against his will, to change. He considered the theological explanation of evil to be psychologically more acceptable than the philosophical; but he differed with the theologians over the nature of redemption, for he shared the growing belief, early popularized by Fontenelle, in progress through human reason. In pessimistic moments, even this hope was dimmed. Certain of Voltaire's Swiss friends, Cramer, Tronchin, and the pastor Bertrand, had already protested against the hopeless spirit of the poem. So Voltaire revised the ending and added hope, thinking that he was arguing in very Christian fashion. Bertrand and Rousseau, however, were thinking of hope in a Christian sense, of redemption in a future life after the passage through this vale of tears. This was Voltaire's real dilemma: in his poem he preached resignation and adoration of the Supreme Being, but he hesitated to subscribe to the doctrine of immortality. He was, then, none too happy to have Rousseau emphasize his unorthodox views of hope and combat them with the more consoling doctrine of a future state of blessedness. "I have suffered too much in this life not to expect another," wrote Rousseau in characteristic fashion at the end of his letter; "all the subtleties of metaphysics will not make me doubt for a moment the immortality of the soul and a beneficent Providence. I feel it, I believe it, I wish it, I hope it, I will defend it until my last breath; and this will be, of all the disputes I have upheld, the only

one in which my own interest will not be forgotten." There is little evidence here either of rationalism or of intellectual receptivity. Moreover, Rousseau was not entirely self-inspired, as he asserted,
in writing this long rebuttal. The parties in Geneva
were already choosing their champions; a certain
pastor Roustan had urged Rousseau to reply and
had singled out for special attack a passage beginning:"When death caps the ills that I have suffered,
how splendidly consoling to be eaten by worms!"
Rousseau was thus already serving the ends of people who would have liked to make life miserable
for Voltaire and who succeeded three years later in
having his poem officially burned.

Several other arguments in Rousseau's long letter
explain the characteristic differences between the
philosophies of the two men. He defended the goodness of God and held man solely responsible not
only for moral but also for physical evil. For example, it could not be proved that the violent death
of thousands of victims at Lisbon had not saved
them from lingering ills to come, and moreover, if
men had not been foolish enough to build themselves cities, if they had been content to stay in the
woods like the savages, the earthquake would not
have injured them. He was indignant, too, that
Voltaire, enjoying all the goods of this world,
should take it upon himself to pity the sufferings
of those unfortunate mortals, while he himself,
"an obscure man, poor, and tormented by an incurable malady," found that "all was well." "You

enjoy life," he wrote, "but I hope, and hope embellishes everything." Knowing "Voltaire's irritable pride," he sent the letter first to their mutual friend Tronchin for approval. He had no immediate cause, however, to fear Voltaire's wrath. The latter was too busy writing a tragedy and a general history to carry on the discussion, or he may have felt that the argument could only lead him into deeper waters. He carefully read the long letter, a copy of which is still among his papers at Leningrad, but wrote only a polite note of thanks for Rousseau's attentions. Two years later he replied, in a very safe and impersonal way, under the veil of the fiction of *Candide*. Rousseau admired his patience: "A man who could take my letter as he has done," he wrote to Tronchin, "deserves the title of philosopher, and one could not be more inclined than I am to join to the admiration I have always felt for his works both esteem and friendship for his person."

Two years after the Lisbon episode, Rousseau received a letter full of indignation from Pastor Jacob Vernes, who was forced to break with Voltaire over the charge of Socinianism against the Swiss clergy in the article "Genève" of the *Encyclopédie*. It was not this charge, however, that aroused Rousseau's virtuous indignation, but the paragraph inserted, either at Voltaire's instigation or to please him, in behalf of the establishment of a theater at Geneva. In the white heat of his enthusiasm and with the eloquence of genius, Rousseau wrote his celebrated *Lettre à d'Alembert sur les spectacles*. The letter voiced all the narrow moralism, all the Puritanism of his ardent soul; and in it art was ever confused with artifice and artifice was considered the devil's own handiwork. Voltaire was, to be sure, cajoled, but Rousseau condemned as immoral all plays, even the best of Racine and Molière, and all persons who were in any way connected with their presentation. This was indeed a bitter pill for a former pupil of the Jesuits, lover of all the classic arts, and especially for the dramatist, whose plays suffered chiefly from his own burning desire to moralize and who had the fond ambition of adding a few civilizing touches to the unpolished but honest Calvinists of Geneva. Moreover, on the Genevan battleground Rousseau's book had won the gratitude of those people, who, as Pastor Sarasin expressed it, "could think wholesomely and who were not given over to the love of frivolity and pleasure."

Enough has been reviewed already to explain the essential contrasts between these two men: one was morally "pagan" or epicurean, the other puritanical; one was artistically classical, the other, in theory at least, as he himself confessed, "Gothic and monastic." One, while not neglecting the passions, was willing to give the last word to reason, to the intellect, to the experimental method; the other adopted the emotions and the conscience as infallible guides, to which reason should serve submissively as handmaiden. Moreover, one was in the thick of the hotly-waged battle for freedom of thought and publication; the other, from his solitary mountain, presumed to play the rôle of prophet and mediator. "Rousseau writes only for the sake of writing," said Voltaire, "while I write in order to act." He could not foresee that Rousseau's works were to affect more radically and more immediately than his own the future history of France; but there is much truth in his statement. Already, too, the exchange of works and letters of those early years had proved to Voltaire that Rousseau was on the side of the enemy, of such men as Roustan, whose religious zeal was ever tracking him down, and Formey, who had finally refused his offers of friendship and was to be the first to publish Rousseau's letter on Lisbon. Yet Voltaire never sought new enemies and forbore to attack Rousseau on such slight provocation. Even the impertinent letter of hatred was not enough to arouse him to action; it merely added its store of pressure, awaiting the inevitable outburst.

The first break came in 1761 and was very definitely caused by the problem of the theater and by a question of conduct rather than by a disagreement concerning ideas. By 1759, Voltaire had acquired two pieces of property in French territory near the Genevan border. At Ferney he was to set up his main residence for the remaining years of his life, while at the little theater at Tournay he could indulge his passion for drama without infringing upon the laws of the neighboring state. Private theatricals were the favorite pastime of eighteenth-century society. Even in Genevan territory, at *les*

Délices, the Duke of Villars played his rôles, along
with the heroine, Mme Denis, Voltaire's plump
middle-aged niece, and as audience there came the
best society of Geneva to weep over Zaïre, forgetful
of the prohibitions of the City Consistory. While
the people of Geneva were thus being "civilized"
and the passion for the drama was rapidly spreading, denunciations of Voltaire and his theater continued to be presented to the Magnificent Council.
Custom was stronger than law, however, and the
council, its authority already diminishing, preferred to refer the matter to the clergy.

Voltaire was too busy attempting to crush Diderot's enemies and his own, such devotees of infamous
Mammon as Fréron and Lefranc de Pompignan,
who were on the side of authority and suppression, to give much thought to Rousseau. But
the latter meanwhile was nursing his hatred, which
was as yet unmotivated except by envy or jealousy,
unless we believe that his feverish imagination
truly pictured a Geneva poisoned because a few of
its notable citizens were attending Voltaire's plays.
He continued, however, to spread his hatred over
the pages of his letters to his Genevan correspondents. Often invited to return to his native city, even
by Voltaire, who feared misunderstandings at a
distance much more than he feared intimate personal relationships, he refused to come, and always
for the same reasons. "What would become of me,"
he wrote in 1759 to Jacob Vernes, "in your midst,
now that you have a master of witticism who in-

structs you so well?" And to Moultou, in 1760:"You speak to me of Voltaire? Why does the name of that buffoon soil your letters? The wretch has ruined my country; I would hate him more if I despised him less"; and the letter ends with a general warning to the people of Geneva that they will be "the last victims of this viper to whom they so generously offered an asylum." Voltaire was well informed of Rousseau's continuous efforts to stir up Geneva against him, but refused again to become excited. Even after Rousseau's letter of hate, he had simply written to Thieriot: "I have received a big letter from Jean Jacques Rousseau; he has gone completely mad; that's a pity." He long continued to hope against hope that Rousseau would be saved for philosophy.

The appearance of *Julie, ou la Nouvelle Héloïse* and the subsequent enthusiasm among aristocrats tired of their boredom were not calculated to please Voltaire. He could not have liked this half-erotic, half-moralizing novel in six volumes even if Rousseau had been his dearest friend. The lyrical language was as foreign to him as it was to most of his contemporaries; he was nevertheless moved at times by Rousseau's indisputable eloquence, especially on the subject of suicide. As a rule, he disliked novels, considering them frivolous, and made exceptions only for the short oriental tale provided with a philosophical background. At just this time, too, he was becoming more and more irritated by Rousseau's support of the movement against the theater, as we may judge by his letter to Damilaville:

Now Jean Jacques has entered the political field; we will see if he governs Europe as he has governed M. de Wolmar's house. He is a strange fool. He wrote me a year ago: "You have corrupted the city of Geneva, in payment for the retreat that was given you." The poor bastard of Diogenes wanted then to get himself a reputation among his compatriots by decrying theatricals; and in his false enthusiasm, he imagined that I was living at Geneva, I who have not spent two nights there for five years. He has the insolence to tell me that I have a refuge at Geneva, I who have for vassals several of the magistrates of his republic, among whom there is not one who does not consider him a madman. He offends me in all willfullness, me who had offered him not a refuge but my house, where he would have lived like my brother.

Voltaire was very touchy on the question of his supposed exile, which was, indeed, virtual but not official. After a year's time, he still remembered the sting and for this reason excused to his Parisian friends the severe criticisms that he published on *Julie*, under the name of the Marquis de Ximénès. There can be no doubt that Voltaire offered Rousseau a home and that he long hoped they could live together in peace. But Rousseau had broken with all his most intimate friends—with Diderot, with Grimm, whom he now called "a German named Grimm," and then with the doctor, Tronchin, breaks for which the motives are still not entirely clear.

D'Alembert was especially disturbed at the signs of open hostility between the two men.

Rousseau [he wrote to Voltaire] thinks he is a cynic

[it was D'Alembert himself who seems to have been the first to apply to him the term Diogenes], while he is only inconsistent and ridiculous. Suppose he did write you an impertinent letter, suppose you and your friends do have just cause for complaint; in spite of all that, I do not approve that you declare yourself publicly against him as you are doing, and I have only to repeat your own words: "What will become of the little flock, if it is disunited and dispersed?" . . . Jean Jacques is a sick man who has a great deal of talent, and who has talent only when he has a fever. We should neither cure him nor insult him.

D'Alembert showed here and in other letters a great deal of insight into the characters of the two men. Voltaire would not forgive, however; he declared that he was willing to get himself burned at the stake if the true philosophers would form a society in all loyalty, forget themselves, and turn their attention to crushing "infamy"; that he would even forgive Rousseau's inconsistence and his impertinence; but that he could never forgive him for stirring up the clergy and the Genevan populace against his theater at Tournay.

Again, however, Voltaire restrained his pen, and Rousseau was almost forgotten in the welter of new interests, new publications, new projects. Early in 1762 Voltaire published his *Extrait des sentiments de Jean Meslier*, his first concentrated attack on Christianity, a brief work derived from a long manuscript left by the Curé Meslier on his death in 1729, in which the country curate asked pardon for preaching all his life what he considered an absurd, intolerant, and oppressive religion. Voltaire thus began in all earnest the battle against "infamous superstition" and the infamous spirit of religious persecution. In May of the same year he was extremely busy with the Calas affair, which was to bring him lasting fame as well as the admiration of his contemporaries, and with the *Traité sur la tolérance*, inspired by this atrocious miscarriage of justice. Meanwhile Rousseau's *Contrat social* and *Emile* had been published under the author's name, and real persecution was his expected and desired reward. There is no proof whatsoever that Voltaire had a hand in this persecution. Rousseau and those friends who trusted in his word were solely responsible for spreading the report. The correspondence proves, on the contrary, that Voltaire was preoccupied with other things, that even the theater and its worries were forgotten as he set himself to the main task of his life, the "crushing of the infamous thing," and that Rousseau had again been put out of mind. Finally, in May of the same year, he wrote to Moultou: "I await impatiently Rousseau's letter to the Archbishop of Paris. But I am very much afraid it will prejudice the cause of reason. I have been extremely afflicted by your friend's inconsistencies. I should have liked him to be my friend. Why has he broken so wantonly with all of his?"

A month later, Voltaire had read *Emile* and the *Contrat social*. Meanwhile Rousseau had been condemned both at Paris and Geneva, his books had been burned, and his arrest was decreed. The idea that Voltaire had any part in this persecution is of the utmost absurdity. On the fifteenth of June he wrote to Damilaville:

Jean Jacques' books have been forbidden at Geneva. I don't know what has been done with them at Paris. I have had his *Education* [*Emile*]. It is a hodgepodge of a silly wet nurse in four volumes, with forty pages against Christianity, of the boldest that have ever been written; and by an inconsistency unworthy of that brainless pate and heartless Diogenes, he says as many injurious things to the philosophers as to Jesus Christ; but the philosophers will be more indulgent than the priests.

Admiration and regret, rather than hatred, pierce through the general tone of contempt. Ten days later he believed he was better informed:

The *Contrat social* has been burned at Geneva on the same pyre as the insipid novel *Emile;* and Jean Jacques has been condemned to arrest as at Paris. This *Contrat social*, or unsocial contract, is remarkable only for a few insults coarsely said to kings by the citizen of the town of Geneva and for four dull pages against the Christian religion. These four pages are nothing but clippings from Bayle. It was not worth the trouble of plagiarizing. The proud Jean Jacques is at Amsterdam, where a cargo of pepper is more highly esteemed than his paradoxes.

There is a definite tone of regret in the following lines addressed to D'Argental: "If he had been content to attack 'infamy,' he would have found defenders everywhere, for 'infamy' is being well decried. . . . Happily for him, his little body is difficult to catch. He is, they say, at Amsterdam. I'm sorry for all that. Ah! what will become of philosophy!" He wrote shortly afterward: "Rousseau is punished for the only things that are well written in his bad books." He rejoiced that Rousseau had dared to say what all honest people believe; "but the wretch is only the more blameworthy for insulting his friends and his benefactors. His conduct puts philosophy to shame." Similar sentiments are expressed in passages from later letters: "I will die of sorrow for having seen philosophy betrayed by philosophers and by men who were capable of enlightening the world, if they had been united. But in spite of Judas's betrayal, the apostles persevered."

From now on, indeed, Voltaire worked with all the zeal and faith of the early Christians to crush religious persecution and superstition. The *Sermon des cinquante* followed the extracts from Meslier, and the *Dictionnaire philosophique* was being printed that same year. The main goal was the suppression of persecution and the means were countless treatises which attempted to discredit the historical, theological, and moral foundations of the Christian religion. For the attack he collected and consulted the most scholarly sources, the Church Fathers, St. Thomas Aquinas, Dom Calmet's *Commentaires sur la Bible*—works in Latin and in English as well as in French. He wrote tirelessly himself and kept the presses working even more tirelessly with the printing of manuscripts and the reprinting of tracts which could in any way serve his purpose. "Theology amuses me," he wrote, "for the folly of the human mind is therein contained in all its fullness."

He signed himself "Christmock," and urged Helvétius to join the band of five or six honest men, well united, fully determined to support the side of reason, in this extraordinary effort of propaganda. Rousseau, then, could again be forgotten if not forgiven, and would be spared until he seriously handicapped or endangered the party.

But the next incident restored Voltaire's hopes. The boldness of Rousseau's reply to Christophe de Beaumont, Archbishop of Paris, filled him with delight. Jean Jacques was again counted among the philosophers; "He is Diogenes, but he expresses himself at times like Plato," "He is the greatest little madman in the world," and "There are charming things in the *Lettre à Christophe*." If he had been well-behaved, he would have entered the French Academy; true, he "speaks a bit too much of himself," but "he swears he is a Christian, and makes our holy religion as ridiculous as could be imagined." There was, too, a little word on Omer Joly de Fleury, Voltaire's chief persecutor: "He suspects Omer of being an ass, but that's just a passing remark: Christophe and Christ are his chief aversions." Voltaire regretted the burning of Rousseau's book at Geneva, for it was a check to the remarkable progress of philosophy; he understood, however, that it was "a party affair in the tiny republic," and that the ruling class, prodded by the dominating influence of France, could hardly have done otherwise. His secret sympathies, later to be actively expressed, were on the side of the

dominated "inhabitants" and "natives" whose
political and commercial freedom suffered greatly
in comparison with that of the "citizens" or
"burghers."

While Voltaire was thus expressing admiration
and pity for the hounded Rousseau, the latter's
persecution mania was at work fabricating the
legend that the philosopher of Ferney, enraged with
jealousy, had been the cause of his principal disasters. Chronology is extremely important here. From
the summer of 1763 to that of 1764, Voltaire forgot
Rousseau in the struggle for justice for the Calas
family and in the feverish preparation and publication of treatises against religion and its persecutions. His drama *Saül*, a rollicking satire on the
lechery and treachery of King David, was maliciously published under his name, in violation of the
tacit understanding between him and both Paris
and Geneva that impious works, if anonymous,
would be publicly burned, but their author would
not be molested. He was therefore forced to deny
repeatedly the authorship of this satire. Rousseau's
experience was there to prove how easily his tranquillity might be destroyed. "I'm very willing,"
he wrote, "to be a confessor, but not to be a martyr."
He was busy, too, with the writing of his *Philosophie de l'histoire* and with the publication of his
Dictionnaire philosophique. The latter work was
burned at Paris and Geneva, and the author's ability
to deceive the authorities was worked to the limit.
In the midst of such activities, he suddenly learned,

in June, 1764, that Paris was convinced that he had been Rousseau's chief persecutor. One of the sources of this news was his old correspondent, Mme du Deffand, friend of the Duchesse de Luxembourg, who had been Rousseau's most ardent admirer and protector. His letter of justification is sincere and only occasionally inaccurate. Therein he reviews the entire relationship, Rousseau's frank avowal of hatred, and his charge that Voltaire had corrupted Geneva in return for the refuge that had been offered him.

In a word, [he replied] I don't understand on what pretext Rousseau could write me such a letter. He doubtless felt he had offended me, and he believed that I would seek revenge; but that shows how little he knows me. . . . He writes to the Duchesse de Luxembourg that I have declared myself his most mortal enemy; he sets down in print that I am the most violent and adroit of his persecutors. I, a persecutor! then Jack Rabbit is a thundercloud of war. I, a little Father Le Tellier! what madness! Seriously, I don't think you can insult a man more atrociously than by calling him a persecutor. If ever I have spoken of Rousseau other than to give a very favorable meaning to his *Savoyard Vicar*, for which he was condemned, I'm willing to be considered the wickedest of men. I never even desired to read a single one of the writings against him, in that cruel circumstance in which one should respect his misfortune and esteem his genius. . . . I am so deeply moved that I can write you this time on no other subject.

Voltaire chose to forget his remarks on *Julie*, published under the name of Ximénès; but that outburst of literary criticism is hardly of major consideration. That Voltaire was genuinely shocked and grieved at the charge of persecution and that these emotions were already bordering on righteous indignation is evident. And he still hoped against hope that Rousseau would return to the flock: "Ah! if I were only supported!," he wrote to Damilaville a week later, on the subject of the distribution of his anti-religious pamphlets; "but the brothers are lukewarm, the brothers are not united: the wretched Rousseau is faithful only to his caprice and his pride. He was assuredly the most capable of rendering great services; but God has forsaken him." For a few weeks he still protested and fumed against the infamous charge of persecution. But the spark was still lacking: the explosion was delayed until December of that same year.

Voltaire's situation that winter was extremely delicate. He was publishing works against "infamy" under the very noses of Geneva's burghers; they were having his *Dictionnaire philosophique* burned publicly in Geneva and were at the same time toasting themselves in sociable fashion by the author's fire at Ferney. The one connection that neither party wished to see made was that between impious work and friendly host. Voltaire, moreover, with both the Calas and Sirven defenses on his hands, was admired as the champion of religious freedom and the defender of Protestants in Catholic France. Political tension likewise added to the delicacy of the situation. The citizens of Geneva formed a relatively small and closed class; they alone could vote, hold political office, and engage in commerce; outside this class were the "subjects," or peasants, the "inhabitants" or aliens, and the "natives" or children of aliens, who alone numbered three-quarters of the population. The Republic of Geneva was therefore very definitely a political aristocracy, and it was little wonder that the unenfranchised inhabitants should hail Rousseau, with his democratic principles, as champion. Voltaire, with friends on the council, or almost exclusively among the "citizen class," was considered the opposing champion, and was reluctantly pressed into service—reluctant, because he had always disliked the domineering spirit of governing bodies, because he saw the justice of the cause of the sturdy workers upon whom Geneva's prosperity depended and for whom he later sacrificed his aristocratic friendships.

In November, 1764, then, appeared the *Lettres écrites de la campagne*, by Tronchin, attorney general of the Council of Two Hundred, pronouncing, in reasoned and moderate language, the legality of the decree against *Emile* and the *Contrat social*. Rousseau was urgently requested by the opposing party to reply, and he immediately did so with his *Lettres écrites de la montagne*. These letters resembled, indeed, in their emotional eloquence and turgidity, those mountain torrents whose beauties Rousseau was the first in his century to sing; neither reason nor moderation could withstand the flow of his rhetoric. It was his last and most effective skirmish. Thereafter he retired within himself, like a wounded conqueror, and left the field of battle to his adherents, the "petitioners," to the opposing camp of "negatives," and to their ever watchful neighbor at Ferney. His early unreasoned craving to be whipped had led him to seek and enjoy contempt and persecution; he had lost most of his friends and now he lost completely the respect of Geneva's foremost "citizens." The "natives" continued in vain to enlist his support; but he had seen fit to attack Christian miracles in the course of his effusions and had thus alienated many of the more liberal pastors who had been sympathetic with the democratic movement. He had also seen fit to attack Voltaire. Why, he asked, did the people of Geneva suppress such reasoned books as his own and leave unpunished books full of mockery, contempt, coarse impieties, and blasphemies against religion? The answer was, of course, simple, and Rousseau knew it—Voltaire had merely refrained from signing his name to his irreligious pamphlets.

Then Rosseau committed the unpardonable sin— the act that Voltaire feared more than any other— he proceeded to assign Voltaire's name to these anonymous works, especially to the audacious *Sermon des cinquante*. Now it was extremely important to Voltaire that these works should appear anonymously. In a moment of human weakness he had confessed, thirty years before and juridically, the authorship of the *Lettres philosophiques*, and that confession was still hanging over his head. It was the one most serious legal weapon by which the whole tranquillity of his life was threatened. In comparison with this new betrayal, then, it mattered little that Rousseau charged him again with intolerance and persecution and insinuated that he was an atheist. The spark had finally reached the powder, and Voltaire exploded with all the rancor and malignity of which his impassioned nature was capable. An unjust attack resulted, an attack which was contrary to all his own most cherished principles and which justified then and only then, after so many years of patience, hope, and restraint, the very charge of persecution and intolerance which had occasioned it.

The authorship of the *Sentiment des citoyens* has long been disputed. Voltaire's secretary, Wagnière, did not hesitate, in 1790, to attribute it to his master. The internal evidence of the correspondence is also convincing, for Voltaire was long thereafter attempting to justify his persecution of Rousseau to D'Alembert and other intimate friends who were in a position to know the facts. There is still much that is obscure about the pamphlet; Voltaire had collaborators, and may have contributed merely his pen and his biting style. For a long time Rousseau thought that Jacob Vernes was the author, for Vernes knew the story of his five abandoned children. It was this charge that cut Rousseau to the quick. He denied it in his printed notes to the work, doubtless on the technicality that his mistress, Thérèse Levasseur, had abandoned the children, not he; but later he eased his conscience in his *Confessions*. There were medical data, too, in the treatise, which were very probably supplied by Doctor Tronchin, Rousseau's former friend and counselor, and which were not so far removed from the truth as might at first be believed. Professional secrecy should, of course, have been observed in such delicate matters. It is, I believe, generally admitted that Rousseau was the victim of a persecution mania, induced by organic disturbances which he claimed were hereditary, but which could be more easily and maliciously charged to youthful excesses. The divulging of these most intimate secrets was, to say the least, unkind. It revealed, as does also the correspondence of the period, the rage of the Genevan "citizens," as well as the extent of Voltaire's irascibility, once it had broken through the barriers of restraint. Some of the charges were certainly false; it is not so sure that Voltaire, spurred on by his friends as Rousseau had been spurred on by his, knew they were false. It might even be argued that he was here writing the opinions of the citizens, not his own, just as Rousseau intimated that the *Profession de foi du vicaire savoyard* could not have been his own, as the vicar was a Roman Catholic. But Voltaire should not have lent even the tip of his pen to such intolerant statements, for example, as the following.:

A fool is to be pitied; but when insanity becomes fury, it must be bound. Tolerance, which is virtue, would then be a vice. . . . But madness which blasphemes to this degree can have no other doctor than the same hand that brought to justice his other scandals. . . . After insulting Christ, it is not surprising that he outrages the ministers of his holy gospel. . . . But he must learn that if an impious novelist is lightly chastised, a vile fomenter of sedition is capitally punished.

Voltaire's personal spite cropped out in a paragraph defending himself from the charge of atheism; his anger and fear occasioned by the charge that he had written the *Sermon des cinquante* were likewise revealed in his letters. At the height of his passionate anger, he believed in two teeth for a tooth; and when he put in writing the opinion that blasphemy should be punished by the courts, he was treading on very dangerous ground.

DUPLICITY AND PROTECTIVE LYING

With regard to the party, Voltaire thought that Rousseau's charges might ruin the whole campaign for enlightenment. In the same letter in which he announced Rousseau's attack to Damilaville, he told of police activities in Paris: "Omer is working on a requisition for the *Dictionnaire philosophique*. People continue to attribute that work to me who have no part in it. I think my nephew, who is a councilor in parliament, will prevent him from designating me." Such designation, he said, "would take from me the freedom of being useful." For he considered this dictionary his most useful project. He had been working on it since 1752, when he submitted the first articles to Frederick II, the original sponsor. It was packed both with scholarly criticism and mocking ridicule of what he considered the absurdities of Christian theology and tradition and was permeated throughout with his guiding principle, the "crushing of infamy" in behalf of tolerance.

To add to his discomfiture at this critical moment, a pirated edition of his works was printed abroad by Rousseau's publisher, so he thought, and his name had treacherously been put on the volumes. The time and energy he spent in denying his own works was prodigious. He was a constant double dealer, he lied and believed in lying that he might live to lie again another day. In this way alone, he believed, he could be useful and work for humanity. It was not only his best works that faced two ways, through his skillful use of irony and innuendo, but also the very method of his attack. Nothing appeared to him so foolhardy as Rousseau's insistence upon signing his works. Much earlier in the century Montesquieu was admitted to the French Academy on his reputation for the very bold *Lettres persanes*, which had been published anonymously and which could not be officially mentioned as his. Rousseau's foolhardiness, in Voltaire's eyes, was exemplified by the effectiveness with which he was silenced after the various condemnations of his books and his person. Diderot, with a still different method, kept his most original works in manuscript and left them to posterity. Such policies would not do for such an active fighter as Voltaire, who lived and wrote most intensely in the present. Censorship, repression, and religious persecution are not, of course, keenly felt by people whose ideas are traditional; to men like Voltaire, with radical and reforming ideas, they were forces which had to be met in very practical ways. The absolute moralists will ever condemn him as a liar and a hypocrite, on the principle that the end never justifies the means. The relativists reply that it is again a question of what end and what means, that in our feeble attempts to weigh human values we cannot be dogmatic, that the smashing of the political and persecuting power of religion was Voltaire's greatest gift to humanity, and that it was far better for the world that he should lie and live.

His violent outbursts against his enemies were often entirely contrary to his most cherished principles; his lying and hypocrisy, on the contrary, constituted an accepted systematic, reasoned method. The necessity of such duplicity was early impressed upon him by his many exiles and flights from justice, by two sojourns in the Bastille, and by the bitter enmities he had made in the opposing camp. Threatened with a *lettre de cachet* and imprisonment (at least) for his *Lettres philosophiques*, he denied roundly that he had France or the French in mind when he wrote these intimate letters from England to his friend Thieriot. As a matter of fact these letters on the English nation have no point or value unless they are read with reference to France and her needed reforms, and they were written for the most part with that sole end in view three to four years after Voltaire's return to France.

The issue of hypocrisy was squarely met, too, when Voltaire was a candidate (for many years unsuccessful) for membership in the French Academy. To his enemy Boyer, bishop of Mirepoix, he affirmed that he was a true Catholic—officially to be sure, he was never anything else; he promised Père de la Tour that he would tear up any page of his works that was hostile to the Church and would live and die in her bosom; and he "kissed the pope's slipper" in the dedication of his tragedy *Mahomet*. At the same time, he wrote to D'Argenson on the subject of Boyer: "He is certainly playing a wicked rôle, and he is doing more harm than he thinks. He ought to know that it is a sad business making hypocrites." And to Thieriot, too, he wrote: "Virtue should not be obliged to render homage to fanaticism and hypocrisy." The philosophical tale *Zadig* is a beautiful example of a work that faces two ways; it is not only full of ironical expressions, but the whole work is an ironical review of Voltaire's years at court. The religious party received it, much to Voltaire's surprise, as on the whole orthodox, preaching resignation to Providence. Voltaire's friends read in it the opposite and more typically Voltairean view. Resignation to destiny, yes, but not until after the fight; and as for interpreting the history of human folly and ignorance as the unfolding of God's will, this was the very principle which he attacked so thoroughly that he has acquired the reputation of being the first modern historian. He hated the self-appointed or traditionally appointed agents of God's will, those who assassinated tolerant kings in the name of God and those who merited heaven through the slaughter of the natives as did the Spaniards in Peru. *Zadig* was written for his enlightened friends and was personally presented to them. If the general public believed it an orthodox work, so much the safer. "I am as harmless as a dove, and want to be as wise as a serpent," he wrote later, quoting the instructions of Jesus to his disciples.

During his stay at Colmar, in 1754, he was being closely watched by the Jesuits, who were doing everything in their power to prevent his settling in their proximity. At this juncture he decided it was distinctly better for his health, or at least for the repose of his mind and his body, to receive communion. Perhaps with some exaggeration, one of his secretaries, Colini, described the grimaces he made when presented with the Host. In a letter to his old friend and comforter at Potsdam, the Marquis d'Argens, Voltaire wrote: "I can see how a devil goes to mass when he is in papal territory, like Nancy or Colmar; but you have a right to groan when a child of Beelzebub goes to mass through hypocrisy or vanity."

On the subject of that hatred that he vowed to intolerant and fanatical priests [wrote his secretary Wagnière] I asked him one day what he would have done

if he had been born in Spain? "I would have had," he
said, "a great chaplet, I would have gone to mass every
day, I would have kissed the monks' sleeves, and I would
have tried to have all their monasteries set on fire. I
was not made to live in Spain, nor even in France."

The celebrated *Dîner du Comte de Boulainvilliers*,
one of the most witty and effective of the anti-religious works, will serve as an example of Voltaire's
methods. It was published under the name of Saint-
Hyacinthe. To Panckoucke, his projected editor, he
denied roundly that he himself had written it:

The more you prove to me your friendship, the less I
understand how you can apply to me for the infamous
work entitled *Le Dîner du Comte de Boulainvilliers*. I had
by chance a copy, but I threw it in the fire. It is a tissue
of bitter mockery and atrocious invective against our
religion. This unworthy work has been known for forty
years; but it appeared in Holland only a few months
ago, with a hundred other works of the same nature. If
I were not spending all the last days of my life on a
new edition of the *Siècle de Louis XIV*, enlarged by almost
a half; if I were not using up the little strength I have
left in erecting this monument to the glory of my country, I would refute all those books that are daily written
against religion.

The borderline between irony, propaganda, and
plain lying is but vaguely drawn in this letter; only
the certain knowledge of the degree of understanding at this moment between Voltaire and Panckoucke would permit the classification of this quotation. Four days later, he wrote to Damilaville,
from whom he withheld no secrets: "My desert is
becoming more precious to me than ever. I would

be obliged to quit it, if calumny imputed to me Saint-Hyacinthe's little book." Damilaville, thus warned, was to oppose this "calumny" in Paris. In a letter to a Parisian admirer, Mme de Saint-Julien, Voltaire's tone is entirely serious:

You do me great honor, madame, and mortally grieve me in attributing to me Saint-Hyacinthe's work, printed forty years ago. Suspicions on such a serious matter would be enough to ruin me on earth, in an old age overwhelmed with maladies, which does not permit me to transplant myself. My last days would be most fatally poisoned.

As for Saint-Hyacinthe, Voltaire had had some little unpleasantness with him some forty years before; but he was now dead: "No harm is being done to Saint-Hyacinthe's memory," he wrote to M. Saurin in self-defense, "in attributing to him a joke written forty years ago. What do the dead care about calumny! But the living might die of it." So Voltaire sought Saurin's aid, too, on the ground that the wise must help each other or they will be too severely persecuted by the fools.

Such phrases, which are plainly ironical when he is writing to his friends, are mendacious and hypocritical when he is addressing neutrals and enemies. One of his favorite methods was to quote, word for word, some of the more absurd theological discussions of the age. No comment was necessary; the fact that Voltaire was quoting them gave them all the intended comic effect. The duplicity of his conduct, his works, and his letters is thus partly an ethical, partly an aesthetic, consideration.

His protective lying varied, of course, in direct proportion to the danger and intensity of the activities in which he was engaged. The most marked period follows 1762, when he determined to make the *Extrait des sentiments de Jean Meslier* the first of an endless series in the clandestine trade of anonymous publications. During the same year his activity increased in behalf of the Calas family, and he followed it shortly thereafter by his defense of the Sirven family and finally, in 1766, by his efforts to avenge the Chevalier de la Barre. It was during this period, as we have seen, that after many years of patience and restraint, he blazed forth against Rousseau, who seemed to be jeopardizing, both by his conduct and by his attacks, the sacred cause of philosophy. The aftermath of the Chevalier de la Barre execution brought him sadness and worry. His own *Dictionnaire philosophique* was found in the young martyr's possession, and many people would have liked to avenge themselves on the master as well as on the disciple. His letters were strictly watched and intercepted, and he was obliged to adopt all sorts of subterfuges and pseudonyms in order to keep in touch with his brothers. His taking of communion in the spring of 1768 was a purely defensive measure, but he was nevertheless forced to excuse himself to the "brothers." To D'Argental, his "guardian angel," he gave the following nine reasons for the apparently hypocritical act.

1. It is a duty that I have fulfilled with Mme Denis once or twice, if I remember correctly.

2. It is not the same with a poor farmer as with your Parisian nobles, who can escape with a noonday walk in the Tuileries. I have to render the blessed bread in person in my parish; I am alone of my band against two hundred and fifty timorous consciences; and, when it costs no more than a ceremony prescribed by law to edify them, there is no use making two hundred and fifty enemies.

3. I am situated between two bishops who date from the fourteenth century, and I must howl with these holy wolves.

4. I must be on good terms with my curate, were he an imbecile or a rascal, and there is no precaution that I should not take, after Attorney Caze's letter.

5. Rest assured that if I see a procession of Capuchins passing, I will go to meet them with bared head, during the heaviest downpour. [La Barre had omitted this deference and had been condemned for sacrilege.]

6. M. Hennin, official resident at Geneva, found a chaplain already in office; he is weak enough to keep him. This priest is one of the most detestable and most insolent rascals of the tonsured rabble. He becomes the spy of the bishops of Orleans, Annecy, and Saint-Claude. Since the resident hasn't the courage to discharge him, I must have the courage to silence him.

7. Since people obstinately attribute to me the works of Saint-Hyacinthe, of the ex-Capuchin Maubert, of the ex-Mathurin du Laurens, of Squire Robinet [Voltairean pseudonyms], all people who do not take the sacrament, I am obliged to take it; if I were at Abbeville [where La Barre was condemned], I would take it every two weeks.

8. I cannot be reproached for hypocrisy, since I make no pretense.

9. I ask you please to burn up my reasons, after having approved or condemned them. I much prefer being burned

by you than at the foot of the great stairway [of the Hall of Justice].

The distance from Paris to Ferney had again caused a slight misunderstanding between Voltaire and his friends. But he was as explicit here as he dared to be; the very intolerant bishop of Annecy had indeed written a letter of complaint to the court and asked for the strict application of the Revocation of the Edict of Nantes; so Voltaire, in order to give the Church party no hold on him, obeyed the very letter of the law: "The king wants people to fulfill their Christian duties," he wrote the following year; "not only do I acquit myself of my duties, but I send my Catholic servants regularly to church and my Protestant servants regularly to the temple; I pension a schoolmaster to teach the catechism to the children." And again, to D'Alembert: "However, that rascally bishop, whom I failed to tip, still swears like a devil that he will have me burned in this world and in the other. I lay all that at the feet of my crucifix; and to escape being burned, I am putting in a provision of holy water."

There is, of course, a great deal of truth in his statement that he was no hypocrite in taking communion because he made no pretense of piety. Only a few of the more fanatical wanted to burn him; the others in authority were very glad to have him obey the letter of the law, take the sacrament, and deny the authorship of his books. In this way he prevented what would have been a very unpleasant persecution for all concerned; for he still had crowned heads up his sleeve.

Protective lying and hypocrisy, irony and poetical exaggeration, these traits do not tell the complete story. Much more serious are the lies that can be classed only as willful calumny and libel. It is, of course, easy for a student, two hundred years after the battle, to sit quietly with copies of all the essential documents and convict Voltaire of gross manipulation of facts and texts. He was himself an outstanding victim of calumny and libel; generous souls such as Vauvenargues, men of integrity such as Stanislas, father of Queen Marie, were shocked and disgusted at the Voltariana which made Voltaire's residence in Paris morally impossible; enemies such as the publisher Jore repented later of their share in the calumniation, and Jore received Voltaire's blessing and financial aid. If he had really believed in an eye for an eye and a tooth for a tooth, no inconsistency could have been discovered; but he professed faith in the Silver Rule of Confucius, "Do not unto others what you do not wish them to do unto you," as much more ancient and much less selfish than the Golden Rule. Again he may be said to have observed this rule in great measure; he was never the first to attack, he would have liked to live at peace and without jealousy in the fraternity of men of letters; yet when others wronged him, he returned the compliment in full measure—fuller, perhaps, because of the sting of his mocking genius. There was a trace of maliciousness

in his nature which he admitted early and late:
'By my stars a bit inclined to malice." Nor is there
any doubt but that he enjoyed the battle. On sending his play *Les Scythes* to Cardinal de Bernis, he
gave an account of his activities during the busy
year of 1766:

As for my puny self, I make war up to the last moment,
Jansenists, Molinists, Frérons, Pompignans, to the right,
to the left, and preachers, and J.-J. Rousseau. I receive
a hundred thrusts and give back two hundred, and I
laugh. I see at my door Geneva in combustion over
trifling quarrels, and I laugh again; and God be praised,
I look upon the whole world as a farce which sometimes
becomes tragic. All is the same at the end of the day,
and all is still more the same at the end of days.

Reviewing his life during his eightieth year and
speaking of Piron, he wrote to the Abbé Duvernet,
his future biographer: "My friends have always
assured me that in the only good play that he wrote
he made me play a very ridiculous rôle. I could very
well have returned the compliment; I was as malicious as he, but I was busier." Piron, he thought,
had wasted his talents in frivolity and useless en-
deavor; his own maliciousness had on the contrary
always been set to the service of reason, and he
could therefore die more happily.

Tolerance is, like democracy, a virtue which
should not be considered in the abstract. In discussing Voltaire's acts of intolerance, his persecutions
of his enemies, and his libels against them, it is
clear at the start that distinctions must be made:
that he never contributed to the execution of any

man for religious or intellectual differences and that
he would have done all in his power to save even
Rousseau from the clutches of the Inquisition. It is
also generally accepted that more than any other
one man he contributed to that measure of tolerance
which the world enjoys today. To the Protestants
of Geneva, whom he constantly reminded of the
burning of Servetus, and to the Catholics of France,
who were still persecuting Protestants, he said: "If
you want to imitate Jesus Christ, be martyrs and
not executioners!"; and he was fond of repeating
that Christ had never had anyone burned for his
religious views. His savage attacks on authority
were attacks on men who wielded authority unjustly or inhumanely; he was in a sense a Don
Quixote in the fight for justice, but he wasted little
time on windmills. As Frances Newman put it, "He
had the advantage of a literary début which encouraged his cynical view of his fellow men in the
personally injurious way that is so much more effective than any amount of impersonal imbecility."
He is often accused by friends and by enemies of
having killed the learned Maupertuis, not with the
sword, but with the pen, which is mightier than
the sword, and of being thus both diabolically
clever and an assassin. Again it will not do to
exaggerate. Maupertuis was of a jealous, domineering nature. He had tried to settle an argument
by the force of his authority as president of the
Berlin Academy and had unjustly treated another
noted mathematician and philosopher, Koenig; he

had written a foolish book, thus presenting a fair target for Voltaire's shafts; he was already afflicted with his mortal malady—"But I am sick, too," said Voltaire, "and half in the grave"; yet he survived by some seven years the personal ridicule of the *Diatribe du docteur Akakia*. None of Rousseau's physical or moral sufferings can be laid at Voltaire's door; and Fréron died in comparative poverty, not because he was ruined by Voltaire's *Anecdotes sur Fréron*, but because he spent as rapidly as he earned the relatively large sums of money with which he was rewarded for being Voltaire's wittiest and most insidious opponent at Paris.

It is nevertheless true that Voltaire often besieged the authorities with requests to suppress parodies and libels written against him or against the philosophic group. Here he gives us help in understanding his motives. He was much interested in problems of crime and punishment, preached even more effectively than Montesquieu that the punishment should be proportionate to the crime, and won his most signal victories in the improvement of justice and the abolition of torture. He maintained, however, that justice is based on law and that it is the business of law to punish criminals. "There are insulting books which ought to be burned," he wrote, "because an insult is a civil offense; while the *Contrat social*, being only illogical, ought to be refuted, not suppressed." In 1739 the libellous *Voltairomanie* cut him to the quick:

If the Abbé Desfontaines and those of his temper who

persecute me [he wrote to Frederick] were content with defamatory libels, well and good; but there are no devices they do not set in action to ruin me. Now they circulate scandalous writings and charge me with them; now anonymous letters to government officials, stories forged at will by Rousseau and consummated by Desfontaines. The religious hypocrites join them and hide under religious zeal their furious desire to wound me. Every week I am afraid of losing my freedom or my life; and languishing in solitude, powerless to defend myself, I am abandoned by those very people whom I have helped the most and who think that it is in their interest to betray me.

In appealing to civil justice he had to contend with the hostility of the pious group who surrounded the Queen and often supported his enemies and with hostile courts whose Jansenist members could not forgive his defense of the Jesuits against Pascal. Often he was obliged to secure the Queen's permission before taking the case to court. Parodies, too, were written with the direct purpose of ruining his plays and his reputation; laws protecting authors against piracy and parody were nonexistent or ineffective; his struggle for protection was thus again inspired by his desire for essential justice.

The Queen had Mme Luynes write me that parodies were customary [he complained to D'Argental] and that Virgil had been travestied. I reply that it was not a compatriot of Virgil who wrote the *Enéide travestie* [sic], that the Romans were incapable of it; that if a burlesqued *Enéide* had been recited to Augustus or Octavia, Virgil would have been indignant; that this folly has been reserved for our long unpolished and ever frivolous nation; that the Queen was deceived when she was told that parodies were still customary; that they have been forbidden for five years; that the French theater is part of the education of all the princes of Europe, and that Gilles and Pierrot are not fit to form the minds of the descendants of Saint Louis.

When, in 1767, his efforts to rehabilitate the Sirven family, persecuted for Protestantism, struck a snag, he suspected again his calumniators, especially La Beaumelle, who had so atrociously beleaguered him at Frederick's court.

I am sending you, my dear Huguenot philosopher [he wrote to pastor Vernes] a little philippic that I was obliged to write. Friend La Beaumelle is maltreated. The ruler of the province threatened him somewhat, by order of the king, with the cell that he deserves. I am very tolerant, but not with calumniators. I have to defend innocence with one hand, and crush crime with the other.

For his most intimate views on tolerance, it is well to avoid the *Traité sur la tolérance*, a work that admittedly "faced two ways" and was carefully designed for its effect on the public, and to quote from a letter written to D'Alembert a passage which explains in some measure this essay. The author worked, he declared, only with the advice of two very learned men:

It was long debated, in composing this work, whether we should limit it simply to the preaching of indulgence and charity, or whether we ought to be unafraid of inspiring indifference. It was unanimously agreed that we were forced to say things which would lead, against

the author's will, to that fatal indifference, because it
can never be brought about that men will be indulgent
in fanaticism and because they must be taught to despise, to look even with horror on the opinions which
they now uphold.

You cannot stop being a persecutor until you have
first stopped being absurd. I can assure you that the book
has made a great impression on all who have read it
and has converted some. I know well enough they say
that the philosophers ask for tolerance for themselves;
but it is very foolish and silly to say that "when they
have accomplished this, they will tolerate no other
religion but their own"; as if the philosophers could
ever persecute or be in a position to persecute! They
will certainly not destroy the Christian religion; but
Christianity will not destroy them, and their number
will ever increase; young men destined to high places
will learn from them, religion will become less barbaric,
and society more refined. They will prevent priests from
corrupting reason and manners. They will make an
abomination of fanatics, and a laughingstock of the
superstitious. Philosophers, in short, cannot help being
useful to kings, laws, and citizens. . . . Such is our present
situation that we are the execration of the human race
if we do not have noble-minded people on our side; we
must have them at any price; work then in the vineyard,
crush infamy. What can you not do without compromising yourself? Do not leave such a handsome candle
as yours under the bushel.

Voltaire thus saw very clearly that it would not be
for the philosophers to persecute. The champions of
justice in human affairs are still relatively few in
each generation: they realize that the goal can never
be attained in any absolute sense, and that it must

be fought for anew with each succeeding generation. Yet since he lived and wrote, many abuses have been definitely eliminated, and the battle has not always been so arduous. Only after serious efforts of understanding, then, should his lukewarm followers attempt to criticize his methods.

Voltaire looked on libels and calumny as very practical legal matters and on intentionally vicious parodies as matters that the law should consider in any civilized country in which literature was to be held in esteem. Tolerance itself was an entirely practical matter, signifying the abolition of persecution; intolerance on the part of philosophers was thus a purely academic question, for how could they be intolerant unless they had an army, a police force, and courts to allow them to persecute? Intellectual intolerance is another thing, or rather is a phrase without meaning, for if a man has an intellect he will naturally agree or disagree with expressed opinions; the whole question is whether he could be friendly to those with whom he disagreed. Voltaire was very capable of this sort of tolerance. "There are as many opinions as there are heads," he wrote to M. de Pomaret two years before he died: "And I, sir, who agree with you on questions of morality, am unfortunately very far from the sentiments that you are obliged to profess [belief in certain doctrines of Christianity]; but that is for me only one more reason to be attached to you, and to be with all my heart, sir, your . . ."

It is hard to deny, however, that, in his *Sentiment*

des citoyens against Rousseau, as well as in his *Ancedotes sur Fréron*, he took unjust advantage of his anonymity. Both pamphlets contain vicious untruths, some of which at least, we may assume, Voltaire knew to be untrue. The anecdotes were furnished on request by his Parisian friend, Thieriot, and published as anecdotes. They may fairly be compared with the *Voltariana* from which Voltaire had himself suffered so grievously. Fréron was the successor and eulogizer of the Abbé Desfontaines— to Voltaire the pamphlet was pure retaliation, not persecution; the difference was that Fréron was well supported by civil and religious authorities in his regularly insidious criticisms of Voltaire, while the latter deemed himself defenseless against the calumnies heaped upon him. He could and did pardon his enemies when they were in trouble and needed his help: "I have heard," he wrote, "that the Abbé Desfontaines is wretched; I pardoned him at once"; twice Voltaire rescued him from prison, and once he intervened to save him from execution on conviction of homosexuality; his reward had been black ingratitude. The attack on Rousseau in the *Sentiment des citoyens* fits in very ill with Voltaire's general nature and principles, especially the admonition there expressed that blasphemers should be dealt with by the law. That opinion was indeed held by many of the citizens, but it was not at all Voltaire's. Either this work is a flagrant abuse of anonymity and a very black mark on Voltaire's record, or some details are still missing from the picture; it was not included in his printed works until fifty years after his death, and the best evidence of its authenticity is the testimony, nearly thirty years after it appeared, of his secretary, Wagnière, usually trustworthy. We know that Voltaire was not responsible for all of it; whether he gave his sanction to it in its final form, that perhaps we shall never know. In any case, it was an exceptional rather than a typical act.

In the interests of truth it is unfortunate that prejudice and malice, often omitting necessary distinctions and extenuating circumstances, have made so much of a few incidents of this nature. For as a general rule Voltaire practiced and preached the virtues of justice and tolerance which are recognized as fundamental to the civilized human state. He could have purchased complete personal integrity only at the price of martyrdom.

CHAPTER V

Voltaire and His Friends

ONE of the most curious phenomena in the Voltaire tradition has been the persistence of the legend that he was incapable of friendship, and this in spite of the opinions of the most reliable critics and in the face of evidence so overwhelming that most mortals who have lived before or since would appear indeed friendless in comparison. The correspondence is alone sufficient proof. Some eighteen large-sized volumes of letters had been collected by 1885, and it is estimated that an editor today could collect nearly as many again. These letters were by no means business letters, or rather business was so mixed with pleasure that the general tone of friendliness is predominant. Both in number of friends and in length and quality of friendships his record is remarkable. Fidelity in friendship was indeed his outstanding virtue; through the stormy years of his life he ranked friendship second only to love of justice, and toward the end, when there was ever so slight a lull in the fight, he fell back on the comforting thought that he still had friends. Often betrayed himself, he was never the betrayer; and often he forgave those who had been personally disloyal. Friendship was the greatest of his virtues in theory as well as in practice. He even wondered why he found so little evidence of it in the New Testament.

From the lifelong friendships contracted with his schoolmates, from his youthful association with Thieriot and his touching poem on the early death of La Faluère de Génonville, whom he had so generously forgiven for stealing his mistress, from the years at Cirey with Mme du Châtelet and the stormy sessions at the French and Prussian courts to the final tranquil years at Ferney, his letters show his great need of friends, his readiness to form lasting ties, his naturally affectionate nature, and his true appreciation of the need for forbearance, patience, and loyalty. In the first letter preserved, written when he was seventeen to his absent schoolmate Fyot, Marquis de la Marche, the tone of friendship is already predominant. Its roots are distinctly classic, emanating from Cicero, Horace, and the great writers of the pagan world. His letter to another former classmate must be quoted again:

My dear Cideville, what a delightful life it would be to live together with three or four men of letters, with talent and without jealousy! To love one another, to live peacefully, to cultivate our arts, to talk about them, and to instruct one another! I think I shall live some day in this little paradise; but you must be the ruling deity.

Cideville became an even closer friend and a regular correspondent for more than forty years. He was a minor author who exchanged letters in prose and in verse with his greatly admired school-mate and frequently sought his advice; he had also been Voltaire's host at Rouen and had greatly aided the clandestine publication of many of the earlier works. In this exchange of letters we find Voltaire in his most charming lighter vein. At the age of about seventy, however, Cideville was living in Paris and had become very pious. By 1767 the letters had ceased, and Voltaire wrote to Mme du Boccage: "I think it's because of my heresy that Cideville writes to me no longer; he has left me flat like a criminal. Pray be merciful to me; I must not be everywhere excommunicated."

It was not always easy to be friendly with such an active and great man as Voltaire, who was so often at the center of the important controversies of his century. His enthusiasms carried him much farther along the way than his friends were willing to follow. D'Argental and D'Alembert were con-tinually trying to calm him down, while he just as continually sought to spur them to action. He used his friendships, too, in the great battle of enlightenment, never being able to explain to him-self cynicism and lack of courage on the part of his friends. When they failed, however, to come to his support, his capacity for resignation and patience was astounding; he also accepted gracefully and sincerely all criticisms of his works or activities that were offered in a friendly way and was very depen-dent on such services. When he was attacked by Saint-Hyacinthe, who contributed to the scandals of Desfontaines's *Voltairomanie*, he wrote to Lévesque de Pouilly, a friend during his early studious days in Paris, asking his intervention: "My dear Pouilly, I have no claim on your brother other than that of the esteem that I am unable to refuse him; but I have perhaps some claim on you, because I have loved you tenderly for twenty years." Saint-Hyacinthe's retraction was never obtained; but ten years later Voltaire sought and found comfort at Pouilly's house in his misery over Mme du Châtelet's death. In the same affair, the unworthy Thieriot betrayed him abominably; but he was later forgiven, and from that time until his death he was one of Voltaire's most intimate friends.

During Voltaire's long efforts to substitute in France the physics of his hero Newton for that of Descartes, it was a serious blow to him that Mme du Châtelet was converted to the opposite camp by Koenig; yet his affection and loyalty for that learned lady never faltered: "We must love our friends," he said, "no matter to what party they belong." His friendship for Vauvenargues, a genius who died young, after having written some of the most valued critical and moral essays of the eighteenth century, was very genuine:

I have been saying to myself for a year [Voltaire wrote to him on receiving his first publication] that you are a great man, and you have revealed my secret. I have as yet read only two-thirds of your book; I am about to devour the third part. I have carried it to the antipodes whence I shall promptly return to embrace the author, to tell him how much I love him, and with what transports I appreciate the grandeur of his soul, the sublimity of his reflections, as well as the humanity of his character. I found things which were contrary to my philosophy; can one not adore the Supreme Being without becoming a Capuchin? No matter, all the rest enchants me; you are the man I dared not hope for, and I beg of you to love me.

The noble and sensitive Vauvenargues had made a definite contribution to the rehabilitation of the passions, but was not for that reason a romantic; he, too, like Voltaire, revolting against Jansenist repressions, believed not only in the beneficence of the passions but also in the classic principle of control.

In exile in England, in 1726, Voltaire lived with Sir Everard Falkener and become his intimate friend. He kept in touch with him by letter until Falkener died in 1759, and the letters, written in Gallic English, show a genuine friendship:

Dear sir [he wrote in 1748] Your letter has afforded me the most sensible satisfaction; for when my friendship for you began, it was a bargain for life. Time that alters all things, and chiefly my poor tattered body, has not altered my sentiments. You acquaint me you are a husband and a father, and I hope you are a happy one. It behooves a secretary to a great general to marry a great officer's daughter; and really, I am transported with joy to see the blood of Marlborough mixed with that of my dearest Falkener. I do present your lady with my most humble respects, and I kiss your child.

Commenting on his refusal of Frederick's offer of a pension, he continued:

The court of a king is not comparable to the house of

a friend. I have lived these twenty years since with the same friends; and you know what power friendship obtains over a tender soul, and over a philosophical one.

I find great delight in opening my heart to you, and in giving you thus an account of my conduct. I will tell you that being appointed also Historiographer of France, I write the history of the late fatal war. . . . My history shall not be the work of a courtier, nor that of a partial man, but that of a lover of mankind.

I am now, my dear friend, at the court of king Stanislas, where I have passed some months with all the easiness and cheerfulness that I once enjoyed at Wandsworth: for you must know that king Stanislas is a kind of Falkener—he is indeed the best man alive. But, for fear you should take me for a wanderer of courts and a vagabond courtier, I will tell you that I am here with the very same friend whom I never parted from for these twenty years past, the lady du Châtelet, who comments Newton, and is now about printing a French translation of it; she is the friend I mean.

I have at Paris some enemies, such as Pope had at London; and I despise them as he did. In short, I live as happy as my condition can permit:

Excepto quod non simul esses, cætera lætus!

I return you a thousand thanks, my dearest and worthy friend. I wish you all the happiness you deserve; and I'll be yours for ever. Voltaire.

Correspondence and memoirs alike give the most convincing evidence of Voltaire's deep despair over losing Mme du Châtelet. More than all else this perennial bachelor needed the companionship of women in his home and in his daily life. Long before he became associated with Mme du Châtelet he had sought feminine protectors. At an early period Mme de Mimeure, a friend whom he had left for Mme de Bernières, desired his presence and recalled him during an operation for cancer. "Mme de Mimeure," he wrote, "underwent the operation with the courage of an Amazon; I couldn't help going to see her in such cruel straits." But Mme de Bernières was jealous and reproached him; "It must be because you like to reproach people," he replied, "that you scold me for visiting a poor dying woman who had her parents beg me to come. You are a poor Christian not to want people to make up on their deathbed."

After the return from England, he found refuge with Mme de Fontaine-Martel until that good lady's death in 1733; then he lived for sixteen years with Mme du Châtelet. His greatest criticism of Potsdam was the absence of women from the court of the misogynous Frederick: he had accepted orders and pensions only in the hope of establishing there a "home" with his niece, the plump, grotesque, and widowed Mme Denis, only to find that she could not persuade herself to leave the Paris establishment which he had arranged for her before his departure. She met him at Frankfort on the frontier as he was leaving Germany just in time to confirm her convictions that all the territory east of France was inhabited by barbarians. But from then on she stayed with him and cared for him during his wanderings and his retirement at Ferney. Often she amazed him greatly: several times she betrayed him, once he sent her off to Paris after she had helped La Harpe to some of his most preciously guarded manuscripts; but she was always forgiven and ever cherished—quite undeservedly according to most witnesses. Mme d'Épinay's testimony is especially spicy:

You would die laughing at Voltaire's niece: she is a fat little woman, like a ball, about fifty years of age, an unbelievable woman, homely and good, lying without meaning to and without malice; devoid of wit, yet seemingly witty, noisy, peremptory, talking politics, versifying, reasoning, unreasoning; and all that without pretensions, and especially without shocking anyone; and over all that a slight varnish of masculine love which pierces through the reserve which she has imposed on herself. She adores her uncle both as an uncle and as a man; Voltaire cherishes her, makes fun of her and reveres her: in short, the house is a habitation of contrasts and a charming spectacle for those present.

But Mme Denis's lovers were too much for the fond uncle—first the Marquis de Ximénès and then La Harpe. Both were occasions for the loss and subsequent publication of manuscripts, both were eventually forgiven and reappeared at Ferney. When, at the second betrayal, he bundled off his niece to Paris, his emotions were in unusual turmoil. In his dejection he planned even to sell Ferney, to change entirely his mode of living and become a hermit. He felt that she had been ruining him with her balls, her banquets, and her extravagant parties. Moreover, he had become "the innkeeper of Europe," it was time to call a halt—for many curious travelers "unlike Don Quixote, who mistook inns for châteaux," mistook Voltaire's château for an inn. He needed the money, too, not for self-indulgence, but to further the progress of his model colony. Mme Denis's letters from Paris were pathetic, revealing the pettiness of her character. She enjoyed a very generous pension from the still fond uncle and labored hard and long to arrange his return to his native city. When that effort failed she abjectly proposed conditions for her return to Ferney. She recalled in a letter the scene of her departure (Voltaire had torn his hair and had kept asking if her trunks were ready). She had loved him like a father for thirty-two years, she protested, and had left him "with death in her soul." The very memory of the moment of leave-taking was poison to her soul. She would come back and greatly diminish her train—a personal maid, of course, and a real Parisian valet "in white shirt and cuffs"—not a stinking peasant from Ferney—also a coachman and two horses; and if her uncle insisted, she would set up a separate household. It was evident that Voltaire could not be satisfied to live alone with Father Adam, ex-Jesuit, and Durey de Morsan, a young straggler of noble family whom he had taken in out of pity. He regretted having sent his niece away, and after a year and eight months' separation, he capitulated: "They say old men are hard," he wrote; "I am unfortunately as tender-hearted as if I were twenty years old."

There was, too, a very affectionate exchange of letters between Voltaire and his younger niece, Mme de Fontaine. His love for his sister, the mother of these girls, had been great, and the news of her death when he was in exile in England brought him very genuine sorrow. When the younger sister, too, became a widow in 1756, Voltaire gathered her into the family fold and later married her to the Marquis de Florian. The story would be long to tell of all the young men and women whom he befriended and for whom he found suitable mates. The best-known case is that of Mlle Corneille, distant, poor, and ignorant relative of the great Corneille, who learned her letters and her catechism under his watchful and amused eye and for whose dowry he published his critical edition of Corneille's works. To Fréron and his devout readers, the young girl was "falling into strange hands," was being brought up by an old irreligious reprobate and his licentious niece. From every purely human standpoint, however, she could hardly have fared better. Fréron misrepresented and slandered Voltaire's family in the pages of his journal and joined a cabal to get the Corneille girl out of his hands. "Well and good," replied Voltaire; "the devout ladies will doubtless prepare for her a more brilliant future in this world and in the world to come, but I shall have had no cause for self-reproach." Fréron very seriously misunderstood or willfully maligned Voltaire's character when he wrote: "It seems that M. de Voltaire is not accustomed to give such proofs of his kind heart and that it is most extraordinary to see him looking tenderly upon a young unfortunate girl." There is actually no trace of the old lecher in Voltaire, while the story of his philanthropies, his financial aid to struggling young poets, his rescuing of wayward souls and dowerless daughters, his open door ever hospitable to the wretched and the persecuted is unmistakably recorded in his correspondence.

Fréron had children. Why, complained Voltaire, don't the philosophers have sons to carry on the uneven battle? Diderot had only a daughter, D'Alembert was unmarried, as was Voltaire. He himself could produce philosophers only vicariously. After marrying off Mlle Corneille and her sister-in-law Mlle Dupuits, Voltaire was again made happy by the marriage at Ferney of Mlle Varicourt to the Marquis de Villette. She was a young girl in a family of eleven children, whose father, for reasons of economy, planned to send her to a convent. Voltaire had been touched by her despair and had taken her in as a guest in his already numerous household. She was beautiful, innocent, and gay, greatly delighting by her presence the old philosopher, who nicknamed her "Belle et Bonne." The Marquis de Villette had fled from Paris to avoid the scandal of an abortive duel. He could not resist the young lady's charms and asked for her hand. With the young wife's aid, Voltaire was able to convert the reckless young nobleman. He was delighted with the marriage and with the young married couple: "My lovers are a joy to see," he wrote during their honeymoon at his château; "they are working day and night to make a little philosopher for me."

It was perhaps only natural that he should have cherished family ties; that he provided as early as the Berlin trip for the future of his nieces and nephew; that he even gave a pension to a maternal cousin twice removed. Only on these grounds can he be forgiven for leaving his factories and farms at Ferney in the profligate hands of Mme Denis. His fondness for the simplicity of family life and for the presence of children which such a life entails has very rarely been mentioned. On his arrival near Lausanne in 1755 he became very intimate with the Pictet family and very fond of the Pictet daughter. This was another enduring friendship. Years later he was greatly entertained by the Pictet grandchildren; "They come and play in his library," wrote a contemporary, "and there they mount astride the great stuffed leopard, open his books, look at his prints, and plunge June bugs into his inkwell." And Wagnière, his secretary, wrote, in his memoirs, of his master's affection and patience:

When my children, still very young, pressed him with their questions, even while he was dictating something to me, and I tried to hush them, he would say to me: "Let them alone; we should always give honest replies to children, give them reasons for their questions according to their lights, and not deceive them." And he was kind enough to treat them accordingly. . . . I dare hope [added the honest Wagnière] that the reader will excuse these little details.

The modern reader would have pardoned him for many more. A painting by Voltaire's frequent visitor, the celebrated artist Jean Huber, shows the "old man of the mountain" in the meadows of Ferney telling stories to a group of peasants with their children. The whole community, Huguenots and Catholics, had come to revere him and often honored him with rural festivals: "I know no more beautiful spectacle," he wrote after one of these celebrations, "than that of public joy. There is no opera that can approach it."

These family and neighborly relations show clearly enough Voltaire's essential warmth of heart and humanity: his intellectual relationships confirm these traits and bring out his keen sense of loyalty in friendship. He was convinced that he had always been loyal to Frederick and that the king, on the contrary, had broken his promises. Of mutual misunderstandings, there were a great number. Voltaire left France in 1750 because he had been treated with indignity; because Louis XV did not share his long-cherished notion that philosophers could be useful as mentors to kings; and because he needed time and freedom to publish his *Siècle de Louis XIV*. The prospect of true and loyal friendship was dim before he went to Frederick's court, and Voltaire knew it well —his French friends even better. Frederick had been disturbed because the French philosopher had played the double rôle of friend and official messenger on his visit to Berlin in 1743. Voltaire was doing his best, as he always did, to bring the two countries together in mutual understanding. During his attempts at diplomacy, without ever betraying his own country, he believed he was working in Fred-

Courtesy of the Moos Gallery, Geneva

VOLTAIRE TELLS A TALE

erick's best interests. The uncollected correspondence with the Prussian Count Podewils is very revealing on this subject. Frederick perhaps believed that thereafter any conduct was justifiable. In any case, he believed too readily the calumnies of the *Voltariana*, and at least twice he betrayed Voltaire in an effort to blacken him at the French court, to force his departure or exile, and thus to conquer through treachery. "Here is part of a letter from Voltaire," he wrote in 1743 to one of his agents at Paris, "which I beg you to pass on to the bishop of Mirepoix by indirect channels. . . . My intention is to embroil Voltaire so thoroughly with France that he will have no choice but to come to me." The bishop of Mirepoix was Voltaire's most powerful and persistent enemy, and no act on Frederick's part could have more seriously damaged Voltaire's standing at court or with the Academy than this revelation to the bishop of his secret thoughts. Again, in 1750, Frederick succeeded in embroiling Voltaire with his close friend and protégé Baculard d'Arnaud by the simple trick of circulating a poem with the preposterous statement that "Volatire's sun is setting and D'Arnaud's is at its dawn." Voltaire was justifiably insulted and enraged. Worse still, the young D'Arnaud took the compliment seriously and acted toward his former benefactor and teacher with disloyal insolence. Voltaire knew well this malicious side of Frederick's character; referring to this poem he replied in kind, asking if Frederick "scratched with one hand while he caressed with the other."

He had consented to leave France "on the express
condition that you deign to love me a little, for
otherwise I die in Paris." It is indeed difficult to
reconcile Frederick's assurance of love and esteem
in his reply with the very unjust estimate of Voltaire's character sent only a few months before to
Voltaire's friend Algarotti:

It is too bad that such a flabby soul is linked with
such a noble genius. He has all the caressing ways and
the maliciousness of a monkey. I will tell you what
he has done when I see you; but I will let nothing appear, for I need him in the study of French elocution.
One can learn even from a rascal. I want to know his
French; what does his moral integrity matter?

This letter was of course unknown to Voltaire, but
it would have completely confirmed his fears aroused
by the story, relayed by La Mettrie, that Frederick
had said: "I will squeeze the orange and throw
away the rind."

Voltaire arrived in Berlin in the summer of 1750,
sick at heart: "This decision is a cruel blow for a
heart as susceptible to friendship as mine," he wrote.
By Christmas, he was desperately homesick, as
appears in the following words to his niece:

I write to you close to a stove, with heavy head and
sad heart, glancing upon the river Spree because the
Spree flows into the Elbe, and the Elbe into the sea, and
because the sea receives the Seine, and our house in
Paris is not far from the banks of the Seine. My dear
child, why am I in this palace, in this study overlooking
this Spree, and not by our own hearthside? . . . How
remorseful I am, my dear child! and how sad it is to

seek happiness far from you! and what remorse if one finds it!

Maupertuis was already decidedly unsociable and hostile; D'Arnaud had betrayed him to Fréron; Frederick had written with one hand a letter of condolence to Darget on the death of his wife and with the other an epigram against the deceased. "That gives cause for thought," wrote Voltaire; "there are three or four of us foreigners here like monks in an abbey. God grant that the Father Abbot be content with mockery!"

Before the end of that same year Voltaire had involved himself in a rather shady speculative transaction with the moneylender Hirschell. Early the following year, only seven months after his arrival, he received a thundering letter from Frederick enumerating the vindictive, deceitful traits of his character. From then on, friendship could be no more than a pretense; Frederick had broken his word, had treated him as would a king, not a friend, and had revealed an absolute lack of affection. In disgrace, Voltaire humbly admitted his wrongdoing in the Hirschell affair and showed that it was his passion for justice that had led him to injure thus his own reputation. Peace and freedom to work were again his consolations: "Work is necessary," he wrote to President Hénault; "it becomes in the end the greatest of pleasures and takes the place of all lost illusions." His illusions were indeed gone. In October of the same year he decided that when kings lack respect for their inferiors and love them not, the

only recourse is to lack respect for kings in return—
very gently, of course—and to leave them—also
gently. So he bided his time and worked diligently,
with the consolation of his friends D'Argens and
Algarotti. Only a fitting occasion was now wanting
for the break; when Maupertuis, with Frederick's
support, unjustly accused Koenig of forgery and had
him dismissed in disgrace from the Academy, the occasion was supplied. Voltaire foresaw his fate the very
day that he read Koenig's defense and saw the injustice of his conviction: "I'm secretly putting my
affairs in order," he wrote to his niece. He knew he
would be obliged to leave, he had long wanted to
leave, and perhaps he welcomed the coming battle.
As he watched later from his window the flames
and smoldering embers of his witty satire, the *Diatribe du docteur Akakia*, publicly burned by the King's
orders, he must have smiled sardonically at the
pettiness of kings. In December, 1752, he wrote to
his niece:

Since I haven't in this world a hundred and fifty thousand moustaches in my service, I have no idea of making
war. My sole idea is to desert honorably, to take care
of my health, to see you again, to forget this three-
years dream. I see that "the orange has been squeezed";
I must try to save the rind. I'm going to make, for my
own edification, a little dictionary for the use of kings.
"My friend" signifies "my slave." "My dear friend"
means "You are more than indifferent to me." Understand for "I will make you happy": "I will endure
you as long as I need you," "Have supper with me"
signifies "I will make fun of you tonight." The diction-

ary may be long; it's an article to put in the *Encyclopédie*. But seriously, it's enough to break your heart. Is all I have seen possible? To rejoice in embroiling those who live together with him! To say the most tender words to a man and to write pamphlets against him! And what pamphlets! To snatch a man from his fatherland by the most sacred of promises and to maltreat him with the blackest malice! What contrasts! And that's the man who wrote me so much on philosophy and whom I thought a philosopher! And I called him "the Solomon of the North"!

Gone are the illusions, indeed! Rousseau passed a similar judgment on Frederick's character, when he called him "an unprincipled man who tramples on all human rights, and who has no faith in virtue." Voltaire's difficulties at Berlin cannot, at least, be justly charged to his incapacity for friendship. Yet it is from just such situations that the unjust charge presumably arose.

Voltaire was not able to desert as neatly as he had hoped. True, he had obtained a farewell supper with the king, in order to persuade the public that he was not leaving in disgrace. But at the border he was held up by Frederick's agents and treated by official-dom with more than usual inhumanity. Doubtless he lost his head entirely at these renewed marks of authority and injustice, and for years afterward he sought to avenge the insults heaped upon him and upon his niece Mme Denis and his secretary Colini. His wrath finally cooled; and as his fame increased, Frederick again paid him court, and the exchange of letters continued with ever-increasing warmth. Voltaire had won a new sense of dignity from the indignity of his sojourn in Prussia. He was after all much greater than Frederick the Great, and Frederick needed him much more than he needed Frederick. The King, too, could not help being humanized by the contact.

The reconciliation was very gradual. In 1766 Frederick chided Voltaire for his pamphlets against the unfortunate Rousseau; the following year he consented, but rather coldly, to let Voltaire and company run the printing presses of the enlightenment freely in his territory; in 1770 Frederick completely capitulated:

As for a good old philosopher in his dotage [he wrote to Voltaire] who lives in a neighboring vineyard, he has ordered the Lorrainer [Frederick's secretary] to assure you that he misses very much the patriarch of Ferney, that he wishes it were possible still to give him a welcome at his dwelling and to associate with him in his studies; that at least this patriarch may rest assured that no one better appreciates his merit or has more love for his fine genius.

Frederick still wanted to become a philosopher and still sent his manuscripts to that best of all judges, Voltaire. Voltaire was not himself completely appeased; he wanted to reach the ideal friendship, which was to be loved for himself, not only for his genius. From a letter of 1775 it is clear that the Maupertuis episode still bothered him considerably, and he blamed that "chimerical geometer and calumniator" for his separation from Frederick. Frederick was now willing to admit that Maupertuis had been brusque, but he believed him possessed, nevertheless, of certain good qualities. Voltaire was not entirely appeased. There was still a reproach in a letter to the King later in that same year:

We hope in France [Voltaire wrote] that philosophy, which is near the throne, will soon be upon it; but that's only a hope: and hope is often deceitful. There are so many people whose interest it is to maintain falsehood and folly, there are so many titles and so much wealth attached to this business, that it is to be feared that hypocrites will always win out over the wise.

Frederick's letters became ever more affectionate, more sincere, more humane: " 'Luc' seems to have changed for the better," Voltaire wrote to D'Alembert. Meanwhile Voltaire's protégé Lekain visited Frederick and reported that Voltaire, too, had changed for the better; and the French actor delighted the King with presentations of his royal host's favorite plays, which were of course Voltaire's *Oedipe*, *Zaïre*, and *Mahomet*. The following year, when Voltaire was eighty-two, the reconciliation was completed. Voltaire sent to a friend in Paris a copy of a letter he had written to Frederick and asked to have it made public: "It's rather fun, too," he added, "to let people know how much this monarch and I, poor thing, have pardoned each other: *Amantium ira amoris redintegratio*." The route may have been long and the climb arduous, but Voltaire had now greatly elevated the dignity of the philosopher and the man of letters and had become, on his own terms, the friend of kings.

Other friendships had been more durable, more intimate, and more serene. In 1752 he wrote to Frederick:

You are not ignorant of the fact that my heart is fashioned for persevering friendships, that I have lived twenty years with the same person [Mme du Châtelet], that my friends are friends of more than forty years, that I have lost some only through death, and that my love for you has made you the master of my destiny.

The old friends to whom Voltaire here referred were his schoolmates, D'Argental, for so many years his "guardian angel," Cideville, amateur poet from Rouen, the D'Argenson brothers, Abbé d'Olivet, Fyot de la Marche, not to mention President Hénault, the obsequious Thieriot, and the Duc de Richelieu, to all of whom Voltaire was early united by the unusually strong ties of youthful friendship. The D'Argenson brothers belonged to a family distinguished for its official positions—the father was long the first lieutenant of police, and it was he to whom it fell to arrest Voltaire and put him in the Bastille in 1717. The elder son was appointed ambassador to Portugal in 1737 and became, in 1744, secretary of foreign affairs. The younger brother was second lieutenant of police and later secretary of war. Both preserved true and lifelong friendship for Voltaire; both defended him against the persecutions of the Abbé Desfontaines.

Voltaire's longest intimate friendship was with the Comte d'Argental, son of the elder sister of Mme de Tencin and Cardinal de Tencin, both of whom were among Voltaire's bitterest enemies; if we add Voltaire's friendship for D'Argental's brother Pont-de-Veyle and for D'Alembert, illegitimate and abandoned son of Mme de Tencin, the members of this celebrated family could be counted, with a fairly even distribution, among his greatest friends and his greatest enemies. Their choice was thus made between philosophy and religion,—between Voltaire and the Church,—with Mme de Tencin and her brother left to intrigue in behalf of Rome and the English Pretender.

The correspondence between D'Argental and Voltaire began in 1715 and ended with the latter's death, in 1778. Their friendship dated from their schooldays of 1710–1711. The letters of the first twenty years have been lost, but from 1734 to 1778 they give us a more complete and more glorious picture of Voltaire than do any other letters, and they reveal a friendship such as is rarely encountered in the annals of men. These letters were not written for posterity, but they reveal above all the steady daily give and take between two men who understood and trusted each other thoroughly. D'Argental was not himself a brilliant writer; he was, however, a man of excellent literary judgment and Voltaire's most severe and respected critic. His position at the court and connections with the theater were of great service to the absent poet. More than anyone else, D'Argental was hurt when Voltaire left France for Berlin, and more ardently than anyone else he desired and worked for his return. Only on rare occasions thereafter did the two men meet—at the watering place, Les Plombières, occasionally, and finally, in 1778, in Paris. The letters are for that reason more regular and more complete during the fullest years of Voltaire's life. He constantly addressed D'Argental and his wife as his "divine" or "guardian" angels, and that indeed was the rôle they played in Paris. No summary can be given of this correspondence, because it represents Voltaire's whole life and activity, with especial emphasis on the theater. Several extracts will serve to illustrate the friendly tone.

The first letter that has been preserved is dated 1725. Voltaire was working on a play, *Mariamne*, concerning which D'Argental had asked him some questions.

I am working night and day [replied Voltaire]; I write a few lines and erase a great many. Otherwise, dear sir, you would see me more often at your house and at Mme de Ferriol's, to whom I beg of you to pass along the word. I cannot therefore reply with precision to your letter; all that I can tell you is that I am beginning to revise the second act. I beg of you, be more severe than I; be indulgent only for my failings; have no indulgence for my verses. As a matter of friendship, your indulgence will be useless to me.

Once again it is apparent that Voltaire in no wise reacted adversely to friendly criticism, even the most severe, but rather sought it; it was only the malicious attacks of a Desfontaines or the insidious praises of a Fréron that enraged him, because they were both malicious and unjust.

Fifty years later, in 1774, Pont-de-Veyle died, and Voltaire sought to console the younger brother:

My dear guardian angel [he wrote] I didn't expect that your brother would pass on before me. I am ashamed to be still alive, when I think of all the victims who are falling about me. My heart says to you: "Live long, my dear guardian angel, you and Mme d'Argental"; as if the thing depended on you. We are all, in this world, like prisoners in a little prison courtyard; each awaits his turn to be hanged without knowing the hour; and when the hour comes, it is found that we have led a very useless life. All reflections are vain, all reasonings on necessity and on human misery are nothing but wasted words. I shall miss your brother, and I love you with all my heart; that is all I can say to you.

When Louis XV died, in that same year, D'Argental begged Voltaire to come back to Paris; four years later Voltaire yielded to the temptation, and the two octogenarians had a chance to discuss again the pranks they had played in their youth on their Jesuit masters.

Friends Thieriot and Mme du Deffand, D'Alembert and Diderot merit special attention; others can only be mentioned in passing—some fifty-five years of serene friendship, for example, with President Hénault, whom Voltaire met in the Society of the Temple and a lifelong friendship with the Duc de Richelieu, nephew of the Cardinal and a haughty aristocrat, warrior, courtier, and rake. Voltaire's strong youthful attachment for him, his extraordinary gift of loyalty, his need of a hero of whom to sing in order to satisfy his classical conception of the poetic function, and his need also of a defender and protector in his dealings with the Parisian theater were responsible for the preservation, in the face of many obstacles, of the genuine friendship between them. When D'Alembert, for example, gave explicit proof of Richelieu's deliberate slighting of Voltaire, the latter replied that he had nothing to say on the matter and added: "I hope you will pardon me for respecting an ancient attachment." Richelieu, formerly a lover of Mme du Châtelet, gave his blessing to her union with Voltaire, and the couple reciprocated by fostering the Duke's marriage to a woman beneath his station. It was at Richelieu's château that Voltaire learned of the threatening *lettre de cachet*, occasioned by the publication of the *Lettres philosophiques*, which forced him to seek refuge in Bâle to escape imprisonment or worse.

Thieriot's friendship was of an entirely different order. A parasite and gourmand, Nicolas-Claude Thieriot, like Rameau's nephew whom Diderot so cleverly analyzed, "reduced all the prodigies of evaluation, all the operations of genius, all the devotions of heroism . . . to their lowest masticatory terms." He had the honor of being Voltaire's most intimate and in many respects most ungrateful friend. For Thieriot traveled from house to house, or rather from table to table, accepting meals wherever his unscrupulousness in the underworld of letters rendered his services valuable. There is no doubt of his great usefulness to a friend whose books usually had to be published surreptitiously; but his lack of principles was carried into his friendship, even into his relations with the man who had the most befriended him. He betrayed Voltaire on many occasions and failed him in one of the most critical moments of his career: he was too piggishly obstinate to say the friendly word that would have counteracted the worst charges in Desfontaines's *Voltai-romanie*. "To hear all over Paris that you are giving your friend the lie," wrote Voltaire, "to hear that you are sparing Desfontaines, that is a dagger-thrust for a heart as sensitive as mine." Yet it was against Voltaire's own principles to break with his intimate friends. "Two friends who quarrel dishonor each other," he maintained. And again: "I am unshakable in friendship and in my opinions." Nor was it entirely a question of principle, for Voltaire loved Thieriot with all the affection that is bestowed on friendships formed in the sentimental years of early youth. For some fifteen years after this major betrayal, which took place in 1738, Voltaire gradually withdrew from Thieriot his confidence, but not his enthusiastic support. Two years later he had him appointed Parisian agent to Frederick, nor was it due to any lack of zeal on his part that Frederick forgot, as usual, to pay for services rendered. But the ties were too strong to be sundered. Thieriot kept also, in his own equivocal way, a sort of canine loyalty to the master by whose hand he had so often been fed.

Thieriot had rendered great services to Voltaire.

It was he who supervised at Rouen the first secretly printed edition of the *Henriade*, and he who, with Adrienne Lecouvreur, nursed Voltaire through a serious case of smallpox. It was he who served as Voltaire's agent in England after Voltaire's return from exile and who prepared the English edition of the *Letters on the English Nation*. In connection with both publications Thieriot absconded with funds upon which Voltaire was counting and when charged with the fraud brazenly replied that his friend had exaggerated—he had pocketed not a hundred subscriptions, but only eighty. The publication of the *Letters on the English Nation* before the signal had been given forced Voltaire's hand and made a French version imperative in view of the threat of pirated translations. Hard beset, Voltaire, realizing that persecution could not reach his friend in England, declared that Thieriot was the author. Thieriot was not loyal enough to accept the honor in a sporting spirit and nursed his grievance; nor were matters bettered when soon afterward at the house of Mme de Bernières he became the table companion of the treacherous Abbé Desfontaines. The Abbé's ingratitude was perhaps contagious, or rather there existed between the two parasites a certain sympathy of digestion, and that tie was more real to Thieriot than the memories of past favors. Voltaire, too, had abandoned Paris for Cirey and his old friends for Mme du Châtelet. When the *Voltairomanie* was published, in 1738, it appeared to Thieriot that Voltaire's reputation was on the wane; it simply did not seem to be to his advantage to estrange his present friends by telling the truth.

By 1754 the situation had changed. Mme du Châtelet had died, and Frederick had been snubbed. Voltaire's star was definitely in the ascendant. Thieriot became again his confidential agent, and his confidence was once more well rewarded. So he sent Voltaire books, informed him of the prevalence in Paris of the manuscripts of *La Pucelle*, helped spread abroad faked copies of it, supervised the publication of the poems on natural law and on the Lisbon disaster, of which he distributed copies to Diderot, D'Alembert, and Rousseau, and engaged in many other undertakings mutually profitable to Voltaire and to himself. It was perhaps he who gave the manuscript of *Candide* to Lambert for the first edition. At any rate, it was he who first hailed its publication. In a letter to Voltaire he wrote:

Oh most cherished Candide, most excellent author and inventor of quips and jests! Your book is snatched from hand to hand. It so delights the heart that those who usually laugh with tight lips are forced to laugh with open mouths. . . . Why, you have every right to call yourself the best old comic fool that ever was seen on this earth, where you will live a hundred years, more like Lucian, Rabelais, and Swift than all three put together.

This effusion had double merit: it was from the heart of a friend, and it was better literary criticism than most of the early reactions to Voltaire's masterpiece.

In 1762 Thieriot was persuaded to leave his beloved Paris for a visit of three months at Ferney. He brought with him many of the golden memories of youth which Voltaire cherished and a power of digestion which his sixty-eight-year-old contemporary could only envy. Seven years later this master talent failed the aging Thieriot. He wrote asking to be inscribed on the list of the philosopher's "charitable works." Voltaire sent him money and many a wise counsel concerning the benefits of diet, during the last three years of lingering illness. Thus the intimacy of the earlier years was renewed and lasted until Thieriot died, in 1772, supported to the end by Voltaire's benevolent hand. It is a pity he was too lazy to leave us a picture of his benefactor "in slippers." At the time, any such intimate portrait of Voltaire's youth might well have appeared disloyal and dishonoring; but posterity would have forgiven him, and Voltaire himself would today be more real, more understandable, more lovable. As in the case of the friendship between these two men who withheld no secrets from each other, complete understanding brings plenary indulgence. *Tout comprendre, c'est tout pardonner.*

The correspondence with Mme la Marquise du Deffand was friendly, intellectual, philosophically speculative, artistic. Few exchanges of letters during the eighteenth century can be found of a more interesting and revealing nature. Both writers venerated the seventeenth century in which they were born, the great age of Louis XIV, with its classical conceptions of art and of life; in many respects both were more truly classical, more essentially pagan in their philosophical acceptance of life and death, than their forebears. Voltaire especially had opened up to genuine classicism the fields of philosophy, science, and religion; Mme du Deffand represented his narrower side, dealing with the more limited aspects of literary taste. Pascal was thus to them the great model for prose—but not for philosophy or religion. Mme du Deffand was pessimistic and resigned in the blindness of her old age; Voltaire was the consoler, amazing her, often shocking her with his activity in the struggle for enlightenment. She would have liked him to forget Calas, Sirven, and the Old Testament, to devote himself to pure literature; but that was beyond the realms of possibility. His works delighted her for their technique, their classical style, even when they shocked her by the modernity of their ideas. The two had long known each other; but their friendship ripened only in old age and after their separation. Both, too, had much to overlook. When Julie de Lespinasse, for whom D'Alembert burned with unrequited love, left Mme du Deffand's salon and carried off a considerable number of her habitués, the blind old lady could hardly forgive either Julie or D'Alembert. Her distaste for D'Alembert prejudiced her against the *Encyclopédie*, against philosophers in general, and she was suspected of supporting Palissot in his attacks upon them. Voltaire's two best friends were thus definitely at odds with each other; his tact in defending the philosophers before Mme du Deffand and in preserving her friendship, while at the same time soothing D'Alembert's ruffled feelings, was remarkable.

It is from Mme du Deffand's letters that we find the most intimate expressions of Voltaire's philosophy; his manner of accepting life and of envisaging death, his metaphysical speculations and skepticism, his intense struggles in behalf of humanity, and his periodic moments of mystical resignation. By 1732 Voltaire was devotedly attached to the Marquise; four years later he thanked her profusely for her praise of his "American" play, *Alzire*, and showed his appreciation of her intellectual capacities by writing her his frankest early criticism of the philosophy of Pope's *Essay on Man*. She was much more to him than an intelligent correspondent, however; she was a firm friend, who remained loyal to him throughout the battles of Paris, Berlin, and Geneva and throughout the main battle of life itself. From Berlin, for example, he wrote how much he missed his friends in Paris, President Hénault, D'Alembert, "whom I regard as one of the best minds that France has ever produced," and the Duchesse du Maine, at Sceaux. In a letter to Mme du Deffand herself he concluded:

Take care of yourself, don't eat too much; I predicted, when you were so ill, that you would live a very long time. Especially, don't be disgusted with life, for in truth, after much reflection, one finds nothing better. I will keep during the whole of mine my feelings of devotion to you, and I will always love Paris, on account of you and the small number of the elect.

Twenty-six years later she came to the ardent defense of Voltaire against another intimate friend, Horace Walpole, who thought he had detected some inconsistencies in Voltaire's manner of dying.

In 1754, when Mme du Deffand had became blind and had brought Julie de Lespinasse to Paris to grace her salon, Voltaire wrote her a very moving letter:

Your letter, madame, moved me more than you can imagine, and I assure you that my eyes were a bit moist on reading what has happened to yours. I had judged from a letter from M. Formont, that you were in twilight, and not entirely in the night. I thought you were in somewhat the same condition as Mme de Staal, but having the added advantage of being free, of living at home, and not being subjected, in the train of a princess, to a restricted manner of life which smacks of hypocrisy; and finally of having friends who think and talk freely with you.

So I regretted, madame, only the loss of the beauty of your eyes, and I knew you were enough of a philosopher to find consolation; but if you have lost your sight, I am infinitely sorry for you; I shall not propose to you the example of M. de S. . . . blind at the age of twenty, always gay, and even too gay. I agree with you that life is not good for much; we endure it through the force of an almost invincible instinct that mother nature has given us; and she added to this instinct the bottom of Pandora's box, hope . . .

This letter was written in Voltaire's most despondent year, while he literally had no home to call

his own. Yet for twenty-four years thereafter he
continually played the rôle of consoler, poet, and
philosopher to this blind aristocrat who fought
boredom, self-depreciation, and pessimism throughout a grand old age. When Voltaire returned to
Paris at the age of eighty-three, most of his contemporaries had died — the long-lived Moncrif,
President Hénault, with whom Mme du Deffand
had been associated for forty years, the D'Argenson
brothers, Cideville, and Thieriot. D'Alembert and
Diderot were, relatively speaking, still youngsters
of sixty-one and sixty-five years, respectively. But
Mme du Deffand was still there to talk with him
of the glories of the decline of the great classical
age of Louis XIV. This friendship and mutual esteem,
which had endured at least fifty-three years, resulted
in a correspondence of inescapable charm and of
inestimable value in appreciating both Voltaire and
the literary and philosophical movements of his
century. To it we must return in discussing Voltaire's views of death.

The correspondence with D'Alembert is even more
friendly and at the same time more philosophical in
the active sense of the word—more political than
reflective. Here we find Voltaire in the very midst
of his energetic campaign against intolerance, persecution, and superstition, the undisputed chief in the
movement to "crush infamy," the infamous thing
being the power of the Christian Church, upheld by
superstition, to affirm intolerance and to persecute.
To D'Alembert, as would be possible only to the

most trusted of friends and as much as the censorship of the mails would allow, he revealed the meaning and the secrets of his campaign, that is, the nature of his own pamphlets, his opinions on the anti-Biblical and antireligious books that were being produced so rapidly during the sixties and seventies, and the titles of the works that he believed worthy of republication and dissemination. D'Alembert was in essential agreement with Voltaire's point of view, but, like Diderot, he was at Paris "under the monster's claw," was drawing a pension from the court, and did not dare to compromise himself. He was likewise more cynical—less sure that mankind was worth the trouble of enlightening. Along with Frederick and Mme du Deffand he tried to calm down "his dear master," and proposed as a model the smiling aristocratic philosopher, Fontenelle, who once said that even if he had his hand chock full of truths, he would yet take care not to open it—Fontenelle who had a remarkably clear historical view of the slow march of human progress and did not believe in forcing the pace; or else, as Voltaire suggested, having once ventured to open up his hand, he had received a deterring rap on the knuckles.

I have written a supplement to the *Destruction des Jésuites*, [wrote D'Alembert in a similar spirit of caution] in which the Jansenists, the only enemies that are left to us, are treated according to their merits; but I don't know when, where, or how I am to publish it. I would like to serve reason, but I want much more to be left in

peace. Men are not worth the trouble one takes to enlighten them; and the very ones who think as we do
persecute us. Adieu, my dear master; I embrace you with
all my heart.

When I see all that goes on in this world of ours [he
wrote later] I should like to go and pull the Eternal
Father by the beard and say to him, as in an old farce
of the Passion: "Eternal Father, what a shame!" And
so forth. 1 am deeply grieved and discouraged. I shall
end, and very soon I think, by taking no further interest
in all the follies that are uttered and in all the atrocities
that are committed from Petersburg to Lisbon and by
finding that all will be well when I have digested well
and slept well. I divide the human race into two parts,
the oppressors and the oppressed; I hate the former and
despise the latter. Why am I not by your fireside pouring
out my heart to you! I am very sure that we would agree
on all points.

Voltaire was wiser than his more cautious friends.
Frederick and Mme du Deffand maintained that
superstition was so firmly rooted in humanity that
it was useless to try to eradicate it; D'Alembert
believed sometimes that humanity wasn't worth the
struggle and that the age of reason was making such
progress, all by itself, that effort was superfluous.
Voltaire was no naïve believer in perfectibility, he
believed only that the fight against the usurpations
of the Church would make life a little more tolerable, and he lived long enough to see convincing
evidence of the soundness of his belief. Cynicism
was with him a literary device, not a deep-seated
conviction. It was quite the contrary, in fact, for
his letters were constantly urging his cynical friends

to love humanity. As early as 1741 he wrote very frankly on this subject to Frederick that "his greatest fear was lest the King learn to despise those featherless, two-footed creatures that people this earth." As for D'Alembert, whose intelligence and whose style, modeled on that of the great Pascal, could produce such telling blows, all he needed was more love and more zeal, plus the advantages of anonymous publication, which the master was ever offering him. A few noble-minded people could suppress "infamy" if they would only league together against the already over-organized enemy, but "one of the greatest misfortunes of honorable people is their cowardice." Yet "the secret testimony of the conscience," after even an anonymous contribution to the destruction of error, "is surely one of the greatest joys." "Your cowardly Fontenelle," he wrote to the wavering brothers, "lived only for himself; live for yourself and for others as well. His only thought was to show his wit; use yours to enlighten the human race. I embrace you in the communion of the faithful." "I am not like Fontenelle," he declared to brother Helvétius, "because I have a warm heart." So Voltaire wished that D'Alembert, one of the geniuses of the century, would abandon mathematics—"except for some twenty theorems useful to mechanics or astronomy," he said, "all the rest is but a tiring satisfaction of curiosity." He urged him to write something for the good cause: "The late Boulanger's name will appear on the title-page. You owe an account of your time to human reason. Hold 'infamy' in execration and love me; remember that I deserve it through the love I shall have for you until the day that I surrender my body to the four elements."

D'Alembert may not always have been a zealous warrior, but he was ever the most loyal of friends. It was to him that Voltaire wrote some six months before his death: "I embrace you with all my might, and I am sorry it is at such a distance"; and D'Alembert replied in kind: "Farewell, my dear and illustrious friend; I embrace you tenderly, and am more than ever *tuus ex animo*."

The friendship with Diderot was much less intimate and yet even more emotional than that with D'Alembert. Diderot and Voltaire met only during the latter's final months in Paris, in 1778. In 1749, before leaving Paris for Cirey, Voltaire praised Diderot's *Pensées philosophiques* and cordially invited the author to a philosophical dinner. Diderot was very independent and very anxious not to fall too completely under Voltaire's influence. He evidently refused the dinner invitation. When he was imprisoned later that same year, Voltaire urged Mme du Châtelet to use her family relationship with the chief warden to make his imprisonment at Vincennes as agreeable as possible. Voltaire left for Berlin the following year. In 1760 he wrote to Palissot, who had joined the enemies of the philosophers:

I don't know M. Diderot at all; I have never seen him. I know only that he has been unhappy and persecuted:

that reason alone should have made the pen drop from
your hand. I regard, moreover, the *Encyclopédie* enterprise as the most handsome monument that could be
erected to the honor of science. . . . Without ever having
seen M. Diderot, without finding his *Père de famille*
amusing, I have always respected his profound knowledge. And at the head of the *Père de famille* there is an
epistle to the Princess of Nassau which seemed to me the
masterpiece of eloquence and the triumph of *humanity*:
let me use the word. A score of people have assured me
that his heart is in the right place. I would be very
sorry to be mistaken, but I wish to be enlightened.

Voltaire was again caught between two fires—
Palissot had been his friend and literary adviser, his
guest at *les Délices*; but certainly, thought Voltaire, he had no right to join in the persecution of
the Encyclopedists. With tact again, but in all
loyalty, Voltaire strove to cool his ardor. Palissot
was unable to prove that Diderot's heart was not
in the right place. And Diderot, finally spurred to
action, wrote Voltaire a letter himself which settled
the matter. Voltaire then strove tirelessly and cease-
lessly to have Diderot elected to the French Academy
and ardently wished success to the *Père de famille*,
not because he liked it, but because such a victory
on the side of philosophy "would deal a mortal
blow to fanaticism." To befriend Diderot because
he was also the friend of humanity, Voltaire sacrificed many literary principles; for in theory, at
least, Diderot was a much more dangerous opponent
of the classical ideal than was Rousseau—in literature
a pronounced and romantic apologist of the strong

emotions and of Shakespeare, in philosophy and religion a materialist and atheist. It was the question of atheism that most effectively held the two men from complete intellectual communion—that and the fact that Diderot was a poor correspondent. Late in life Voltaire wrote to Diderot on the occasion of the death of their mutual friend and go-between Damilaville: "This friend knew," said Voltaire, "that we were not so far apart and that nothing more than a conversation would have been necessary to bring us together." For Damilaville, like Diderot, could not accept Voltaire's conviction that there is a guiding intelligence in the universe. "But we were nevertheless good friends," remarked Voltaire, and he very explicitly forgave them their "bad" metaphysics for their humanity. "If God had permitted 'Brother Plato' [Diderot], you, and me to live together," he wrote to Damilaville, "we would not have been useless to this world. But we will have to end, like Candide, by cultivating our gardens." Diderot was an energetic opponent of superstition and fanaticism, and his heart was in the right place. No amount of disagreement concerning abstract ideas could keep the two men from mutual admiration and respect.

Adieu, great brother [wrote Diderot at the end of a letter in 1762], be of good health, take care of yourself for the sake of your friends, for philosophy, for literature, for the honor of the nation, which can count only on you, and for the good of humanity, to which you are more essential than five hundred monarchs all together.

You don't know how much those rascals who, ever doing harm, got the idea that they alone were elected to be public benefactors, suffer to see you the friend of men, the father of orphans, and the protector of the oppressed. Continue to write great books and to do good works and let them die of spite. Farewell, sublime, honest, and dear antichrist.

Many of Diderot's most intimate friends, D'Holbach, Grimm, and Naigeon, were incapable of understanding Voltaire. This effusion is therefore all the more remarkable; Voltaire finally conquered Diderot, as he did also the pastors of Geneva, by his works.

The final chapter of this friendship was written in Paris, in 1778, when Voltaire came home to die. Many anecdotes have been collected from the meeting of these celebrated figures. Diderot, still jealous of his intellectual independence and ever ready to display his exuberant eloquence, did not miss this occasion, and Voltaire was forced to accept the unaccustomed rôle of listener. This led to one of his better-known witticisms: "This man is certainly intelligent; but nature has refused him one talent, and an essential talent: that of the dialogue." And it is reported that after seeing the eighty-three-year-old patriarch, Diderot likened him to an old fairy castle, fallen in ruins, but still inhabited by some old sorcerer. Much truer to the general tone of their friendship, almost perfect in its representation of the character of the two philosophers, is Diderot's own account of the meeting:

I have taken the liberty [he wrote] to contradict M. de Voltaire by word of mouth and in writing, with the respect that I owed to that great man's years and superiority, but also with a frankness suitable to my character, and that without offending him, without receiving any disagreeable replies. I remember that he complained bitterly one day of the stigma put upon books and authors by the magistrates: "But," I added, "do you not know that time effaces that stigma which so grieves you and turns it back upon the unjust magistrate? The hemlock was worth a temple to the philosopher of Athens. . . ." Then the old man, throwing his arms about me and pressing me to his bosom, added: "You are right, and that is what I expected of you. . . ." Others have experienced the same indulgence.

Voltaire, affectionate, too great to be always affectionately loved in return, again took the initiative, indulgently awaited the word he could heartily approve, and embraced the man who had fought so many battles with him in the common cause of humanity.

CHAPTER VI

The Final Years

AT EIGHTY-TWO

THE preceding paragraphs represent merely the more colorful types of Voltaire's friendships. Only a reading of his entire correspondence can give one an accurate impression of the large number of his friends and of the intimacy and tactfulness of his relations with them. A brief survey of the letters of a single year will add to the evidence. For the year 1776, in which fell his eighty-second birthday, somewhat more than two hundred and ninety of his letters have been collected. His correspondents included kings, queens, princes, cardinals, marshals, dukes, marquises; many notable men of letters, men of science, and politicians; and many humbler people who were also friends. The majority of the letters are militant, concerning the liberation of the county of Gex from taxation and oppression; the fall of Turgot from power; the necessity of filling the French Academy with faithful brethren; the rehabilitation of Lally and of Morangiès; the establishment of the persecuted Delisle de Sales; fulmination against Shakespeare, who had been represented by his translator, Le Tourneur, as vastly superior to all French dramatists past and present; the reply to the Abbé Guénée, who had questioned in three volumes Voltaire's Biblical erudition. D'Argental, Richelieu, and Cardinal de Bernis were friends of more than fifty years' standing, and D'Argental was still the favored correspondent. Not quite so old were the friendships with Frederick the Great, Diderot, Marmontel, and especially with D'Alembert, who received some sixteen letters in the course of the year; and among the more favored recent friends were Turgot, Condorcet, Mme de Saint-Julien, Dupont de Nemours, Comte de Tressan, and La Harpe, and also De Vaines, who had taken the place of Damilaville and Thieriot as Parisian agent and to whom some thirty-six letters were addressed. During the year friendly letters were also written to Hennin, French resident at Geneva, Jaucourt and Morellet, of Encyclopedic fame, and Cramer and Panckoucke, his publishers. Among Voltaire's candidates for the French Academy were Turgot, La Harpe, Condorcet, and Morellet. La Harpe was elected during the course of the year. He discussed political economy with Dupont, archaeology with Le Gentil, biology with the Abbé Spallanzani, philosophy with D'Alembert and Condorcet, and the theater with Thibouville and D'Argental. The "old owl of Ferney" was ill, very ill, and very conscious of his failing strength. His secretary Wagnière did the actual writing of all except the most intimate letters.

Thibouville had discovered a beautiful and talented actress and wanted Voltaire to write a tragedy for her, so he painfully started his last play, *Irène. Mais c'est montrer Vénus toute nue à un castrat*, said he.

His physical frailties seem to have affected the keenness of his mind very little; and yet old age had made him sadder and wiser. He still professed, as he professed in *Candide*, that the sorrows of this life outnumber its pleasures. He no longer felt the exuberant optimism of his youthful *Mondain*, in which, he confessed, he had performed the miracle of changing water into wine. Long and bitter struggles had convinced him that there was no immediate cure for human ills.

Governmental abuses [he wrote to Condorcet] are the patrimony of so many powerful men that they come to be regarded as fundamental laws. Almost all princes are brought up with profound respect for these abuses. . . . All we can do is to enlighten little by little the youth who may some day have a share in the government, and to inspire them gradually with more wholesome and tolerant maxims.

He himself had become much less aristocratic and much more sympathetic with the people, without at the same time believing that democracy would solve all their problems. To M. Gin, who had defended the monarchy against Mably, he expressed his somewhat guarded approval: "You do very well to show that the monarchical government is the best of all; but that is true only if Marcus Aurelius is the monarch: for otherwise what does it matter to a poor wretch whether he is devoured by one lion or a hundred rats.''

Revolution was in the air during this year 1776. Prince Frederick, Landgrave of Hesse, was sending for Voltaire's approval a composition of his called *Pensées diverses sur les princes*, while at the same time he was selling troops for slaughter in America, much to the disgust of his uncle Frederick the Great. And it was reported that Dr. Benjamin Franklin's troops had suffered reverses at the hands of the English. Did this perhaps add to the bitterness of Voltaire's attack on Shakespeare? The English were conquering everywhere—on the American continent as well as in the sacred domain of drama. And Voltaire, like a good patriot, was trying to stem the tide, praising Chamfort's *Jeune Indienne* as "pure Racine," and proclaiming that outside of Racine there was no salvation.

Many of the old personal quarrels had run their course. Rousseau, for example, had been completely forgotten. He was anxious that Paris should know of his reconciliation with Frederick. Fréron died this same year and Voltaire, in letters to D'Argental and to Thibouville, had his final word: "Do you know, my guardian angel, that I received an invitation to Catherin Fréron's burial and besides that an anonymous letter from a woman who might well be his widow? She wants me to take in Fréron's daughter and marry her off, since, she says, I married off Corneille's grandniece. I replied that if Fréron had written the *Cid*, *Cinna*, and *Polyeucte*, I

could easily make a match for her." A recent critic
has made this incident the basis for a major attack
on Voltaire's character. The Fréron family was
indeed indignant at the suggestion that the widow
might have written the letter. Yet Voltaire had
been wantonly calumniated by Fréron at the very
time of his kindness to Mlle Corneille; and this
anonymous letter gave him the irresistible occasion for a sally in letters to two of his friends. To
judge from this episode that Voltaire, like a black-
guard, persecuted and grossly insulted the bereft
Fréron family, is indeed making a mountain out of
a molehill.

The year 1776 was also the year of Turgot's fall.
Turgot was the very close friend of Condorcet,who
kept Voltaire informed of events. Admiration for
Turgot made Condorcet somewhat unjust toward
Necker, and Voltaire, won over by Necker's praise
of his own hero, Colbert, was obliged to temper
his friend's hatred. He expressed, however, the
warmest praise for Condorcet's edition of Pascal,
found "something divine in this miscellany of Blaise
Condor," and expressed this interest in making
personal annotations, later published as his *Dernières remarques sur les Pensées de Pascal*. At the end
of his life, as at its beginning, Voltaire admired
the mysticism and the style of his great predecessor,
and at the same time he saw in him the doctrinaire
whose influence it was most important for him to
combat.

The letters show again the paradoxical fact that

the men who call themselves pessimistic, who see most realistically the ills that beset the human race, are the very ones who fight abuses the most energetically and hopefully. Voltaire's hopeful tolerance is still apparent in a letter to the Protestant Moultou, in which he disagrees with the Protestant view that the Catholic Church must be, or could be, entirely destroyed; for "What is founded on so much money and so many honors is founded on a rock. We are claiming only to moderate the spirit of those who enjoy that money and those honors. We have begun this great work and we hope it will work out its own fulfillment."

There was certainly nothing rabid, nothing fanatical, nothing intolerant about this eighty-two-year-old lover and champion of humanity. Wit is ever cruel, often unfair in its emphasis, sometimes untimely, just as all art is in a sense propaganda and a distortion of reality, whether it be idyll or caricature. Wit was Voltaire's chief sin, if sin it be; and to many temperaments, such as the serious-minded Rousseau's, it was his unpardonable sin. His early cynical view of his fellow men had produced many an artistic masterpiece and his use of innuendo had brought him many a triumph. Such literary methods became so deeply ingrained in him that he could not free himself from them even when his essential love for humanity became the dominant trait in his character. It is precisely this rare combination of wit and humanity which explains to a great degree his superiority over Piron, who was witty and futile, Pope, whom he termed cold, and Swift, who was essentially misanthropic.

THE BENEVOLENT DESPOT

The facts of Voltaire's life have tempted many writers and delighted many readers because of their dramatic nature. There was an ever-swelling crescendo of activity and interest in the life of this man who began at sixty-five to live in earnest, whose final months in Paris form a magnificent climax to his career of unflagging energy, whose last conscious words were a generous tribute to a family for whom he had been able to secure long-denied justice, and who lived, as his influence even now lives, as a vital force in French culture. He was not mistaken, at least, in the assurance that posterity could not ignore him.

The twentieth century has witnessed the publication of many books on Voltaire's final years, books which have the undoubted advantage of being founded on documents rather than on prejudices. The basic study has been Fernand Caussy's *Voltaire, seigneur de village*. Paul Chaponnière has at last atoned for Genevan injustice in his *Voltaire chez les Calvinistes*, while Léon Kozminski has laid the ghost of the charge of avarice in his *Voltaire financier*. Even Desnoiresterres was forced to admiration, grudgingly it would seem, as he prepared the final chapters of his monumental biography, while Morley and Brandes have been eloquent in their unstinted praise. Voltaire himself had a judicious mind. Could he then have been so very much mistaken in his sincere conviction that he had lived the good life? Many biographers and critics are coming to share that conviction.

In the modern village of Ferney-Voltaire there is a shady public park, with benches where the patriarchs of today while away the sunny afternoons. The "one in the straw hat" is reputed to be a local authority on things Voltairean. Whether or not he goes to mass he does not say—it is possible. At the entrance to the park is a statue of Voltaire with the following inscription:

To the Benefactor of Ferney.

Voltaire built more than a hundred houses. He gave the town a church, a school, a hospital, a reservoir and a fountain. He loaned money without interest to the neighboring communities. He dried up the swamps of the countryside. He established fairs and markets. He nourished the inhabitants during the famine of 1771.

It was at *les Délices*, close to Geneva, that Voltaire began to cultivate his garden; a play garden, however, a suburban garden such as should be maintained by a wealthy resident having a coach and four. He soon felt cramped there both morally and physically—he needed to get farther away from his aristocratic Calvinist friends, and above all, he needed more land. Four years later he acquired two properties, Ferney and Tournay, on French territory between Geneva and the Jura mountains. Here he found a new employment for his capital and a new freedom to test out his utilitarian philosophy. He was the wealthy landlord, to be sure, but a resident landlord and one who finally succeeded in making himself beloved by his villagers and esteemed by men of good will.

Voltaire's great desire was to establish and maintain a profitable and exemplary agricultural economy, "to make two blades of wheat grow where only one had grown before," to surround himself with a happy, prosperous, and ever-increasing community. A rich and influential landlord alone could buy the necessary agricultural machinery and defend his people against the rapacity of the tax collectors. Inspired at first by the doctrines of the physiocrats, he planned to make his farms as self-sufficient as possible and to live on the products of his "rustic establishment." "I am only a peasant," he would tell his Parisian and English guests, and he would take them to his stables and barns, urge them to drink his milk, and show them the cleanliness of his poultry yards. He changed heaths into pasture lands and planted twenty thousand seedlings—chestnut and walnut, plane, hornbeam, and elm. Many of the seedlings died, in spite of the greatest care, because of the harsh winds and poverty of the soil; but Voltaire kept on planting them even to advanced old age, at a time when he described himself as "ridiculous for not being dead." "I have planted more than twenty thousand standing trees," he wrote to the inspector general of the Royal Nurseries, "which I got in Savoy; almost all of them died. Four times I bordered the main highway with walnut and chestnut trees; three quarters of them perished or were torn up by the peasants; however, I have not given up; and old and infirm as I am, I would plant today even if I were sure I would die tomorrow. Others would enjoy them."

The soil was indeed so poor that many fields had to be remade with transported loam and fertilizer. To save the expense of transportation, he had the brilliant idea of penning cows at night on the less-favored lands. On the subject of agriculture in the *Dictionnaire philosophique* he wrote: "A sovereign could thus change the nature of a vast tract of land by having cavalry camp upon it and consume forage drawn from the neighborhood. Whole regiments would be needed but in the long run another great tract of good land would be won from nature."

The physiocratic system of Quesnay, the subject of some correspondence between Voltaire and Dupont de Nemours, emphasized the powers of nature as the only proper source of public wealth and advocated the necessity of noninterference with natural laws affecting the relationships and processes of society and industry. But Voltaire attached much greater importance to experience than to systems, with regard to economics as well as to metaphysics. It did not take him many years to learn that mother nature could not be pushed beyond a certain degree of productivity. The fine market for wood in Geneva

not only threatened to denude the slopes of the Jura
mountains but also was a constant menace to Voltaire's newly planted trees. Since the profits from
sale were spent in the commercial establishments
of Geneva, Voltaire was not so sure that the free
movement of nature's bounties constituted a source
of public wealth to the Ferney neighborhood. The
woodlands of Tournay would have kept him warm
in winter, and would have also yielded him a profit;
but President de Brosses, before leasing the property
to Voltaire for life, had already over-exploited
them, and he cleverly left to his tenant the plant-
ings rather than the cuttings.

The dairy business was indeed profitable, and to
a certain extent the raising of wheat. Beyond these
enterprises, however, the capital that Voltaire was
investing brought ever-diminishing returns. Not
only was the soil poor, but the industries at Geneva
drew away the native sons in increasing numbers,
until it was necessary to import less efficient farm
hands from neighboring Savoy. Geneva was the
natural economic capital of the Gex countryside,
and neither national boundaries nor political laws
could change that situation. Faced with these facts,
Voltaire returned to his old faith in the economic
theories of Colbert—to the establishment and support of national industries through state aid and
protective tariffs. Beginning in a small way, he first
avenged himself on De Brosses by thoroughly exploiting a quarry on the Tournay estate, the stone
from which made it possible to construct many

new houses for the growing population of his village. A profitable tile works was established to
provide building materials. To these industries was
added a tannery, a natural industry in a cattle-
grazing country.

Thus the occupations of Ferney kept Voltaire so
busy that he gradually lost touch with his aristocratic friends at Geneva. He soon estranged them still
further by supporting the underprivileged in their
struggle for suffrage and representation. The civil
disorders occasioned by these political struggles
gave him his chance to grant a refuge to the skilled
artisans who fled from the city and to establish
them on French soil at Ferney and at Versoix. He
thus became an industrial promoter and added to
his other productions silk stockings, "blond" lace,
and Swiss watches.

At Tournay he had remodeled one of the build-
ings for a theater, where he had hoped, through
the drama, to smooth and to polish the angular
traits of his Calvinist neighbors. With more serious
occupations now at hand, he gave over his play-
house to the production of silk. He was soon sending
sample stockings, accompanied by delicate compliments, to Catherine the Great and to the wife of
Choiseul, Minister of Foreign Affairs; not entirely
out of friendship but also in the interest of the
promotion of sales. He depended, too, upon his
friends at court to launch the sale of his watches,
hoping with Catherine's aid to find a market even
in China. It was Choiseul, too, whom he interested

in the colony at Versoix, a port on the lake in French territory, which would free the county of Gex from too great dependence on Geneva. The Revocation of the Edict of Nantes had brought to Geneva an influx of artisans who furnished the city's industries with cheap and servile labor. The eighteenth century had seen the rise and success of the Levantine Company, which introduced luxuries into the formerly frugal city and made the uneven distribution of wealth more noticeable. Resistance to the artisans' or "natives' " demands for suffrage brought on the "War of Geneva," while France stood by, expecting to profit from the internal dissensions, whatever the outcome. The more bellicose watchmakers were finally exiled from the city, and Voltaire attempted to settle them at Versoix and at Ferney. The Versoix project was not yet ready for the accommodation of so many families; and Choiseul's fall soon completely ruined it. Voltaire brought the remains of the colony to Ferney with great publicity and great expense. Houses were built as rapidly as possible, and soon a thriving watch factory was operating at Ferney. It must be admitted that success was due largely to Voltaire's skill as promoter. Five years after his death the industry returned to Geneva, its more natural economic habitat. An offshoot, founded by one of Voltaire's partners, took root in France, however, in 1790, at Besançon, which has since been the center of French manufacture of watches.

During these final years at Ferney, Voltaire was

especially concerned with the tax problem. Taxes in France were, as is well known, heavy, complicated, and unjustly distributed. The mere enumeration, from head tax to salt tax, would confuse even the modern taxpayer. Here again Voltaire began his crusade from primarily selfish motives, but he was able soon to generalize his motives and finally to bring relief to the whole district of Gex. By buying Ferney in the name of Mme Denis, widow of an officer of the king, he was able to secure certain exemptions which were enjoyed by the lords of the neighborhood. A heavy tax which he was forced to pay for the leasing of Tournay made that acquisition an even worse bargain than had at first appeared. Customs regulations were so burdensome and rigid that only by yearly application could he get permission to sell his wheat in Geneva, while bands of armed smugglers overran his border territories. The salt tax was perhaps the meanest and most despised of the levies. Moreover he had under his eyes a general tax collector who was amassing an immense fortune, and who had neither his own spirit of social benevolence nor the desire to found a model economic community. After many years of struggle and during the ministry of his former friend, Turgot, Voltaire finally succeeded in freeing the district of Gex from the French tax system. This grant was obtained, to be sure, in return for a single annual contribution exacted by the tax collectors, which Voltaire thought much too heavy.

He had an idea, however, which would have lightened the burden. If the community could run its own salt monopoly, the sum could be obtained, and salt would still be cheaper than under the former system. Fabry, the general tax collector, enticed by the opening of a free market for salt, had had a similar idea, and had already made arrangements to corner the market for his own personal enrichment. But Turgot, true to his physiocratic principles, had meant to establish an entirely free market, and the plans of both Fabry and Voltaire came to naught. There was also much discussion of how to pay the levy, increased considerably, moreover, to meet the expenses of the abolition of the *corvées*. The physiocrats had advocated a single tax on land. In spite of his enthusiasm for Turgot, Voltaire, who was one of the large landholders of the region, could not see the justice in thus taxing agriculture and exempting industry and commerce. A compromise was reached, and as a general result of the whole arrangement the more privileged 40 percent of the population paid the entire tax and the 60 percent of impoverished citizens were exonerated—quite contrary to custom in pre-Revolutionary France. Just as Voltaire had established relationships with the Genevan aristocracy, only gradually to abandon them in order to champion the unfranchised artisans, so, after first claiming exemptions commonly allowed to the nobility, he finally came to the support of the fourth estate in their taxation grievances and joined the farmers and artisans and curates in their struggle against the tax collector, the Parliament at Dijon, and the privileged nobles of his neighborhood. The breath of economic freedom was in the air. Voltaire certainly did not originate it, but he was intelligent enough to feel and accept its implications. It would indeed have been surprising if this champion of religious and political justice had been totally blind to the nascent, often unrealistic, demands of economic justice. Lord of his village, he was fond of saying that after all he was nothing but a peasant.

The aptness of the title "benevolent despot" depends upon the relative emphasis put upon benevolence and despotism. His wealth and his influential position as a man of letters, with friends in all the principal courts of Europe, put considerable power into his hands. All his life, too, he had desired that freedom which was now for the first time his to use. Possessed of indomitable energy, quick to act and to react, and believing that the hope of the people was in the enlightenment of their rulers, he ruled at Ferney in a manner that has seemed to many commentators despotic. A Jesuit, François Cornou, in the course of his recent study of Fréron, Voltaire's greatest tormentor, speaks of the patriarch's slaves at Ferney. It is alarming to find such willful misrepresentations in a book crowned by the French Academy. Voltaire may not have consulted his workers when he made his decisions; he did, however, consult their interests, and through his good will and benevolent acts he won their affection. The memoirs of his secretary Wagnière are full of instances of this affection, as were the accounts of many travelers from all parts of Europe who visited the patriarch at Ferney. Voltaire was deeply touched by the tribute of Mme Suard: "How moved I was," she wrote, "to find you always as perfectly good as you are great, and to see you doing all about you the good that you would have liked to do for all humanity."

Voltaire comprehended fully the social responsibilities conferred on him by his power and his wealth. Inequalities of wealth he accepted as the natural concomitant of the inequality of talents. To picture him dashing off to distribute revolutionary literature to the populace is of course absurd. At Ferney he was surrounded by a wretched peasantry, mostly illiterate. True, he established a school as well as a hospital and boasted that he had abolished abject poverty in his village. But as a practical problem he had little faith, at first, in the reformation of society through the agency of the people. He was not, of course, the first to say that "the poor we have with us always." He was, however, by temperament an aristocrat, and a champion of an aristocracy founded not on the hazard of birth or on political favor, but on good taste, good will, and a capacity for reasoning.

The aristocratic tone of the following letter to his friend Damilaville has often been used against him by modern socialists:

I think we misunderstand each other on the question

of the people, whom you deem worthy of receiving instruction. I mean by "people" the populace, who live by brawn alone. I doubt if this class of citizens ever will have the time or the capacity for instruction; they will die of hunger before they will become philosophers. I deem it essential that the ignorant poor exist. If you were exploiting a farm, as I am, and if you had ploughs, you would agree with me. It's not the worker that we must educate, but the good bourgeois, the city dweller; that enterprise is great and difficult enough.

Voltaire added that he would prefer to train orphans to be farmhands rather than theologians. Damilaville evidently thought this view too harsh, for Voltaire wrote again, praising the spread of wise philosophy and somewhat softening his opinion:

The lower classes [he said] will certainly be more worthy when the principal citizens cultivate wisdom and virtue: they will be restrained by example, which is the strongest and best of teachers. It is certain that pilgrimages, miracles, superstitious ceremonies will never make gentlemen. Example alone makes them and by example it is best to instruct ignorant villagers. It's therefore the leading citizens who must first be enlightened. . . . Reason is making great progress, but only among a small number of intelligent people. . . . Let us be consoled that the number is growing every day and is composed everywhere of the best people of each nation.

However, when Linguet used the same arguments the following year in a letter to Voltaire criticizing the educational influence of the Encyclopedists and writing that "all is lost as soon as the people are taught that they, too, have intelligence," Voltaire replied in very different fashion. He would now distinguish between the artisans, who require an honest education, and purely manual laborers.

Parisians would be surprised [he wrote] if they saw in several Swiss cities, especially in Geneva, that almost all those employed in manufactures pass in reading the time that cannot be devoted to work. No, sir, all is not lost when the people are taught that they have minds. All is lost, on the contrary, when they are treated like a herd of bulls, for sooner or later they will gore you with their horns.

Never again, Voltaire believed, would the people fall so easy a prey to fanaticism as they had during the days of Cromwell or of the religious wars of France.

In the colony that Voltaire drew around him at Ferney, as well as in that which he had started at Versoix, his liberalism was religious rather than political, and religious toleration interested him much more than democratic equality. He was delighted to see his Protestant and Catholic villagers living together in peace and he hoped that the pastor and the priest would bowl together on the green after the preaching was done. "We have no desire to destroy you know what [the Catholic Church]," he wrote during the last years of his life. He often repeated that he did not wish to keep lackeys from going to mass, and he was delighted when Protestants joined with Catholics in the celebration of Corpus Christi. As lord of his village he was glad to recognize the restraining power of religion in the policing of his domains. Economic liberalism and genuine democracy, he believed, would never be feasible until the Enlightenment had broken the powers of religious fanaticism. When the issue was joined, his common sense often demanded a sacrifice of principle.

Both as gentleman farmer and as industrial promoter, he acted always in what he thought were the best interests of his people. In a very interesting letter to the physiocrat Pierre-Samuel Dupont de Nemours, Voltaire described his conception of an ideal farm, flattering himself that Ferney, after ten years of occupancy, resembled somewhat his description. Here, and often thereafter, he repeated his belief that the landlord should reside on his farm at least nine months of the year, as was the custom in England: "Not only would the possessors of great domains through their generosity of heart bring aid to those who suffer, but through necessity (the very fact of residence) they would help those whom they would put to work. Whoever puts men to useful employment renders a service to his country." Voltaire's theories have a familiar ring today; but these words were written in 1769, in the France of the Old Régime, when the profits of agriculture were almost universally spent in the pursuit of pleasure in Paris by nobles and abbés many of whom had never seen the land from which their income came. Five years later, tempted to go to Paris, he found he could not leave Ferney: "My

VOLTAIRE VISITS HIS VILLAGERS

colony," he wrote to D'Argental, requires my real
presence." And in the same year he wrote to tell
Mme du Deffand how sorry he was he could not
come to see her in Paris: "Frivolous as I may have
been, I have eight hundred people to guide and sus-
tain. I am a founder in a wild country; I have
changed its nature, but I cannot absent myself
without having everything relapse into chaos."
Two years later, writing to ask for money that was
due him, he said: "A poor man of letters should
never have founded a fine city in which five hundred
thousand francs' worth of trade is transacted yearly.
My insolence makes me see at least what benefits
the lords could bring to their provinces if they
would only live at home. They prefer to spend a
hundred thousand crowns at court in order to obtain a pension of two thousand. My folly is better
than theirs. I started too late, my dear friend, to
accomplish this little act of beneficence." The pessimistic tone, through which pride penetrates, was
due of course to the fact that he needed the money.

DEATH IN PARIS

When finally, in February, 1778, Voltaire was
persuaded, at the age of eighty-three, to visit Paris,
the cares of Ferney were so heavy upon him that he
hardly knew three days before his departure whether
he could really leave. And after his first serious illness in Paris, hardly more than a month before his
death, he planned to go back to care for his flock.
"I must leave in two weeks," he wrote D'Argental,

his "guardian angel," "otherwise everything will go to ruin at Ferney. I hope by September never to leave again the protection of my angel's wings." His fears were only too soon to be realized. Mme Denis, who inherited Ferney, had nothing of her uncle's benevolent spirit and no desire whatever to reside on the frontiers of France. With Voltaire dead, the experiment in model government was over, and Ferney shared the vicissitudes of the stormy years to come without special privilege. France owes at least to her great man of letters the retention of the village of Ferney-Voltaire within her boundaries. She has yet to show her gratitude by turning the château at Ferney into a national monument.

By his works shall the artisan be known, and Ferney was indeed a monument to a man's devotion to his ideas. The immensity of human suffering impressed him so profoundly that he was benevolent and charitable. With the wilfully lazy and debauched he was often harsh. But the unfortunate and oppressed could count on his generosity. If possible, he established them in some useful occupation, for hard work had been the remedy for his own moments of weakness and despair. The widows, the orphans, and the aged he cared for.

Voltaire's devoted secretary, Wagnière, who accompanied his master on the fateful journey to Paris, says that the people of Ferney were filled with grief and consternation at their lord's departure, weeping and seeming to foresee the impending disaster, while Voltaire himself wept from emotion. He promised them he would be back in a month and a half, and that was his intention, for he had neglected to put his papers in order. On the trip it was impossible for him to maintain his incognito, and his coach and the inns where he stopped were besieged by his admirers and the curious. On the afternoon of the sixth day the coach reached the boundary of Paris. The customs agents asked if it was carrying anything against the King's orders. "Gentlemen," replied Voltaire, "I believe there is no contraband here but myself." By that time the agents had discovered the identity of the wizened face under the immense wig and begged Voltaire to continue on his way. Wagnière relates that his master was a gay traveling companion, now reasoning with him, now telling stories that made his sides shake with laughter.

The day after his arrival, he wrote the following brief note of greeting to Mme du Deffand: "I arrive dead and I want to rise again only to throw myself at the feet of Madame la Marquise du Deffand." From that moment on, he was overwhelmed with the love and adoration of old friends such as Mme du Deffand and D'Alembert and newer friends whom he had never seen. There were touching interviews with Diderot and with Franklin, who brought his grandson with him for Voltaire to bless with the words: "For God and Liberty." The French Academy sent a special delegation to visit him; the actors of the *Théâtre Français* came in a body; and the Eng-

lish ambassador also paid his respects. The court
at Versailles was alarmed and looked in vain for
judicial papers of banishment. Voltaire had been
right, there was no *lettre de cachet* against him, nor
had he been legally exiled. What mattered it, after
all, that in 1778 the court of France chose to snub
her greatest citizen?

Such a busy life was a great contrast to the tranquillity of Voltaire's existence at Ferney. Ten days
after his arrival in Paris, Dr. Tronchin was alarmed
and declared that since his patient had been in
Paris he had been rapidly exhausting his reserve
strength. His legs had begun to swell, and by the
end of the first two weeks the first violent hemor-
rhage occurred. A certain Abbé Gautier had been
hoping to win from him a last-minute confession.
Voltaire was torn between his desire, as a matter
of taste, to die within the forms of the religion of
his birth and his fear of shocking his brothers in
philosophy. He wrote with his own hand a statement to the effect that "he wished to die in the
Catholic religion in which he was born and asked
pardon of God and the Church if he had offended
them." Soon after he signed for Wagnière another
declaration which read: "I die adoring God, loving
my friends, not hating my enemies, and detesting
superstition."

During the month of March, following his partial recovery, he received new honors and new
glories. He visited and addressed the French Academy, exhorted the members by word and by exam-

ple to work on their dictionary, and was received as an honorary member into the Masonic Lodge of the Seven Sisters. The greatest triumph was, however, that of his tragedy *Irène*. At the sixth performance the author was wildly acclaimed, his statue was crowned with laurel upon the stage, and the people drew his coach home in triumph through the streets of Paris.

Before the final performance of *Irène*, Voltaire, discovering that some of his verses had been tampered with, flew into a high rage, more violent than his secretary had ever witnessed and lasting ten hours. "If that didn't kill you," observed Wagnière to his master, "nothing will unless we knock you down with a bludgeon." Voltaire's friends had been very critical of his text and had elicited from him very humble, almost pathetic letters, in which the aging author expressed his hope that the pit would be indulgent. It was chiefly for the performance of *Irène* that he had made up his mind to come to Paris.

After the triumphs of *Irène*, the month of April came, and Voltaire's thoughts turned to Ferney. Dr. Tronchin strongly advised him to return, and Wagnière, too, believed that his master could not long endure the excitement of Paris. They had not counted, however, on the natural desire of Voltaire's friends to keep him in Paris nor on Mme Denis's long-standing dislike of Ferney and her determination to live in Paris. To please his niece Voltaire secured a house in a more quiet section of the city and offered to go back to Ferney alone to settle his affairs. Mme Denis at first accepted but afterward realized that she could not thus abandon her uncle without opprobium. She therefore made greater efforts to keep him in Paris. Voltaire himself was not fooled by the acclamations of the populace nor by the quiescence of the court. When his niece asked why he must return, he replied, "Because I adore the country, and it gives me life."

Wagnière, who gives the most authentic account of these events, was always afraid he would bore his readers with trivial episodes. In a note, however, he recounts a very touching incident. The coachman, who had been called from the country to make the return trip to Ferney, brought a handsome dog that Voltaire was very fond of. The dog also showed an abundant affection for the patriarch. Voltaire sent for the dog that evening in Mme de Villette's presence. "The animal, entering the apartment, ran to M. de Voltaire and caressed him. 'You see, now,' he said, 'that I am still loved at Ferney.' At the same time the tears streamed from his eyes. From that moment, they did not let the dog enter the house."

Voltaire's friends finally persuaded him that he should not run away from persecution. Wagnière thus went back to Ferney alone to get some much-needed papers and books. Whether Voltaire would have lived longer if he had returned too, no one, of course, can say. That he could not live long in Paris was evident at least to his doctor and to his secretary. The second attack came early in May and was evidently aggravated by an overdose of an opiate which Voltaire was urged to take without his doctor's knowledge. Uremic poisoning set in, followed by gangrene, and the illness was incurable. Wagnière has very possibly exaggerated the neglect with which Mme Denis treated her uncle and her desire to keep the secretary from him as long as possible. Voltaire himself finally wrote demanding Wagnière's return. It was too late. As Wagnière was entering Paris, the body of the patriarch, upright in a coach, was being secretly removed from Paris, where Christian burial had been denied. Voltaire thus was deprived of the consolation of his secretary, to whom he was affectionately attached, and posterity was deprived of a reliable eyewitness of his last moments.

Wagnière foresaw, however, the stories that would be circulated by the pious about the death of a man whom they regarded as the personification of impiety. He therefore took great pains to collect all the information possible from those who were with Voltaire at the end. Atrocious stories did in fact appear and have been republished even in our present age—stories which illustrate, as clearly as any Voltaire himself could have found, the disease of fanaticism.

CHAPTER VII

On Life and Death

VOLTAIRE VERSUS PASCAL

VOLTAIRE held very definite views on life and death which were in direct contrast to those of the Jansenists. Like early Protestantism, Jansenism explained human nature in terms of the divine through the theological doctrines of the fall and the redemption, predestination, and grace. Pascal was considered the most gifted and most influential interpreter of these views and Voltaire recognized in him the redoubtable champion of a way of life directly opposed to his own. Voltaire published his *Remarques sur les Pensées de Pascal* in 1734. Yet Pascal's ideas continued to preoccupy his mind and his final commentaries were published as late as 1777. Voltaire's views are clearest when they are thus set in opposition to Pascal's.

Influenced by Montaigne's skepticism concerning the powers and uses of reason, Pascal maintained that the "heart has reasons which Reason comprehendeth not." By the "heart," Pascal seems to have meant not only the vague emotional sensations which have not yet developed into verbal expression but also that higher intuition, or attribute of genius, which is the sudden, often unconscious, revelation of the rational experience of the past through a happy invention of phrase. Pascal believed that it was by intuition, not by reasoning analysis, that man might comprehend and be comprehended. A precociously great scientist on the threshold of one of the greatest of scientific ages, Pascal turned his back on science and sought the comfort and peace of his own heart in the consolations of authoritative religion. His early death prevented him from arranging and completing his *Pensées*, which he seemed to have collected for the purpose of writing an apology for the Christian religion. Voltaire was quick to see the logical weaknesses of these brilliantly conceived thoughts. He was also able to point out, as if he were writing from the orthodox Catholic and Jesuit standpoint, their heretical nature: a perfidious method, some would say, but under no other conditions could he have safely opposed the Jansenist doctrines.

Man, according to Pascal, is not an animal like other animals but is unique—a fallen angel; "a finite creature with the ignominious mark of the infinite upon him"; more wicked than other creatures because alone among them he is endowed with reason; more unhappy because he has within him the vision of perfection and because he is destined ever to search restlessly and in vain for the Absolute; bafflingly incomprehensible to himself because of the two natures of good and of evil that he perceives, when in the anguish of meditation he dares look within himself. What better explanation could be given, thought Pascal, for this double nature of man than the theological doctrines of the fall and the redemption? And is it not man's obvious duty to forego the pleasures of this life, to prepare his soul for the escape from the body, and to hope for grace, which is the indication that an abode of eternal happiness is prepared for him?

It is obvious that Voltaire did not have to go out of his way "to attack this giant," for he found him lying directly across his path. Man is not unique, he countered, but differs from the other animals only in degree. He may be best understood, not by the sharp division into the two absolute categories of good and evil, but as an animal, imperfect like other animals, but more finely organized, with more passions and desires. He is intellectually superior and less necessarily a prey to his passions; a mysterious creature, to be sure, if we insist on knowing his beginnings and his ends and the nature and interaction of his spirit and body, yet not incomprehensible to those who seek in good faith to know him. In spite of the brilliant ideas of Plato and Pascal concerning the double nature of man, human reason gives no support to any such dichotomy. Nor can "inconceivable man" be rendered more conceivable, so Voltaire's argument runs, through the inconceivable doctrine of original sin. "The misery and wretchedness of human life," Voltaire thought, "in a philosophic sense no more proves the fall of man than the misery of a cab horse proves that horses were formerly all big and fat and were never subjected to the whip.'' Such a doctrine can be accepted only as revealed truth, not as reasoned truth.

Moreover, is man after all so utterly wretched? Voltaire wrote his sparklingly joyous and ebullient poem *Le Mondain* two years after his first comments on Pascal, and there is an obvious connection between the two works. In *Le Mondain* one finds the celebration of life's pleasures, physical and intellectual: the pleasures of food and wine partaken in the pagan spirit of Rabelais or in the more refined epicurean spirit of Saint-Evremond as well as the joys of the arts and letters. Apart from its economic defense of luxury, broadly conceived, the poem is indeed a part of the pagan revolt against Christian asceticism, a reassertion of the essential natural goodness of man—not in his natural state, to be sure, for Adam and Eve had no scissors to cut their black fingernails, no beds on which to rest their weary limbs, and nothing to eat but acorns; but rather in his naturally civilized state, as a participant in the gay life of Paris, with its champagne, its actresses, and its operas.

Voltaire was here forcing the note for the sake of the argument. The twenty years between this poem and the *Poème sur le désastre de Lisbonne* brought many disillusions. Never again could this particular kind of optimism appeal to him. Yet he accepted human life in its fullest and lived on good terms with it to the end. He had sought and found his earthly salvation through the exercise of a generous heart and a tireless mind. Before the idea was definitely formulated by Beaumarchais, Voltaire had discovered that we must laugh at human affairs lest we be obliged to weep over them.

Being intellectually curious, he was tormented by the problem of evil. The list of his works that deal with the problem is long and includes many of his best: *Le Mondain*, *Les Discours sur l'homme*, *Zadig*, *Le Désastre de Lisbonne*, and *Candide*, not to mention the *Dictionnaire philosophique* and countless prose pamphlets. He knew as well as Pascal that the universe is mysterious, he felt the same awe, though not the same dread, in contemplating its mysteries. He was sincerely shocked that Pascal should abandon the rational arguments which seemed to him satisfactory proofs of the existence of God or of a Supreme Intelligence and should leave the question to be settled by a wager. "Your reasoning," he remarked, "would serve only to make atheists, if all nature did not cry out to us that there is a God, and with as much force as there is weakness in these subtleties of yours." "The heavens declare the glory of God," he asserted, in a burst of righteous indignation; the very Scriptures were wiser than Pascal knew. It is amusing to find Voltaire thus defending against Pascal, and with quotation from the Bible, the reasonableness of a belief in God. Yet Pascal was perhaps wiser than Voltaire knew in his refusal to accept as a rational proof of God's existence the argument of an ordered and harmonious universe.

Voltaire did not ordinarily trust too much in the efficacy of reason in solving the mysteries of life and death. But above all else, he was intellectually courageous. He was strong enough to live with his doubts and be happy with them. Doubt was for him the beginning and end of wisdom, and he sought no escape in the consoling arms of that revealed religion which Pascal often mistook for intuitive truth. Thus both Pascal and Voltaire sought and found happiness, each in his own way—one by renunciation, the other by the fulfillment of the faculties of natural man living in human society. Voltaire could explain Pascal's way only as that of an abnormal, sick, and tortured soul. Pascal had no chance to reply. Yet how easy it would have been for him to explain that Voltaire's perverse incredulity was due to a soul deprived of grace and predestined to damnation! There is an evident simplification of the issues to be gained by the unquestioned acceptance of certain religious axioms. Voltaire felt he could not afford that luxury, he preferred to remain in doubt, clinging only to those truths that are humanly accessible through purely human means.

Pascal is in Voltaire [wrote J. R. Carré, in the most philosophic treatment yet accorded the study of the two men] and therefore Pascal's definition of man was not so far wrong; at least for great men, Pascal was right: they live with a heart that nothing satisfies. But it is perhaps the precise function of philosophers to know how to live under a leaden sky; and to refuse to betray reason, in the search of euthanasia or beatitude, cost what it may, even if it should mean throwing themselves in the

[213]

arms of the unknowable. Such a betrayal would have seemed to Voltaire intellectual cowardice.

Voltaire was not tortured, when confronted with the unknowable. His skies were far from leaden, even in old age; he was literally and spiritually dazzled by the glare of the bright sun on the brilliant snows of the neighboring Jura mountains. His enthusiasm for life was very influential in determining the emotions with which he viewed its inevitable termination. Pascal, on the contrary, was led by his preconceived notions concerning death and heaven to put man in a very low and precarious position in relation to the universe. In contrast to Pascal's view that contemplation of death is the proper study of mankind, his contemporary Saint-Evremond, in love with the pleasures of life and with no great faith in immortality, considered the deterioration of the body and its final disintegration painful subjects which should be put out of mind as far as possible. Voltaire's views were more in harmony with those of that classical civilization which he so greatly admired. Without Pascal's escape and with no more faith in a future life than Saint-Evremond, he was nevertheless able to face death with equanimity. He prepared himself early for the eventuality and wrote on the subject willingly and with the utmost calm to his various friends, especially to Mme du Deffand, who would seem often to have preferred death to the pure boredom into which her life so often resolved itself.

It might be argued, of course, that Voltaire, never

robust and often in ill health, lived so close to
death for such a long period of years that a certain
degree of intimacy had grown up between them.
This was an observation he had already made at
the age of thirty; and in his old age he remarked
that he had managed to keep on living, but had
nevertheless felt the virtual experience of death
many times. As early as his exile in England, Arthur
Young had satirized his physical appearance in the
terms of a criticism that Voltaire had made of
Milton:

> Thou art so witty, profligate and thin,
> At once we think thee Milton, Death and Sin.

Yet such an explanation is hardly satisfactory. His
biography and his correspondence lead to one conclusion: he was in love with life because he was
living it abundantly and generously. He obviously
did not welcome death; why then did this lover of
life not fear it? There is but one satisfactory answer:
his conscience was clear, he had lived the good life,
he had fought the good fight. Not that he expected
thus to avoid eternal punishment. His God was not
the God of vengeance, the God that encouraged
Dante on his journey through hell to stifle human
pity in his breast, but a God so lofty that he could
pay little attention to the fate of individual man,
no more perhaps than to rats on a sinking ship—the
God of heavens, rather that of heaven and hell.
"It is clear, indeed," he wrote in his *Dernières
remarques sur les Pensées de Pascal*, "that it would be
better to be a Trajan or a Marcus Aurelius, in no

matter what system, than to be a Nero or a Pope Alexander VI. This pope and this emperor, Nero, should fear lest their souls be immortal. Good people have nothing to fear in any system."

But the modern world has been torn since Petrarch between two ideas of immortality, and the pagan conception is the older and perhaps the more tenacious. Voltaire, like Cicero, could face death calmly because he expected to be admired by posterity. The fact that his expectations were in great measure and with great injustice unrealized, he did not, of course, foresee. It was in this respect that he was over-optimistic in his views of reason and human nature. Yet "his spirit still torments half of the world," wrote Paul Chaponnière, "like a fever and like a reproach." Voltaire will always remain the hero of the intellectually curious; while those whose greatest need is consolation will continue to seek it in the direction indicated by Pascal.

IMMORTALITY OR DISSOLUTION?

It was in his correspondence with Mme du Deffand, as we have seen, that Voltaire most frequently touched upon the subjects of life and death. Mme du Deffand could not forget the brillance of her youth nor the gay life at the court under the Regency of Philip of Orleans. In contrast to Voltaire, she was completely unable to share his generous impulses and to adapt herself to the social and literary changes of the second half of the century. Abandoned by her protégée, Julie de Lespinasse, and by many

of their common friends, unhappy in her marriage
and in her relations with her most intimate friends,
such as President Hénault, she had been able to
form no satisfactory philosophy with which
to meet her old age and blindness. The gatherings in
her celebrated salon were her only rampart against
boredom—those and her affection for Mme de Choiseul, her unseasonable love for Horace Walpole, and
her letters from Voltaire.

In 1723 Voltaire, stricken with smallpox, had
been confessed and had made his will. "After that,"
he wrote to Mme du Châtelet's father, "I awaited
death tranquilly enough, regretting only my failure
to put the final touches on my poem and *Mariamne*,
and saddened by having to leave my friends so
soon." That same tranquillity and the same type of
regret characterized his whole career. To Voltaire
the desire for death was entirely unnatural, though
he expressed his wonder in *Candide* that, considering
the extent and depth of human misery, there were so
few suicides in the world, which was evident proof,
he thought, of the tremendous power of the instinct
to live. The first remedy that he proposed to Mme
du Deffand was hope, the bottom of Pandora's box,
the subject of that most beautiful of all ancient
fables. By "hope" he did not mean belief in the
future life—Rousseau and the pastor Élie Bertrand
were soon to challenge him on that definition. Hope
of immortality, he often reflected, was the most
magnificent and consoling chimera devised by man.
Hope meant to him the expectation of a new heaven

and a new earth. Not that he, Voltaire, would live long enough on earth or by a projection of his identity, in heaven, to see them—and what could that sort of hope mean for poor blind unloved Mme du Deffand, whose ideal society was the gay, aristocratic society of her youth? Voltaire tried the remedy of diversion: "I would not commit suicide," he said, "because I am receiving life annuities from two sovereigns and I would be inconsolable if my death enriched two crowned heads."

In trying to dispel Mme du Deffand's pessimism, Voltaire offered no easy optimism:

You ask me, madame, what I think [he wrote]. I think that we are indeed contemptible creatures and that there are only very few people spread over the earth who dare hold to common sense; I think you belong to that small number. What use is that? None at all. Read the parable of the *Brahmin* that I have had the honor of sending you; and I exhort you to enjoy as much as you can life, which isn't much, without fearing death, which is nothing.

The long letter is one of Voltaire's best; Mme du Deffand called it divine. It diverted but did not convert. Her answer showed the same black pessimism: "All conditions and all species seem to me equally unhappy, from the angel to the oyster; the sad part of it is having been born, and yet it may be said of that misfortune that the remedy is worse than the disease."

The continued pessimism of her letters was a real affliction to Voltaire. Was it not enough, he thought, not to be numbered among the imbeciles and the fanatics that people the earth, to have friends, as well as a good digestion?

Upon reflection [he wrote] I think we should never think of death: the thought is good for nothing but to poison life. The real business of life is not to suffer, for, as for death, that moment is as insensible as the moment of sleep. People who announce it ceremoniously are the enemies of the human race; we must keep them from ever approaching us. Death is nothing at all; the idea alone is sad. So let's never think of it, and live from day to day. Let us get up in the morning saying: What can I do today for my health and amusement? That's the final answer for people of our age.

The themes of this paragraph frequently recur, sometimes enlarged upon, throughout the rest of this intimate correspondence. In a letter written somewhat later he agreed with Mme du Deffand that life is very short and often unhappy, but he called attention to one of his relatives who although completely paralyzed by a fall had become accustomed to his lot and was really in love with life. He added:

It is not that there isn't something good about annihilation, but I believe it is impossible really to love it, in spite of its good qualities. As for death, let us reason a bit, please: it is very certain that one does not feel it; it is not a moment of pain; it is just like sleep; it is only the idea of never waking up that is painful; it is the paraphernalia of death that is horrible—the barbarity of extreme unction and the cruelty of people in warning us that all is over.

Why do they come and pronounce our sentence? It will be executed surely enough without the bother of notary or priest. We must make our arrangements early and then forget about them.

[219]

It is sometimes said of a man: He died like a dog; but a dog is very lucky to die without that ceremony with which the last moment of our lives is persecuted. If people were really charitable toward us, they would let us die without telling us anything about it.

And it is even worse to be surrounded with hypocrites to make you think what they don't think themselves or imbeciles who want you to be as stupid as they are; all that is very disgusting. The only pleasure of life at Geneva is that one can die as one likes; many good people don't call priests. They commit suicide, if they wish, without anyone's finding fault, or they bide their time, without being bothered.

But still the very doleful letters arrived from Mme du Deffand. Voltaire tried a new consolation—the fatalistic resignation of the materialistic philosophers of old:

Annihilation has its good points; let us console ourselves, clever people contend that we shall enjoy them. It is very clear, they say, after Seneca and Lucretius, that after our death we shall be what we were before birth. But what shall we do with the two or three minutes of our existence? We are, they claim, little wheels in the great machine, little animals with two feet and two hands like monkeys, less agile than they, just as comical, and better supplied with ideas . . . we are no more the masters of our ideas than we are of the circulation of our blood in our veins. . . . What a sorry state of affairs! you will say. . . . Here is, perhaps, madam, what I would offer as a remedy. . . . You couldn't help writing the very philosophic and very sad letter that I received from you; and I write you, of necessity, that courage, resignation to nature's laws, profound contempt for all superstitions, the noble pleasure of feeling oneself of a different order from the stupid, and the exercise of the thinking faculty are true consolations. This idea, which I was destined to represent to you, recalls in you, of necessity, your philosophy. I become an instrument which strengthens another, through which I am in my turn strengthened. Happy are the machines which can give each other mutual aid.

Voltaire was careful to attribute to other men this philosophy of materialistic determinism. Outwardly, he fought it; but there are many occasions when he appears inwardly to have been tempted by it. Resignation before the unattainable, the ineffable, the unknowable, was at least an early and abiding characteristic of his view of life. It was in this spirit that he wrote later to Mme du Deffand: "I await in all calmness the dissolution of my being, thanking nature very sincerely for having made me live to the age of seventy-four, a little favor that I would never have expected."

It was of Mme du Deffand that Voltaire asked for the details of M. d'Argenson's death, and he again expressed his preference for pre-Christian customs. He wrote:

I would like to know if M. d'Argenson died like a philosopher or like a milksop. Last moments are accompanied in a part of Europe by circumstances so disgusting and so ridiculous that it is very difficult to know what dying people think. They all pass through the same ceremonies. There have been Jesuits impudent enough to assert that Montesquieu died like an imbecile, and they use that as an argument to engage others to die likewise.

It must be confessed that the Ancients, our masters in everything, had a great advantage over us; they didn't trouble life and death with subservient obligations which make them both baleful. In the days of the Scipios and the Caesars, they lived, they thought, they died as they wished; but we are treated like marionettes.

Six months before his death he wrote to Frederick the Great: "I am eighty-four years old today. I have a greater aversion than ever for extreme unction and for those who give it."

Mme du Deffand was perplexed about the problem of a possible existence after death. "What shall we be?" she had asked. "You will no longer be you, and you will be a great loser; I shall no longer be I, and I can't help gain thereby; but once again, what shall we be? If you know, tell me; and if you don't know, think no more about it."

Again Voltaire offered a consolation that he was unwilling openly to claim as his own:

I once knew a man [he replied] who was firmly persuaded that when a bee dies, its humming subsists no longer. . . . He said that nature has so arranged things that we think with our heads just as we walk with our feet. He claimed it was most evident that man is made, like all the other animals and all the plants and perhaps like everything else in the universe to be and to cease to be. His opinion was that this idea is a consolation for all the sorrows of life, because all these alleged sorrows have been inevitable; so this man, when he had arrived at the age of Democritus, laughed like him at everything.

Was this man La Mettrie, author of *L'Homme machine*, whom Voltaire had known at Frederick's

court and from whose philosophy he strove in vain
to save the Prussian king? And was Voltaire again
close to an acceptance himself of this philosophy of
the Ancients, or did he merely consider it an argument of the last resort in his effort to console his
loved and skeptical Parisian correspondent?

There are other indications in Voltaire's letters
to bear out the assumption that his conception of
the afterlife was more in accordance with that of
the sages of antiquity than with the Christian
doctrine. During the last years, too, when he finally
believed in all sincerity that he had not long to
live, when he joked about packing his bag for the
final journey, it was the Elysian Fields of the Greek
and Latin poets rather than the Christian heaven
that he conceived as his destination. In the spring
of 1777 he suffered what he believed to be a slight
stroke, a definite warning that the end was approaching. To La Harpe he wrote that he was on his way
to see Horace and asked if his protégé had any
messages for Jean Racine. To D'Alembert he said he
had received a warning from nature summoning him
to appear soon at the tribunal before which the
rascally Fréron was at that moment showing off his
literary asininity. There is a certain variety, however, in his pronouncements. To D'Alembert he
expressed his delight in Louis XVI's support of
Turgot and declared that the event made him want
to live, but he added: "Nevertheless, I must go and
join the Being of beings." For the Abbé Gautier,
during his first illness at Paris, his words were care-

fully chosen to suit the occasion: "I am going soon to appear before God, creator of the universe."

Voltaire seems thus to have found consolation in the philosophy and in the poetry of antiquity. He believed, like Epicurus, that friendship and work were the best remedies for life's ills: "I find that old age makes friendship very necessary," he wrote to Mme du Deffand; "it is the consolation of our woes and the support of our weakness, even more than is philosophy. How happy are your friends, Madame, who console you and whom you console!" When D'Argental, in one winter, lost his brother, his wife, and a dear friend, Voltaire wrote him a very affectionate letter of condolence:

Your very grief bears with it the most flattering of consolations [he said] for it is the inner witnessing of the fact that you suffer only because you have a beautiful soul. . . . Keep very busy, my dear guardian angel; I know no other remedy for your present state. I am sick in bed, over eighty years old, in the midst of the snows. I keep busy, and that alone keeps me alive.

Voltaire as might well be expected, often joked about his approaching death. It was in a jesting mood that he said he was soon going to inhabit his cemetery in order to give more variety to earth's little theater. Like the death of Swift's Sir Isaac Bickerstaff, Voltaire's death was often announced and rumored abroad before it occurred. To the postmaster at Berne, who had heard such a rumor, Voltaire related in one of his most happily phrased letters the story of Bickerstaff, and he added:

If you wish to bury me, sir, you are indeed at liberty to do so. I am seventy-four years old, I am very thin and weigh very little, and two little boys will suffice to carry me to my tomb, which I have built in the cemetery of my church. You won't even have to have me prayed for, since in your communion you don't pray for the dead. But I will pray God for the conversion of your correspondent who insists that I be in two places at once, which has never happened to anyone but Saint Francis Xavier, and which appears today to several worthy people morally impossible.

On the occasion of Voltaire's communion at Easter, 1768, a certain Abbé de la Bletterie was reported to have remarked that the philosopher had forgotten to have himself buried. Voltaire replied with the following epigram:

> It did not slip my memory,
> My works and I will soon decease;
> But I'm polite, La Bletterie,
> And say: You first, sir, if you please.

> Je ne prétends point oublier
> Que mes œuvres et moi nous avons peu de vie;
> Mais je suis très-poli, je dis à La Bletterie:
> "Ah! monsieur, passez le premier!"

At the much more serious moment when Voltaire knew there was grave doubt whether the clergy of Paris would allow him a Christian burial, he wrote to a friend at court: "I believe that the Abbé de Beauregard, preacher at Versailles, so-called "former Jesuit," would willingly have refused me the rites of burial, which is very unjust; for it is said I would like nothing better than to bury him, and he owed me, it seems to me, the same consideration."

To D'Alembert, he wrote: "The disorders in Geneva amuse me, but I am too ill to be greatly amused. I'm on my way down the highway to the other world, that land from which, as Will Shakespeare says, no traveler has ever returned. Must I die without knowing exactly whether Poissonnier has succeeded in 'de-salting' sea water? That would indeed be cruel."

Neither his own sufferings and tribulations nor Mme du Deffand's pessimism seems to have in any way diminished his will to live or to have implanted within his heart any fear of death. All the arguments for and against, even when he was seventy-eight years old and suffering, were summed up in this final unreasonable conclusion: "For, after all, it is sweet to live."

CHAPTER VIII

Deist, Mystic, or Humanist

VOLTAIRE AND DEISM

"Perhaps humanity, which is the principle of all my ⌐
thoughts, has beguiled me."
—Voltaire to Frederick, October, 1777.

THE discussion of the man Voltaire and his emotions leads inevitably to a more general discussion of his fundamental attitudes and ideas. In analyzing the particular kind of deism to which he subscribed and certain mystical tendencies of a cosmic nature which are occasionally observable in his life and works, it will appear that there was nothing in either his deism or his mysticism contrary to the obvious humanism of his way of life.

Voltaire habitually called himself a theist. The substitution of this term for deist brought out more clearly his lifelong denial of atheism and afforded him a greater semblance of orthodoxy, which was much needed in time of persecution. His freedom to propagandize the public in behalf of humanity depended on his success in not shocking politically influential friends. A neglect of such necessary considerations had early silenced Rousseau, while Diderot was constrained to dedicate his thoughts to posterity in manuscript form. In spite of a careful avoidance of the term, however, Voltaire inherited many of the positive tenets and developed the critical attitudes of the French and English deists.

The deists held such a diversity of beliefs that the term "deism" has come to be descriptive of the period in the history of thought from Descartes to Condorcet as well as of a purely philosophical attitude. We may define it, however, as consisting in the acceptance of a natural religion based on common ideas of morality and including the worship of an impersonal deity, whose laws are plain and engraved in the hearts of all men, as opposed to revealed religions with their supernatural doctrines and specific religious duties. This natural religion was considered "as old as creation," and such favorite heroes as Democritus, Confucius, Socrates, and Cicero were claimed as its exponents. It was, moreover, the logical outgrowth of the classical ideal. It is misleading to say that Voltaire was classical and conservative in literature and revolutionary in politics and in religion. The deists were more consistently and inclusively classical than the seventeenth-century group, who took their religion on faith as something apart. For the latter too often made the mistake of identifying fiction with classical mythology and of divorcing it from truth, which was identified with revealed Christianity. The return of religion to the classical idea of basic, fundamental, universal principles, to common moral principles which God has engraved in the hearts of all men, which are true at all times and in all latitudes, is as essential and as consistent a manifestation of the French classical ideal as are Molière's comedies, La Fontaine's fables, and Racine's tragedies. Deism was the logical deduction from the principle of the oneness of humanity, and in this sense Voltaire was truly a deist. Here, where an eminent critic saw only chaos, lies the essential unity of Voltaire's thought. The modern literary humanists, so-called, have accepted this principle; but, still ogling the divine, they have in general yielded to St. Paul, Augustine, and the Anglicans. They have substituted for the inner harmony of the humanists of all ages and nations an appeal to external authority and have repudiated Voltaire's frank but limited acceptance of the scientific method. They have thus usurped the name of humanism, and their ingratitude to Voltaire has weakened their position and has lost them many disciples.

It is this belief in a universal morality "as old as creation" that lies at the bottom of the deistic movement. "Religion should be in conformity with morality," Voltaire wrote, "and universal like morality; thus every religion whose dogmas offend morality is certainly false." He looked around at eighteenth-century Christianity, he examined the lives of men such as Archbishop Dubois and Archbishop Tencin, and he came to the honest conclusion that Christians were immoral. He examined further the foundations of their religion and decided with equal honesty that these, too, were immoral. If he

[229]

had let Christianity alone, if he had called his
universal morality a "categorical imperative" as did
Kant, and had built a nebulous philosophical system
upon it, he would be revered today as Kant is
revered. He chose the more difficult and the more
dangerous course and laid himself open to the charge
that attacks on religion do not constitute a philosophy. Certainly attacks on Christianity do not
constitute a philosophy, but just as certainly these
attacks were inspired by a pure and consistent form
of classical humanism.

Subsequent centuries succeeded in demolishing a
little too thoroughly the central position of deism.
It is not strange that many modern philosophers,
sifting out what was too naïvely rationalistic, are
again defending natural law on purely humanistic
grounds. Voltaire's personal deism has also been
subjected to varying interpretations. When allow-
ance has been made for concessions to current terminology and, more important still, for compromises
in the interests of personal safety and propaganda,
there will be found little left to offend humanistic
religion.

Voltaire believed in the existence of an intelligent
supreme being who was responsible for the unchanging laws of the universe. Having created and ordered
the world from matter, he gave it a tap to set it in
motion and his job was done; or, as Mr. Kingsley
Martin has put it, he seemed to believe that "God
created the world in six days and has rested ever
since." His arguments in favor of the existence of

God are various. At times he appears to support his belief by an appeal to the clear, intuitive, self-evident ideas of Descartes. "It is evident to me," he says, "that there is a necessary eternal, supreme, intelligent, being; and that is not faith, it is reason." He was nearly forty years old when he first perceived the weaknesses in the Cartesian physics and metaphysics and began to popularize Newton and Locke in France. By the middle of the century the battle was won, but the leader himself could not entirely overcome the habits of thought and the manners of speech of his youthful years. He stated clearly enough, when he was on his guard, that it was not Descartes, but Newton, Hartzoecker, and Nieuventyt who persuaded him of the existence of God. Just as a clock implies a clock maker, so this marvelously ordered and regulated world implies a supreme intelligence. Diderot and his fellow atheists could argue all they liked about chance and trial and error and an infinite number of throws of the dice. Even Spinoza admitted intelligence in the universe, answered Voltaire. But when Diderot, the materialist, reminded him that he had once strongly supported Locke against Descartes and had agreed with Locke that for all we know God might have bestowed upon matter the faculty of thought, he was plainly embarrassed. "Perhaps it is the social admiration for the prudent and law-abiding citizen," writes Professor Morris R. Cohen, "which makes us cling to the old naïvely rationalistic and anthropomorphic doctrine that nature does nothing in vain." Voltaire believed, too, in final causes, but at least with much less naïveté than that displayed by the Abbé Pluche or Bernardin de Saint-Pierre: he could ridicule the belief that noses were created to bear spectacles or that the natural divisions in melons were divinely ordered to correspond to the number of members in an ideal human family.

Concerning the attributes of God Voltaire time and again expressed ignorance. It was impossible for him not to speculate, however. Deism was often merely a useful weapon with which to attack Christianity, and he was anxious, of course, to prove that the God of the deists was intelligent and just and good, while the Christian God was jealous and given to anger:

Who is the impious man? It is he who ascribes a white beard, feet and hands to the Being of beings, to the great Demiurge, to the eternal Intelligence through which nature is governed. But he is only an excusable infidel, a poor infidel with whom we should not be angry.

Even if he paints the great incomprehensible Being borne on a cloud, which can bear nothing; if he is stupid enough to put God in a fog, or in a rain, or on a mountain, to surround him with little round, fat-cheeked, ruddy faces, between two wings; I laugh, and pardon him with all my heart.

Such was Voltaire's reaction to the Christian God as represented in medieval art. He was more severe with the followers of scholastic philosophy: "The impious man who supposes the great being to be jealous, proud, malicious, and vindictive, is more dangerous. I should not like to sleep under the same

roof with such a man." To Voltaire, the God of
the organized Church was still more detestable:

But how will you treat the impious man who says to
you: "See only through my eyes and do not think. I
announce to thee a tyrannical God who has made me
thy tyrant; I am his well-beloved. He will torment
through all eternity millions of his creatures, whom he
detests, in order to make me happy. I will be thy master
in this world, and I will laugh at thy sufferings in the
next world."

Do you not itch to drub this cruel blasphemer? And if
you are born gentle, will you not run west with all your
might when this barbarian utters his atrocious ravings in
the east?

The impious man who also ascribes to the Being of
beings preposterous predictions and acts of injustice
would make me angry, if that great Being had not presented me with reason to suppress my anger. This
fanatical fool repeats to me, what others have said before, that it is not for us to judge what is reasonable and
just in the great Being, that his reason is not like our
reason, and that his justice is not like our justice. But
how, my ranting fool, do you expect me to judge otherwise of justice and reason than by the notions I have of
them myself? Do you expect me to walk otherwise than
with my feet or to speak otherwise than with my mouth?

If God is represented as good and just in ways that
either contradict or surpass human understanding,
we have no right to use those terms; as an English
deist suggested, we should say rather that God is
blictri—a meaningless word for an incomprehensible
thing.

From this last quotation it is evident that this
God of Voltaire's was entirely humanistic or, in a

moral rather than in a physical sense, still purely anthropomorphic. "If there were no God, we should have to invent one," he wrote; and again, "God created man in his own image and man returned the compliment." These expressions are more than mere witticisms. The God of the deists gave man reason and imagination, and it is through reason and imagination that man conceives of the giver.

The process by which the reason apprehends God and his moral law gave Voltaire no little trouble. Temperamentally he was utterly outraged by the domineering dogmatism of the servants of the Church, who claimed to be the agents of God's will on earth. He was revolted by the usual apology for human crimes committed in the name of the Lord. In his *Discours sur l'homme* he had early put into the mouth of one of the partisans of the devil the following words:

> It is not I, it is God who goes back on my word,
> Who burns, rapes, pillages, and kills by my sword.

> Ce n'est pas moi, c'est lui qui manque à ma parole,
> Qui frappe par mes mains, pille, brûle, viole.

And he was fond of repeating ironically Dryden's line:

> Down with him, kill him, merit heaven thereby.

Such manifestations, ancient or modern, of the Christian spirit elicited his sharpest rebuke. Yet he did not quite dare to leave his own faithful with only human instincts, passions, and reason to guide them. Like Montesquieu, he thought that even if there were no God, man would have to deify justice. But it was, after all, only from these human faculties that the ideal and symbol of justice could be created.

For purposes of anlysis we can find the fullest statement of Voltaire's position on the deistic issue in two works addressed to Frederick the Great: the *Poème sur la loi naturelle* and the *Profession de foi des théistes*. In the latter work he wrote: "Our religion is without question divine, since it was engraved in our hearts by God himself, by that master of universal reason, who said to the Chinese, to the Hindus, to the Tartars, and to us: 'Adore me and be just'." When Voltaire speaks of natural law engraved by God in the hearts of all men, he is using the current terminology of deism. To the early deists, justice, goodness, and truth were intuitively self-evident through that common sense which, according to Descartes, was the most equally shared factor in the human make-up. This is, of course, unfortunately not so: Voltaire himself had a sense of justice far superior to that of most men, and the distinction between right and wrong is not so clearly shown in the light of intuitive reason as man might desire and has often maintained. Such an idea is dangerously close to Rousseau's rhetorical glorification of conscience as the infallible judge of human conduct. Voltaire used the terminology of the intuitionists chiefly in his works of evident deistic propaganda, but he never seriously subscribed to their arguments in his own intimate philosophy.

While the appeal to intuition was thus yielding

in the eighteenth century to more scientific and humanly verifiable evidence, often hidden as it was by the retarded change in terminology, primitivism, another fundamental deistic argument, was gradually giving way to the more hopeful idea of progress. The deists had often preached the superior goodness of primitive man in comparison with modern civilized man, the natural goodness of the savage as compared with the corruption of the missionary tainted with superstition and dogma. Voltaire's profession of faith continues as follows: "Our religion is as old as the world, because primitive man could have no other. . . . All nations are agreed on this point—that they originally recognized but one God, to whom they rendered a simple and unadulterated cult which could not have been infected at first by the dogmas of superstition." The restoration of religion to its original purity was an essential part of deistic propaganda. Voltaire was well acquainted with Tindal's *Christianity as Old as Creation, or the Gospel a Republication of the Religion of Nature*. He contributed also to the literary manifestations of primitivism with a novel, *L'Ingénu*, in which he used the primitivistic argument for its literary effect and at the same time not too obviously made sport of it. He went so far as to write in his profession of faith that the deist was of the religion of Adam, Seth, and Noah, outdoing even Rousseau, for whom the state of nature was a psychological or a logical, not a chronological, concept, a contemporary aspect of man abstracted from society rather than a past event in history. Yet he was certainly not himself a primitivist but was writing here for the sake of the argument.

These passages have been deliberately chosen to show Voltaire at his worst, when the campaigning spirit of his propaganda led him to expressions most opposed to the general trend of his personal life and intimate thought.

Our religion, oh great man [he continued in his profession to Frederick], is then the only one that is universal, as well as the most ancient and only truly divine religion. Ye Nations astray in the labyrinths of thousands of different sects, theism is the basis of your fantastic edifices; on our truth you have founded your absurdities. Ungrateful children, we are your fathers, and you recognize us all when you pronounce the name of God.

Voltaire's slip into the kind of rhetoric which he himself called, in condemnation of Rousseau, *déclamation à la Jean-Jacques* reveals his didactic insincerity, employed here in the cause of universal tolerance.

We adore from the beginning of time [he added] the Divinity, one and eternal, rewarder of virtue, avenger of crime; up to that point men are in agreement, all repeat after us this confession of faith. The center in which all men are united in every century and in every land is therefore truth, and divergences from this center are therefore error.

Yet Voltaire's skepticism concerning the existence of the soul and the dependent theory of reward and punishment after death has been clearly revealed in the perusal of his life and letters.

What matters [he asked again] all that has been said and all that will be said concerning the soul? What does it matter that people have called it entelechy, quintessence, flame, ether; that people have believed it universal, uncreated, transmigrant, etc. Of what importance, in these questions inaccessible to reason, are these romances of our uncertain imaginations? . . . We have a thousand testimonies of ignorance and not one that affords us a ray of probability.

This was Voltaire's unvarying personal attitude. He expressed his skepticism in 1734 in his *Lettres philosophiques*, and when he read, in 1777, in Diderot's *Pensées philosophiques*, that "the deist affirms the existence of a God, the immortality of the soul and its consequences; the skeptic is undecided on these points," he wrote in the margin: "No, the deist believes in God but does not believe for that reason, that the soul is immortal. Witness, the Sadduceans." In the recently edited Boswell papers there is an interesting letter that Voltaire, at the age of seventy, wrote in English to the inquisitive Boswell: "You seem solicitous about that pretty thing called Soul. I do protest you, I know nothing of it; nor whether it is, nor what it is, nor what it shall be. Young scholars and priests know all that perfectly. For my part, I am but a very ignorant fellow."

From these considerations it is clear that the *Profession de foi des Théistes* is indeed the deists' faith, but not Voltaire's. He uses the compromising "we"

and rarely does he say "I so profess." It is evident
that this was not his belief but rather what he
desired Frederick to believe. It is curious how many
pages on the deist's faith were written directly for
the consumption of the philosopher-king and how
much of his denial of atheism was instigated by La
Mettrie, who was with him at Frederick's court in
the early fifties and who played the rôle of court
atheist. Voltaire could see that Frederick was dangerously lacking in the moral sense. Like the other
leading moral philosophers of his century, Voltaire,
too, dared not give over morality entirely to purely
utilitarian considerations. Atheistic philosophers,
as history had shown, could be trusted; but atheistic
lackeys, like Diderot's Rameau, and atheistic magistrates need the curb of divine sanction. It was
therefore to Frederick the Great both as a fellow
philosopher and as the symbol of an enlightened
magistrate that Voltaire outlined the full faith of
deism. On another occasion, after expressing his own
personal skepticism, he added:"However, it is a very
good thing to make men believe that they have an
immortal soul and that there is an avenging God who
will punish my peasants when they steal my wheat
and my wine and who will break on the wheel the
judges of Calas and will roast those of the Chevalier
de la Barre." As for the lackeys, even the prevailing
religion might be good enough. He denied that he
wished to keep them from attending mass: and in
the margin of one of his English books he wrote:
"Natural religion for the magistrates; damn'd stuff

for the mob." It was his idea that tolerant deism could be imposed from the top down. History has belied his faith. Since the eighteenth century the magistrates have betrayed the cause, while Russia gives us an example of religious oppression fought from the bottom up.

Frederick was not at all deceived by Voltaire's professions of deism, nor could Voltaire long cherish any illusions on that subject. Frederick early stated his objections to the ideas in the *Poème sur la loi naturelle*, and Voltaire readily admitted the weaknesses in his arguments: that he wrote the poem in behalf of tolerance; that natural religion was merely the pretext; but for the sake of society he begged Frederick to aid him in this self-illusion. "Your reflections are of more value than my work, . . ." he wrote. "You terrify me; I am much afraid, for the human race and for myself, that you are unfortunately in the right."

Belief in the social and political utility of divine moral sanctions has been more powerful than has personal intellectual persuasion from Cicero to the present day. It was this belief that drove Montesquieu from the irreverent attitude of his *Lettres persanes* to the more politically mature acceptance of an established religion as a police power in his *Esprit des lois*, and that led Rousseau to the intolerant civic profession of faith at the end of his *Contrat social*. Diderot compromised in a different way, refused to let his head follow his heart, and as a result he could not bring himself to write a long-

[240]

projected work on ethics, which he feared might appear to destroy the distinctions between virtue and vice.

It is apparent that Voltaire was not building a system of philosophy; he was seeking a way of life. A belief in a heaven and a hell would hardly have been consistent with his abandonment of the traditional and authoritarian bases for such a belief. It was as a matter of policy that he attacked the views of Frederick's court atheist.

When deistic philosophy is stripped of its more naïve manifestations, its intuitionism, primitivism, and supernaturalism, all of which Voltaire distrusted but professed occasionally for practical reasons, there is still the central tenet of deism, which is purely humanistic and which formed an essential and characteristic part of his most intimate philosophy. Continuing his exposition of the deist's faith addressed to Frederick, he wrote: "The center in which all men are united in every century and in every land is therefore truth, and divergences from this center are therefore error." It is this belief in a universal morality that lies at the bottom of the deistic movement: the reduction of religion to beliefs held in common by all men and the banishment of all theology, which is the eternal source of disputes and crimes. Morality likewise springs from a single universal source. It may vary historically and geographically in its rites and manifestations. It would hardly do for a Frenchman to pass off his wife as his sister for gain, as Abraham represented his, or like

David, assassin of Uriah, to toy with his scores of concubines; nor could he well, as an act of filial piety, eat, like the cannibals, the flesh of his parents. But Voltaire sorrowfully disagreed even with the great Locke in defending his own belief that the idea of justice and injustice is everywhere recognized, that everywhere socially useful acts are considered good, and that socially harmful acts are condemned.

In his *Poème sur la loi naturelle*, he sought somewhat more scientifically the origin of this universal moral principle. Innate ideas will not do, for, according to Locke, all ideas are subsequent to sensation and reflection; of what use are innate ideas if the new-born child forgets them and is obliged to learn them all over again through the play of his senses and imagination? But instincts are inborn, and here, in the instincts of pity and remorse, Voltaire sought the foundation of his principle. The fox does not seek its prey, nor the bee, honey, at the moment of birth; the instincts are nevertheless no less securely planted.

In the preface to the same poem Voltaire gave a case history and added reason to conscience as moral guides:

The wild girl who was found near Châlons admitted that in her passion she gave her female companion a blow, and in consequence the poor wretch died in her arms. As soon as she saw her blood, she repented, she wept, she stopped the blood and dressed the wound with herbs. Those who maintain that this relenting of humanity is only a branch of self-love do that principle a great deal of honor. Let men call reason and conscience by what names they will, they exist and are the foundation of the law of nature.

In appealing to reason and conscience Voltaire seemed to be unwittingly in accord with Rousseau. There was a great difference, however, in their beliefs. To Voltaire conscience was not the voice of God but was the voice of humanity. When he was confessing rather than professing, he made it clear that there was no particular Providence, no good or evil in the eyes of God. Moral concepts and the idea of justice arose from man's having lived in society. In his opinion there was no divine sanction, as the following important quotation reveals: "We have no ideas of justice other than those which we have formed for ourselves from every act useful to society . . . Now, this idea, being only an idea of relationship between man and man, can have no analogy with God." To Sister Fessue, who had prayed God for the recovery of her sparrow, the metaphysician replied:

If *Ave Marias* had made Sister Fessue's sparrow live an instant longer than it was to have lived, these *Ave Marias* would have violated all the laws established through all eternity by the Great Being; you would have deranged the universe; you would have necessitated a new world, a new God, and a new order of things . . .

Voltaire may have been naïve in some respects; in the interests of human happiness and the betterment of society, he was willing to appear much more naïve than he truly was; but he was not naïve enough to believe that God paid any attention to particular sparrows or numbered the hairs of our heads. In devouring the sheep the wolf was merely fulfilling his natural physical functions. Human morality was entirely the affair of men; Voltaire's God was beyond good and evil. Once God had endowed man with reason and the emotions, his part in the moral order was ended.

Although Voltaire expressed himself at times rhetorically in the terms of Platonic idealism, it is impossible to describe his own philosophy as Platonic. The confusion of terms was often deliberate, possibly sometimes unconscious. He had sensed a great moral truth, and he struggled against odds to give it a natural and rational explanation. According to Professor Auer, humanism "does not expect unanimity of results, but it believes that its method of approach to the truth may be used anywhere and by all people." A certain uniformity of results may well be expected, because men everywhere have essentially the same instincts and the same needs, which lead them of necessity into essentially similar forms of society. The passages in which Voltaire voiced the principles of idealistic philosophy must be heavily discounted as discordant with the whole trend of his life and thought. And it must be borne in mind that there are two approaches to the principles of natural law and the essential brotherhood of man, one the humanistic, from human experience up, the other the idealistic, from absolutes down.

His absolute concerned the human race or some other analogous race, if such existed, in the planets. It had nothing to do with transcendental idealism. A. O. Lovejoy has shown that while most of the great thinkers of the eighteenth century were partisans of the theory of the "great chain of being," that Neoplatonic pattern of thought from which so few escaped, "Voltaire and Dr. Johnson, a strange pair of companions in arms, led an attack upon the whole conception."

The French Revolution and the romantic reaction turned men away from Voltaire and the Encyclopedists and left the field to the disciples of Rousseau. Kant had developed his categorical imperative, and humanism was to suffer for a century because of the return to the spacious realms of metaphysical speculation as opposed to the more limited but more fruitful field of human experience. It gave way, too, before a hardly less disastrous empirical pragmatism which sought social panaceas without the moral and spiritual eminence that Voltaire found in reason and nature.

Voltaire was much more nearly in agreement with La Mettrie than he was willing publicly to profess. In *L'Homme machine*, his best-known work, La Mettrie adopted a purely humanistic philosophy, unadulterated with divine sanctions, and gave the only definition of natural law that will meet the tests of modern philosophy. His argument was as follows:

Nature created us all solely to be happy; she gave us all

a portion of natural law. This is a feeling which teaches us what we ought not to do because we would not wish it to be done to us. Would I dare add to this common idea that this feeling seems to me to be only a kind of fear or dread, as salutary to the race as to the individual? For may it not be true that we respect the purses and the lives of others only to save our possessions, our honor, and ourselves; just like those Ixions of Christianity who love God and embrace so many fantastic virtues, merely because they fear Hell! You see that natural law is but an intimate feeling which, like all other feelings (thought included), belongs also to the imagination.

To La Mettrie even animals were subject to remorse and repentance; a knowledge of good and evil was then the result of experience and of imagination. It was not necessary to explain it vaguely or poetically as a law engraved in men's hearts. Voltaire, in his intimate correspondence, favored this conception of determinism and was unconsciously a thorough-going hedonist and utilitarian.

It would be well to avoid a too-rapid and too-sweeping condemnation of Voltaire's practical compromise. Moral freedom within the determinist's system depends upon the relative development of the intellectual faculties, memory, imagination, and especially knowledge; for no man can choose a good of which he is entirely ignorant. Therein lies the entire justification for education. But unfortunately children, lackeys, and even kings are not always intelligent. It is still a supremely important social, religious, and educational question at just what point traditionalism and authoritarianism

[246]

should give way to the knowledge and experience
of individuals or groups as guides for behavior. Nor
is compromise for self-protection unknown today
in a world in which the "idealistic" philosopher
still has a great professional advantage over his
purely humanistic brother. Voltaire's own life is a
brilliant reminder that martyrdom is, as he himself
believed, infrequently efficacious.

The central principle of Voltaire's deism, the
belief in a universal moral law engraved in the
hearts of all men at all times and in all nations, has
suffered a serious eclipse in the face of nineteenth-
century nationalism and historicism. Philosophically
speaking, romanticism sharply opposed classical
universals and abstractions, sought the peculiar,
eccentric, distinguishing characteristics of individuals and of peoples, and discovered romantic heroes
and racial souls. Ends as well as first principles
have lost their interest in comparison with the
factual results obtained by our modern scientists
and inventors and by our empirically minded historians and legislators. The pendulum has swung
too far away from eighteenth-century thought.
Modern philosophers are seriously reconsidering
natural law in the belief that it can be perfectly
well defended on other grounds than *a priori* rationalism. Deism in its less naïve form is not dead,
because reason and nature are not only not dead but
have the habit of recurrently impressing upon us
their vitality.

A definition and a measure for civilization have

generally been found in the relative degrees of justice and of intellectual freedom attained in a given society. Justice is the underlying principle of Voltaire's intellectual activity; intellectual freedom is its necessary concomitant. One of the most understanding tributes ever paid to Voltaire was written by Professor Whitehead, author of *Science and the Modern World:*

The common sense of the eighteenth century, its grasp of the obvious demands of human nature, acted on the world like a bath of moral cleansing. Voltaire must have the credit, that he hated injustice, he hated cruelty, he hated senseless repression, and he hated hocus-pocus. Furthermore, when he saw them, he knew them. In these supreme virtues, he was typical of his century, on its better side.

Professor Whitehead has here sensed Voltaire's essential humanism based on the obvious demands of human nature. And in singling out the principle of justice he has prepared the way for the merging of deism and humanism.

For Voltaire saw in the distinction between justice and injustice the basic principle of his universal moral law. It has no necessary connection with intuition, nothing to do with divine sanction or absolutism in any form. It was the natural outgrowth of the interplay of reason and the emotions wherever man was found living in society. It was universal because there are universal human instincts and universal human needs, arising, as Diderot would say, from the identity of human organisms.

[248]

Voltaire could not believe with the relativists that justice was merely action in conformity with stated man-made laws; for he perceived that no statement of law was possible without a previously conceived idea of justice. Logically, then, this instinctive conception of justice was "natural," and was held by man in his "state of nature."

A modern apology for this deistic belief is found in Professor Cohen's *Reason and Nature:* "The essence of all doctrines of natural law is the appeal from positive law to justice, from the law that is to the law which ought to be; and unless we are ready to assert that the concept of a law that ought to be is for some reason an inadmissible one, the roots of natural law remain untouched." It is Professor Cohen's thesis that much that is valuable in the classical and deistic conceptions of reason and nature should be rescued from the lowly estate into which romantic philosophy has pushed them. "Ultimately," he writes, "all science goes back to the classical conception of nature according to which the variation of phenomena is to be referred to some unitary law." In his analysis and comparison of the two poles of thought represented by classicism and romanticism, his essential humanism inclines him to favor the former:

Even with regard to modern European peoples the mythology of racial souls has obscured the fact that the origin and development of differences in culture can be rationally studied only on the postulate of a common human nature. The practical result of particularism is that while the old rationalistic historians were devoted to the virtue of toleration and the arduous pursuit of enlightenment, the historicism of the nineteenth century was frequently the hand-maiden of nationalistic and sectarian claims.

With regard to the central body of truth that Voltaire found in all the religions he had studied, Professor Cohen concluded, with a bit of Voltairean irony: "The old rationalistic idea of finding the core of truth in that which is common to all the different religions is now generally abandoned. It is inconsistent with the authoritarian claims of every church to be in exclusive possession of the supreme wisdom." Professor Cohen and Voltaire have both drunk deep of the humanistic spring. It was prophesied of Voltaire and Diderot that a few minutes conversation would have settled their differences. A similar prophecy might be made that, in spite of minor disagreements, the Elysian Fields will find Professor Cohen and Voltaire boon companions.

An effort has been made in these pages to distinguish between the deistic beliefs that Voltaire accepted and those which his reason, if not always his heart, rejected. By his own admission he himself accepted only half of the theory of deism; and that half which he accepted, the classical principles of natural law, justice, and essential brotherhood of man, is found to be perfectly defensible in modern philosophy and consistent with thoroughgoing humanism. If deism must be construed as implying belief in primitivism and supernaturalism, exemplified by the noble savage and the judgment day, there can be only one answer: Voltaire was not a deist; he was a humanist.

VOLTAIRE AND MYSTICISM

If there are essential truths common to all religions and if the humanist is to find a religion which he can consistently accept, it must be in the mystical adoration of the mysterious forces of the universe that Voltaire so often and so heartily recommended. Such a "religion" can be accepted, however, only with the reservations that he has indicated. In a section of *Le Philosophe ignorant*, entitled "Incomprehensibility," he expressed his feeling of awe and meanness when faced with the mysteries of the cosmic order:

I find myself suddenly stopped short in the pursuit of my vain curiosity. Miserable mortal, if I cannot fathom my own intelligence, if I cannot know by what I am animated, how can I have any acquaintance with that ineffable intelligence which visibly presides over matter in its entirety? There *is* one, as everything demonstrates, but where is the compass that will guide me toward its unknown and eternal abode?

This is no isolated statement. The same spirit of awe before the unknowable pervades his philosophical works, his letters, and even the philosophical tales with which the world is most familiar. It is therefore difficult to attribute to anything but unconscious prejudice the statement of M. Lanson, in most respects his best critic, that "Voltaire had no sense of religion, no sense of the mysterious nor of the infinite." Voltaire's obvious mystic sense, obscured for many years by the common notion that religion means faith, and that faith, for Western Europe, means faith in the Christian doctrine, has been recognized only within the last decade. "But if one may conceive of religion as the expression of awe in the presence of the great Mystery, or as an 'intuition of the Absolute'," says Professor Morehouse, "I contend that Voltaire was religious, and that at times his inner consciousness was attuned to the mysterious spiritual forces of the universe." This judgment is certainly true if we omit the "intuition of the Absolute," which might require explanation, and the adjective "spiritual," which seems to limit unnecessarily the mysterious forces that Voltaire so much admired.

A truer comprehension of Voltaire's religion is due perhaps to the recent popular works of the modern mathematical physicists. Studying religion from its beginnings as a satisfaction of human needs and feelings, Albert Einstein, in a discussion of religion and science, finds that the first primitive religion was one of fear, exemplified in the earlier parts of the Old Testament and stabilized by an alliance of priests and princes. A second source of religion appeared in the social feelings of families and communities and in their need for social and moral guidance. The God of this form of religion is the God of providence and of love. The development from the first form into the second is seen in the New Testament. The forms are often mixed, but the moral conception of God predominates in the higher levels of society. Common to these forms is the anthropomorphic character of the idea of God. Only exceptionally gifted individuals and especially noble communities rise *essentially* above this level to the higher form of cosmic religion resting on a cosmic religious sense. Mr. Einstein finds indications of this higher form in many of the Psalms and in the Prophets, in Buddhism and in the philosophy of Schopenhauer. The religious geniuses of all times—for example, Democritus, St. Francis of Assisi, and Spinoza—have also been distinguished by this cosmic religious sense, which does not necessarily recognize either dogmas or God made in man's image.

Strange as the idea may at first appear, there is no escape from enrolling Voltaire, too, among the mystics. The eighteenth-century reading public was just discovering that Galileo was right, that the earth was a very unimportant part of the universe, which was governed by certain fixed and immutable laws. Newton had explained what some of those laws are, and it was Newton who dazzled Voltaire with the unifying principle of gravitation and reduced him to moods of silent adoration. The scientific discoveries had given Voltaire telling arguments against belief in an orthodox heaven but had opened up at the same time the expanse of the infinite heavens and the mysteries of the universe. Many people are aware of these mysteries without for that reason being mystics. But Voltaire was especially gifted. He was conscious of enjoying a genuine mystical experience and was often "ravished to the third heaven," as he expressed it. At times his inner consciousness was attuned to the mysterious forces of the universe.

The intense feeling that this world and its inhabitants were relatively insignificant was the theme of Voltaire's delightful tale *Micromégas*, which seems to have owed its conception to the author's studious preparation for the writing of his *Eléments de la philosophie de Newton*. During the decade immediately following his return from exile in England we find in his works the first positive indications that he had a sense of the cosmic. The epistle addressed to Mme du Châtelet on Newton's philosophy, written in 1736, contains his clearest expression in verse of the mystical experience throughout its customary stages: first, contemplation of the mysteries of the heavens; then meditation, followed by rapture, illumination, and finally resignation and tranquillity. Several verses may be translated as follows:

The all-powerful charm of philosophy lifts a sagacious mind above envy. Tranquil, high in the heavens which have surrendered to Newton, it knows no longer whether it has any enemies. Space, which contains God's immensity, sees the limited universe rolling in its bosom, that universe which seems so vast to our feeble perception and which is nothing but an atom, a point in infinity. . . . How beautiful are the celestial bodies! How the soul, purified, flies to these truths by which it is enlightened! Yes, in God's bosom, far from this mortal body, the spirit seems to listen to the voice of the Eternal.

In similar language Saint Theresa described the flights of her spirit and the attendant obscurity of the senses and "the soul never so alert to things divine and never more gifted with light and recognition of the grandeur of divine majesty."

Nor is the spirit of these verses mere poetic fancy on Voltaire's part. In 1747 he was returning to Cirey from Paris in his coach with Mme du Châtelet. The roads were poor, and the ground was covered with snow. In the middle of a starry night, far from any town, the rear axle broke, and the coach was overturned. Voltaire was pinned beneath Mme du Châtelet, her maid, and countless packages, unable to move until the lackeys and postilions had succeeded in pulling the women and their bandboxes up through the window. No one was seriously hurt, but it was hours before help could be obtained. While waiting for the carriage to be repaired, Voltaire and Mme du Châtelet, in need of consolation, sat on pillows on the snow-covered highway and contemplated in rapt admiration the beauty of the heavens.

It is known [wrote their secretary Longchamp] that astronomy was always one of our two philosophers' favorite studies. Entranced by the magnificent spectacle spread out above and about them, they discoursed, shivering, on the nature and the course of the heavenly bodies and on the destination of so many immense globes scattered through space. They lacked only telescopes to be perfectly happy. Their souls lost in the depths of the skies, they no longer perceived their sad position on earth, or rather on snow and surrounded by broken ice.

This incident befell Voltaire at the time that he was writing *Zadig*. Now Zadig represents Voltaire's ideal for himself, what he would like to have been if his passions had not so often blinded his reason. Zadig tried to live according to virtue and wisdom but was rewarded by a series of calamities and finally was forced to flee by night from his native city, Babylon. Voltaire continued the story as follows:

Zadig directed his course by the stars. The constellation of Orion and the brilliant Dog Star guided him toward the port of Canopus. He gazed in admiration at those vast globes of light which appear to our eyes as so many little sparks, while the earth, which is in truth nothing but an imperceptible point in nature, appears so great and so noble to our fond imaginations. He looked upon men as they truly are, insects devouring one another on a little atom of mud. This true picture seemed to annihilate his misfortunes, by showing him the nothingness of his own being and that of Babylon. His soul reached up into infinity and, detached from his senses, contemplated the unchanging order of the universe.

This sensation Voltaire describes as a tide of sublime philosophy. It is the same cosmic sense that Einstein finds in Buddhism and in the Bible—the same tone as in the beautiful nineteenth Psalm, which Voltaire often quoted with praise, beginning: "The heavens declare the glory of God, the firmament sheweth his handiwork. Day unto day uttereth speech and night unto night sheweth knowledge." Zadig, like the psalmist, found his consolation in the contemplation of the heavens and came to the same conclusion: "What is man that thou art mindful of him, or the son of man that thou visitest him."

The same cosmic sense is expressed again at the beginning of his justly celebrated article "Religion," written in his old age and now included in the *Dictionnaire philosophique*: "I was meditating last night; I was absorbed in the contemplation of nature; I admired the immensity, the course, the harmony of those infinite globes which the vulgar do not know how to admire. I admired still more the intelligence which directs these vast forces. I said to myself: One must be blind not to be dazzled by this spectacle; one must be stupid not to recognize the author of it; one must be mad not to worship Him." The entire article is a perfect example of the steps in the mystical experience. After the contemplation of the heavens, Voltaire meditates upon the uniformity of light and of the forces of gravity throughout the universe and decides that moral forces must likewise be uniform. In the midst of these meditations, "one of the spirits that fill the intermundane spaces" came down and carried him off. Then follow the vision and the enlightenment, and finally the consolation: "The vision disappeared, and I was left with a clear conscience."

Again the literary expression is based upon personal experience. The article might well have been written during that same winter in which *Le Philosophe ignorant* was composed, in a mood which Voltaire described to Mme du Deffand as follows:

So, in the midst of eighty leagues of snowy mountains, besieged by a very hard winter and my eyes refusing me their service, I have passed all my time meditating. Don't you meditate, too, Madame? Don't there come to you, too, sometimes, a hundred ideas on the eternity of the world, on matter, on thought, on space, on the infinite? I am tempted to believe that we think of all these things when our passions are spent and when everybody is like Matthew Garo, who is trying to find out why pumpkins don't grow on the tops of oak-trees.

Voltaire was the first to mock at his own mystical experiences. He felt no kinship with St. Theresa or with St. Catherine, or with St. Francis of Assisi, because these mystics confused their experiences with the special doctrines of Christianity, while the central phenomenon is, of course, independent of creed. Voltaire did feel a certain kinship with Democritus, Newton, and Spinoza, even at times with Plato in spite of the latter's "sublime dreamings," and also with Blaise Pascal. Less than a year before his death he read Condorcet's edition of Pascal's *Pensées*. He found "something divine in that mixture of Blaise Condor," but it was "the sublime metaphysics and the great subjects presented in Blaise," not Condorcet's comments, that translated him to the third heaven. He admired the sublime in Plato and in Pascal, but he attacked them because they "mistook their visions for truths." Nor had he any use for mysticism as an escape from life. He kept his feet on the ground and refused to let his cosmic musings run away with him. The constant maxim of his intellectual life was: "Everything must be reduced to moral philosophy." Gazing at the starry firmament and trying to satisfy his metaphysical curiosity could be a pleasure, and to some minds, as it was to his, a comfort, a consolation, even a source of energy; but there was always present in his mind this human society of ours which had been rendered almost intolerable through superstition, fanaticism, and stupidity. Like Zadig, he felt "the ebb and flow of sublime philosophy and overwhelming grief." He could burst into peals of Homeric laughter with the inhabitant of Sirius at the puniness of this world and the folly of its inhabitants. But the morality and consequent happiness of human beings was ever his chief concern. Newton had revealed the heavens to Voltaire, but Locke was there to demonstrate to him the limits of human understanding and to discourage him from attempting to rebuild human nature with materials beyond human reach.

For mysticism has no necessary connection with asceticism or monasticism. It is probably much more widespread than is commonly supposed. In its purest form it is not a withdrawal from human realities, but an attitude which gives men more power to face them. Nor has it any necessary connection with revealed religions. Voltaire could well be just as hostile to the Christian Church as the

Church has often been to mystics. Nor should it be allied with any specific intellectual content—a fact that would seem to be indicated by the diversity of thought held by the mystics mentioned in Einstein's list, to which might well be added Voltaire, Havelock Ellis, and Einstein himself. It pertains to emotional rather than to rational man. And finally there is no necessary relationship between mysticism and the divine or the Absolute. The humanist, the materialist, and the atheist may share the experience with the Neo-platonist and Buddhist.

It cannot be denied, however, that the mystical experience has often been closely associated with transcendental idealism and with the intuition of the Absolute. It seems evident, too, that Voltaire himself was somewhat confused with regard to the relationships between his deism, his mysticism, and his humanism. His admiration of the nature and courses of the stars made him postulate harmony and purpose in the universe, a supreme intelligence, and a general providence. His mysticism undoubtedly made him cling obstinately to his belief in an intelligence and to seek rational proofs that quite shocked D'Alembert and Diderot, his mathematical and scientific friends. His idea that providence was general, the source "from which has emanated through all eternity the law that governs everything, just as light springs forth from the sun," resolved itself, in his correspondence, into a belief in human progress without divine intervention. Otherwise the universe appeared to him anything but benevolent. The connection that he made between his mysticism and the uniform laws of deism was rhetorically couched in a terminology which closely resembled that of idealistic philosophy. Many intellectual difficulties, however, attended his desire to encourage the belief that moral laws were as uniform and as invariable as physical laws. On these very points, closely linked to his mystical experience, the emotional Voltaire appeared at times to dominate the rational Voltaire, and on these points interpretations of his beliefs have been difficult and varied.

VOLTAIRE AND HUMANISM

In spite of the various conceptions of the term "humanism," its application to Voltaire's way of life is so apt that the meaning of both the term and the man seems to emerge more clearly. According to Voltaire, God's sole command to man is "Adore me and be just." Adoration was seen to have resolved itself into a satisfying and restrained form of mysticism; justice was found to be a basic principle of natural law. Voltaire's natural law was not the intuitive law of the deists, however; it was supported by no divine sanction, by no principle superior to humanity, by no system of values of which man is not the measure. Once these elements are removed from deism, the residue is pure humanism.

Even when Voltaire professed, against his inner convictions, the divine sanctions of the deists, he was moved by humanistic considerations. In a gen-

eral scheme of things in which man's happiness is
of primary importance, such formulas as "truth for
truth's sake," "art for art's sake," or "virtue is its
own reward" are meaningless. Voltaire may have
been mistaken in his judgments of things useful to
human happiness, but his motives are beyond cavil.
One suspects, too, that even humanism must make
compromises if it is ever to appeal, as does Christianity, for instance, to the average man. Yet the
personal convictions which Voltaire sometimes sacrificed to social utility were not scientific truths;
they were rather hypothetical solutions of scientifically unsolvable problems, such as the existence
of God, immortality, and the existence of evil.
Very rarely has a great author kept so well in mind
the public to which he was writing and been able
at the same time to address himself to such varied
groups.

It is strange that this essentially humanistic quality in Voltaire has received so little stress. But
humanism itself as a method of philosophy and a
way of life is still struggling for respectful consideration. It has often been accepted in practice and has
insinuated itself in varying degrees into every theistic system. It has proudly asserted its superiority
at well-defined intervals during important periods
in the history of thought, and it is not by chance
alone that at least one such period is called the
Renaissance, and another the Age of Enlightenment. The proponents of humanism have ever been
dubbed negative thinkers and destructive critics by

the orthodox, who often forget that every negative statement is posited on a previous affirmation. Voltaire was clearly the greatest humanist of the Age of Enlightenment. Diderot was in some respects more profound, but his philosophy was already tainted with that exaggerated romantic individualism which Jean Thomas, author of *L'Humanisme de Diderot*, seems often to confuse with humanism. For Voltaire satisfies the essential definitions of "humanist" to a remarkable degree. In philosophy his principal interest was ethics, its most human branch, which was for him the science of human happiness. He must be credited, too, with writing the first important social history in which the arts and the sciences are more important than wars and dynasties and events are explained entirely by means of human and natural causes. In literature he upheld the classical conception of man by which individual or racial variations are referred to universal moral law. And he reacted against dogmatism in the field of science as strenuously as in the domain of theology. In international politics, humanism is cosmopolitan, and Voltaire was the most cosmopolitan of French writers. Narrow nationalisms had their birth in the romantic reaction against Voltaire and eighteenth-century philosophy.

The conceptions of hedonism and utilitarianism, which Bentham found implicit in the works of Helvétius, were taken for granted by the whole school of philosophers of that period and, of course, by Voltaire. The chief obstacles to human happiness he considered to be stupidity, intolerance, and fanaticism. The causes of these major evils were the dogmas and doctrines of revealed religion, as well as the lust for power and the domineering nature of its earthly representatives. The apologists of these evils were the systematic philosophers, the theologians, and the political theorists. As a matter of historic record, Christianity has been the chief obstacle to humanism, partly because of the very richness of its own humanistic appeal. In Voltaire's day the theistic elements had yielded very little to the humanistic, and he was quick to see the enemy. His conception of natural law, with its bearing on ethics, has been defended in the chapter on deism, and in discussing his mysticism we have seen how speedily he returned from his metaphysical flights to moral considerations. Instead of running away, as did the Absolutists and the Transcendentalists, from the sphere in which practical problems arise, Voltaire was ever forcing himself back to it.

The difference between seventeenth- and eighteenth-century ethics is not only between individual and social morality but also between theism and humanism. The individual in the former age was responsible, at least in theory, to abstract theological, moral absolutes; in the latter age he was responsible to human society, of which he felt himself a unit. The individual moral conduct of the eighteenth-century philosophers was certainly higher than that of the seventeenth-century courtiers who followed Louis XIV to mass; added to that they had a nobler conception of humanity and of the individual's responsibility in furthering human happiness. The unselfish motive of *bienfaisance* displaced the selfish motive of personal salvation. Piety, thought Voltaire, has no ethical value. He is strictly in accord with the humanists of all ages in considering ethics a purely human, social, and rational science. It was, in fact, the discrepancy between theory and practice in the seventeenth-century all-Christian France that led Voltaire's precursor, Pierre Bayle, to the conclusion that religion had no bearing whatsoever on morality. The modern humanist uses slightly different terminology; he says that the Absolute can furnish no answer to difficulties arising in the field of human experience.

It is clear, too, that from the point of view of the individual Voltaire bases moral distinctions on reflection, reason, and knowledge. Through these faculties only, man can be said to be morally free, differing thus in degree only from the other animals. This moral freedom of man is in no wise inconsistent but is rather concomitant with the theory of determinism which Voltaire adopted as the basis of his moral psychology. In his dictionary article "Liberty," he discusses in the form of a dialogue the problem of free will:

A. It makes you ill to be free like your dog. Do you not eat, do you not sleep, do you not propagate in essentially the same manner? Would you like the sense of smell otherwise than through your nose? Why should you desire freedom of a different sort than your dog's?

[265]

B. But I have a soul which does a great deal of reasoning, and my dog reasons very little. He also has nothing but simple ideas, and I have a thousand metaphysical ideas.

A. Well, then, you are a thousand times more free than he: that is, you have a thousand times more power to think than he; but you are free only in the same way as he.

Voltaire then shows how ridiculous is the belief in free will and the accompanying expression "I will will," when it is so evident that we will necessarily in consequence of the ideas which present themselves to our minds.

It is strange that now, nearly two centuries after Voltaire, many humanists are wary of this essential postulate of the humanistic position. A little reading of Voltaire would help, for he went through the same struggles that confront the present-day seeker. Determinism is implicitly accepted in the practical world of human experience. This is another case in which metaphysical speculation beclouds the issue. Voltaire himself was finally quite clear on the subject:

An inevitable destiny is then the law of all nature, and this was felt by all antiquity. The fear of taking from man some vague false liberty [free will], of despoiling virtue of its merit and crime of its horror has sometimes frightened tender souls; but once they have been enlightened, they have soon come back to this great truth that everything is linked together and that everything is necessary.

Man is free, once more, when he is able to do what he wills; but he is not free to will. It is impossible for him to will without cause. If this cause does not have its infallible effect, it is no longer cause. The cloud that would say to the wind "I don't want you to push me" would not be more absurd. This truth can never do any harm to morality. Vice is always vice, as sickness is always sickness. The wicked will always have to be repressed; for if they are determined to evil, we shall tell them that they are predestined to punishment.

Voltaire's real belief in determinism coupled with his long life spent in ardent propaganda should be in itself a sufficient answer to those who still confuse determinism with fatalism, which leaves man a prey to outside forces, or with predestination, which makes him the puppet of a foreseeing God. On the plane of human conduct, knowledge and reason are vital links in the chain of necessity, as we implicitly recognize when we surround our children with the best possible influences and when we choose for them the best schools. In fact, when education is (as it should be and too often is not) the attainment of knowledge, it is the most humanly directable factor in the search for the good life. Voltaire was "determined" that in the realm of ideas which through the mechanism of choice necessarily influence our decisions the ideas of the humanist's way of life should be presented for consideration.

Voltaire's literary, moral, religious, political, and social thought is all based on the same fundamentally humanistic principles. The threads are so intricately interwoven in the central theme that it is extremely difficult to separate them into their individual categories. His conception of history, for example, is closely connected with the rôle played by knowledge in the determination of human conduct.

To Voltaire the object of history was, not the satisfaction of curiosity or the endless piling up of facts, but the search for material and ideals useful in controlling the future. In his emphatic application of this principle he revolutionized the writing of history. His most ambitious work was the *Essai sur les mœurs et l'esprit des nations*, the first truly universal history of man. His predecessor Bossuet wrote history in the ancient theo-teleological manner, proving after the fact that human and national affairs are merely the unfolding of God's will and that the Roman Empire fell because it was God's will to convert the world to Christianity. Voltaire entirely eliminated the supernatural element and attempted to explain history as the result of human conduct, of human passions, and of human reason. Modern historians cling to the notion that history can and should be purely objective; that the historian's job is to pile up facts—to make bricks with the idea that some day somebody will build a house of them. They then delight in throwing the bricks, with the charge of superficiality, at the Voltaires and the Wellses, who try to build something with them. There are, however, the so-called "new historians," James Harvey Robinson, the Beards, Harry Elmer Barnes, and, in England, J. B. Black, whose conception of history is entirely Voltairean. And the movement is spreading.

Humanism bases its claims on a certain universality of human needs. It employs a method which should prove useful at all times and in all places. And Voltaire, in his search for ideals, looked to the past, especially to the period of pre-Christian thought, in the hope of retrieving some of the best values of the pagan world. He often corrects some of the vagaries of the modern humanist movement. "Fifteenth-century humanism," writes Professor Auer, "looked back in the hope of restoring some of the lost values of the past; twentieth-century humanism looks forward, creating its values as it progresses. It is a new thing and it would be better served if we could find a new name for it." Let us hope that here Professor Auer is wrong. For humanism, with its method of reasoning from the known to the unknown, has more need for the past experience of mankind than has any other philosophy. Sixteenth-century humanism, like modern scholarship, may have been too busily concerned with collecting data to apply them to human problems; but nevertheless its driving force was a glimpse of a new way of life dimly viewed in the past. Nor should eighteenth-century humanism, with its Voltaire and its Diderot, be left out of consideration. These men best appreciated the uses to which history might be put in the development of the mind and in the search for knowledge and happiness.

Voltaire has often been accused of a lack of historical sense, of failing to understand the cruder civilizations of primitive times, of measuring all things by eighteenth-century standards. It is true that he often accepted as universal the customs and eccentricities of his own day. This is indeed very difficult to avoid and very easy to criticise from the viewpoint of another age. It is at the same time true that rarely in the history of man have individuals approached more nearly the universal type than did these eighteenth-century philosophers. It was to some extent for the sake of the argument that Voltaire stressed, for example, the story of the Biblical David and Bathsheba and his many other concubines. He might have attempted to justify such conduct on the grounds of primitive behavior. But to him it was just as immoral to use piety as a cloak for treachery, licentiousness, and murder in David's day as it was in his own.

But it will not do to leave Voltaire and humanism entirely in the hands of the historians. No one seriously questions, writes Professor Cohen, the value of history as a genuine method of extending the span of experience. But the romantic school, accusing Voltaire of naïve rationalism, had an even more naïve faith in the omnipotence of the historical method. Professor Cohen rightly concludes that no one has been able to refute Sidgwick's argument "that the history of ethical opinion or practice cannot be the decisive factor in determining its validity." Voltaire, too, believed in the moral insufficiency of history and in the necessity of recourse to imaginative literature. But he put it this way:

The beautiful fables of antiquity have this great advantage over history, that they present a comprehensible morality: they are lessons in virtue, while almost all history is a succession of crimes. . . . I know how much history can teach us, I know how necessary it is; but truly it needs much help if one is to draw from it any rules of conduct. . . . As far as events are concerned, history seems to accuse Providence, while fine moral fables justify it. It is evident that we find in literature the useful and the agreeable: those in this world who are neither the one nor the other cry out against it. Let them talk and let us keep on reading Homer and Ovid as well as Livy. Taste leads to preferences, fanaticism to exclusions. . . . History teaches us what human beings are; literature teaches us what they should be.

It could not be more clearly stated that the history of ethical opinion or practice cannot be the decisive factor in determining its validity or more clearly implied that a universal law of nature must be assumed if we are to conceive of man as he ought to be; both these ideas are purely classical, and purely humanistic. The natural law that Voltaire defended was the logical deduction from the classical persuasion of the oneness of humanity.

It was entirely logical, therefore, that Voltaire should have recourse to imaginative literature. His literary theories were an essential part of his humanism. In a philosophical sense he completed the ideal of classicism—and in a literary sense also, in spite of the fact that his plays were not as good as Racine's. *Candide* is a classical masterpiece in every sense of the term. Pure classicism is in no sense antagonistic to humanism; it is rather its chief source. The neoclassicists of the French seventeenth century made some serious blunders in interpretation. Voltaire's often-noted innovations were much less a movement toward romanticism than a reaction against the dogmatism and the absolutism of this school. His conception of man, whereby variation of phenomena was to be referred to some unitary law, remained distinctly classical. He reacted especially against the idea held by the neoclassicists that ancient mythology was the sole subject suitable for fictional treatment to the exclusion of truth (Christianity). His plays *Zaïre* and *Alzire* brought Christian problems back to the stage.

Another tenet of literary humanism is the belief that "through fiction we arrive at a higher reality." Voltaire's agreement with this principle is apparent in his defense of mythology against the Jansenists of his century who would gladly have abolished fiction and all the arts in the name of their "truth." The modern literary humanists have especially laid themselves open to his charge that "taste leads to preferences, fanaticism to exclusions." Their betrayal of humanism is all the more regrettable because much of their criticism is excellent. Their reaction to scientific dogmatism is distinctly Voltairean. It is a pity that they do not find their "inner check" in philosophical humanism without recourse to supra-rational intuition and theological dogma.

Of the relationship between science and humanism something still remains to be said. In religion and ethics, subjects which seemed to be ill-adapted to laboratory experimentation, Voltaire clung to the rational principle of natural law. In science, however, he revealed his interest in the following striking passage from his contemporary Diderot:

Experimental philosophy [wrote Diderot] knows neither what will come nor what will not come of its labors, but it labors on incessantly. On the contrary, rational philosophy weighs the possibilities, makes a pronouncement, and then lets the matter rest. It says boldly enough, "Light cannot be decomposed"; experimental philosophy listens and is silenced for long centuries. Then suddenly it brings forth the prism, and says, "Light *is* being decomposed."

Voltaire not only approved but also practiced. During the middle period of his life he worked arduously with Mme du Châtelet in the laboratory which they set up in their château at Cirey. He even wrote for the Academy of Sciences a very creditable tract on the nature of fire, the result of his own experiments. At this time, too, he mastered Newton and introduced both Locke and Newton to the French reading public. After the turn of the century, however, scientific interest was captivated by two new sciences, geology and biology. Voltaire did not keep abreast of his times in these subjects. When Needham spontaneously produced "eels" in barley water, Voltaire tried to laugh the eels out of court —they were being used too readily both by the theologians and by the materialists in the interests of dogmatism. Voltaire was wrong: the eels were there. But he was right also, as Pasteur proved a century later: they were not spontaneously produced. Again the scientific world was startled by the discovery of cockleshells near the tops of the mountains between France and Italy—proof, said the theologically minded geologists, of the Biblical account of the flood. Voltaire was disturbed that science should seem to confirm such an incredible fable. So he did his best to explain that cockleshells were known to have been worn by French pilgrims on their way to Rome and that they had undoubtedly been dropped along the way. He was again wrong; yet he was right in thinking that these shells in no way proved the Biblical account of the flood. It is a commonplace in the history of science that English geology might have been advanced half a century if fossils had not from the beginning been associated with the flood. Voltaire thus kept reason and common sense as a court of higher appeal, even in the field of the applied sciences.

It has been stated also that Voltaire was a very poor psychologist. We should not judge, however, on the basis of several poorly constructed plays that he had no psychological insight. If psychology means the knowledge and science of the workings of the human mind rather than the elementary reactions of the paramoecium or the artful antics of the ape, valuable as such studies are slowly proving themselves to be, then he was a great psychologist. His works are in themselves a veritable encyclopedia of human relations. As a humanist he believed that it was the human mind in its most distinctly human aspects that counted. Professor Cohen has suggested that the statesman, the business man, and even the physician may obtain more practical information from a moralist like Balzac, for instance, than from most scientific psychology, "since the latter deals with elements, whereas in conduct we deal with whole situations." Modern psychology draws much of its information from abnormalities. Voltaire, consistently enough, considered normal intelligent man as the chief object of his interest.

It has ever been the lot of humanism, as of deism, to be obliged to attack the prevailing social prejudices. Voltaire's essential humanism has thus often escaped notice, partly because it is more often expressed in negations than in affirmations, partly because the affirmations have been peculiarly modified for publication and do not agree with those implied in his negative criticism. The negative side of deism will appeal to men as long as men appeal to reason, or, as Voltaire would say, as long as men contrive to be men, the highly developed reasoning faculty being the sole distinctive claim of humankind. He steadfastly refused, therefore, to accept any authority but reason, and he sought to destroy the authoritarianism of religions and philosophies based on the supernatural or the Absolute. The prime object of his attack was the persecuting spirit of the Inquisition, which would gladly have burned him, as it was burning others, for the greater glory of the Christian God. The appeal for toleration was nevertheless an appeal to reason. It must not be forgotten that he was the leader and inspiration of a group of philosophers who gave the death blow to the Inquisition in France, freed science from theology, humanized civil and criminal law, and made liberal democracy possible. Heine remarked that in the great war for the liberation of humanity, Voltaire's name would always stand first. For he unified the best thought of his age, clothed it in beautiful prose, and set it in motion. If negation can effect such reforms as these, let us have more negation. Voltaire believed that man's mind, like his body, was fallible. Errors and false steps develop naturally in the growth of civilization, just as disease is a natural concomitant of human growth, and, like disease, they should be eradicated.

Like the attacks of the modern humanists, for the same reasons and in the same terms, Voltaire's attack was directed primarily against Plato and the theologians:

All the metaphysicians, all the theologians of antiquity, were necessarily charlatans who could not agree. The very word indicates this: *metaphysics*, above nature; *theology*, knowledge of God. How can we know what is not natural? How can man know what God has thought and what he is? The metaphysicians necessarily have said only words, since the physicists said nothing else, and yet dared to reason without experimentation. . . .

The obscure Plato, wordy rather than eloquent, a poet rather than a philosopher, sublime because he was with difficulty understood, got himself admired among the Greeks, the Romans, the Asiatics, and the Africans, by his dazzling sophisms.

Plato's sublime nonsense, Voltaire continued, won him the title of "divine," just as the Italians call "divine" their charming fool Ariosto, who was, nevertheless, much more intelligible than Plato. Voltaire charged Plato with being the first to speak of a purely spiritual being, with spreading nonsense after nonsense about the Trinity, and most serious of all, with being the true founder of Christianity. He showed more than once that he could appreciate the purely human qualities of Jesus, but not at all Plato's metaphysical reveries. He felt that Plato's mythical account of ideas as reminiscences of a previous existence had as little basis in fact as Descartes's innate ideas. "Humanism," says a modern exponent, "seeks the source of anti-humanistic speculations in Platonism, and in criticizing this system it passes judgment upon the derivative systems as well."

Voltaire's main attack, however, was directed against the religion with which he was forced to deal at every moment throughout his long life. He objected not only to its organized form but also to Christianity itself in so far as it was a revealed religion. The great bulk of his deistic or rationalistic writings consisted in witty and satirical diatribes on its mysteries, doctrines, and traditions and on its historical and moral foundations. To many readers today this part of his work reads like an old story. It is often little more than the application of the critical method to religious and church history. The method and results have since been popularized by Thomas Paine, Ingersoll, and Bernard Shaw, and transformed, in one branch at least, into the science of exegesis. The more modern theological schools have nearly caught up with Voltaire—with the humor lacking. His voracious reading and genuine scholarly method have raised the argument to a more elevated plane than that on which he found it. If the Emanuel prophecy is enacted in our churches today, it is not because the pastors are ignorant of the fact that the prophecy has literally nothing to do with the Christ, but because tradition demands it.

To a great many other readers, however, this part of his work is distinctly distasteful—it shows bad taste, they say, because it attacks some cherished notions and blasphemous because it makes light of what they consider sacred. Until we are willing to let our children begin their religious instruction on a higher plane, Voltaire will always be a shock to youthful minds. Relatively few are even the universities where students are invited to read freely these arguments from the pen of the world's greatest champion of intellectual liberty.

Voltaire's library, now preserved in Leningrad, bears witness to the seriousness with which he undertook his critical works. From the works of the English deists he gleaned many arguments against the miracles, the prophecies, and the morality of the Biblical heroes; from the German scholar Fabricius he learned of the apocryphal gospels and pious forgeries of the early Church; from the French rationalists, by book or by manuscript, he was informed of countless contradictions and inconsistencies in the scriptural record as well as in the subsequent history of the Church. The most voluminous and orthodox sources did not discourage him. He was acquainted with the works of the doctors Grabe, Mill, Cave, and Huet, as well as with the unending commentaries of his Benedictine friend, Dom Calmet. Neither language nor aridity deterred him; not even the "bad taste" of the theologians or of a Thomas Aquinas:

Let St. Thomas agree with Scotus [he wrote to his friend Cardinal Bernis, who would have liked to make theology reasonable] I have read your Thomas, I have him in my library; I have two hundred volumes on the subject [theology], and what is worse, I have read them. It's like going the rounds of the insane asylums. Laugh and profit by the folly and the imbecility of men.

He was often guilty of literary exaggeration; but that was usually after, not before, he had seriously collected the facts. The impression of superficiality that some readers have got from his works is therefore much more apparent than real and is derived from the brightness of the style and from the bantering tone more than from any lack of knowledge.

It would be much easier to present Voltaire to modern readers if the argument could be seriously made that he was a Christian. A body of Protestant modernists, in fact, who are interested chiefly in the social gospel of Jesus and who would gladly abandon the accretions, Platonic and ecclesiastical, which have so modified primitive Christianity, feel

[279]

a certain affinity with Voltaire. They sense, in other words, his essential humanity, just as he himself appears at times to have sensed and appreciated the humanity of Jesus. This attitude is very dangerous, however, unless the modernists are prepared, as indeed many seem to be, to go the whole road to humanism.

The article "Religion" from the *Dictionnaire philosophique* is the chief source of the argument that Voltaire was himself a Christian. The first paragraphs, already quoted, have shown him lost for a moment in mystical meditation and descending rapidly to the human plane of moral philosophy. At this point a spirit from the intermundane spaces comes down to serve as a guide, in the manner of Virgil in Dante's *Divine Comedy*, to lead Voltaire into the regions of the dead, the exact location of which he refrains from defining. After viewing the huge mounds of the bones of those who lost their lives in religious wars and quarrels, he weeps and thus earns the right to proceed to the graves of the blessed. Here he talks with Numa Pompilius, Pythagoras, and Socrates and finally is brought into the presence of a gentle and compassionate being of about thirty-five years of age, whom the reader recognizes as Jesus. In the ensuing conversation Jesus declares that he is entirely innocent of the persecuting, quarrelsome spirit which accounted for the huge piles of bones, that he never taught any of the rites now celebrated on earth in his name, and that his sole doctrine was to love God and justice and one's neighbor as one's self. When asked by Voltaire: "Did you not once say that you came to bring, not peace, but the sword?," he answers: "That is a copyist's error; I told them that I brought peace and not the sword. I never wrote anything; what I said could have been changed without evil intent." When finally Voltaire learns that Jesus did not institute fast days or pilgrimages or confession he says: "Well, if it be thus, I take you for my sole master."

His attitude toward the Christian religion is here much more respectful than is customary in his writings. Yet even if we take it at its face value, it is the attitude not of a Christian, but of a deist, and it is consistent with his most ingrained philosophical ideas. Voltaire is merely following the lead of the English deists, especially of Matthew Tindal, whose most important work was entitled *Christianity as Old as Creation*. Voltaire was fond of the phrase and the idea. It meant that the only important truths in Christianity were those universal moral truths that are common to all religions because they are the natural outgrowth of human experience and human reason; that everything that has been added to these truths is false; that therefore since these truths are the clearest and most apparent to all men, revealed religions are then not only false but also useless. In this article Voltaire was not showing that a deist is a Christian, as was often attempted in England, but he was doing his best by means that appear heretical to the orthodox to show that Jesus was a deist.

When Voltaire's deism is analyzed, it seems to be composed of rationalism and humanism, with touches of mysticism. His use of reason was definitely held in check whenever he considered such use detrimental to human happiness. Clear in his own mind concerning his acceptance of the theory of determinism, he kept it very much to himself for fear that a misunderstanding of it would have an evil effect on human morality. After accepting a mechanistic conception of the universe as a necessary first principle for scientific research, he maintained against Diderot and others the existence of a Supreme Intelligence behind creation. Diderot's hypothesis was clearly more scientific and just as clearly not a complete account of the physical universe. Normally Voltaire would have been satisfied that the limits of human understanding had been reached and would have agreed with Diderot that the existence of God could not be proved and that the hypothesis of his existence helped to solve no problems of any kind. He was betrayed by his mystical sense to seek a rational proof of the necessity of God as first cause, and he suffered the contempt, on this point, of many of his fellow philosophers. Voltaire's enemies have accused him of reducing God to some vague Supreme Being who had no connection whatever with human affairs. In this they have been very nearly right. For Voltaire's God was beyond good and evil, and his attributes were beyond human comprehension; the mystery of the universe could be sensed only in moments of mystic exaltation. Voltaire's deism as well as his mysticism are thus definitely within the limits of human experience and are in no way contrary to thoroughgoing humanism. Both have their origins and their justification in human nature and human reason. Voltaire's attitude may be called religious only if the customary limitations of that term be expanded to include humanism and the cosmic sense.

It has been very difficult for Christendom to forgive a man who denied many of the attributes of the Christian God—even more difficult because many believing Christians who have understood him have been forced to admire his works. His own life was a dangerous illustration of his conviction that a firm belief in revealed religions was not only not an aid, but an actual detriment, to the good life. Alfred E. Noyes, in his recent study of Voltaire, became convinced of Voltaire's moral integrity and therefore tried to bring him closer to the Church. The argument is not convincing. Voltaire was too clearly hostile to divine Revelation and its interpreters on earth. He liked too well such stories as that of the Swiss captain who prayed: "May god, if there is one, save my soul, if I have one." Voltaire could not bring himself to the Church, but he did fondly hope that the Church would come to him. Humanity may never find its salvation until Voltaire is canonized. Mr. Noyes's book is an indication that such an eventuality is not impossible.

Voltaire did not foresee that the humorless spirit of Rousseau and the prudery of the Victorian age would produce generations for which such mockery as his would be a liability rather than an asset. The more is the pity, for Voltaire has an important message for the present age. His readers in the period preceding the World War were mildly amused or mildly shocked but not deeply moved. The Inquisition had been suppressed, religious wars were practically nonexistent, and civil liberties were being more generally enjoyed through the gradual spread of democracy. Today our hopes are not so sanguine. Christendom seems more bent than ever on its own destruction, religion is again on the warpath, and the very principles of democracy are being challenged. It is in such periods of increasing fanaticism that generations will turn again to the spirit of Voltaire.

Notes

THE voluminous bibliography of writings on Voltaire has been so adequately assembled by Quérard and Miss M.-M. H. Barr that no separate listing is necessary for this study beyond the indication of authors and titles actually cited above. When no author is indicated, the volume and page reference is to the Moland edition (Garnier, Paris, 1877–85) of Voltaire's complete works, of which Volumes 33–50 contain the collected correspondence. The abbreviation PMLA stands for the *Publications of the Modern Language Association of America*.

CHAPTER I

1, 16. world: I, 353.

4, 11. fountain: XXI, 147.

6, 25. Rousseau: Cf. Matthew Josephson, *Jean-Jacques Rousseau*, New York, 1931.

11, 27. nature: See A. Guérard, *The Life and Death of an Ideal*, New York, 1928.

12, 2. Rousseau: A. O. Lovejoy, "Optimism and Romanticism" in PMLA, XLII, 921–45.

12, 12. existence: Morris R. Cohen, *Reason and Nature*, New York, 1931, p. 457.

CHAPTER II

15, 3. Paris: XXXV, 252.

15, 17. paganism: Cf. F. Gaiffe, *L'Envers du grand siècle*, Paris, 1924.

16, 27. disciple: XXXIII, 30–31.

16, 31. teacher: Cf. I. O. Wade, "The *Épître à Uranie*," PMLA, XLVII (Dec., 1932), 1077–81.

18, 6. abundance: XXXIII, 2, 5, 7–9.

18, 11. Bernières: XXXIII, 62.

18, 22. themselves: Quoted by Voltaire, XXXI, 23. Cf. Pascal, *Pensées*, ed. Brunschvicg, Paris, 1904, II, 322–23.

19, 21. people: XXXIII, 103.

19, 27. homosexuality: XXXIII, 111–12.

19, 30. ennobled: XXXIII, 315, 324.

20, 15. morals: XLV, 67.

21, 8. versifies: XXXIII, 39–40.

21, 8. Paris: XXXIII, 46.

21, 17. Maecenas: XXXIII, 40–41.

21, 22. hunt: XXXIII, 42.

21, 25. theologians: XIV, 53.

22, 6. more: IX, 361.

23, 1. grace: X, 467.

23, 20. friend: XXXIII, 26.

24, 1. Lecouvreur: XXXIII, 135.

24, 7. you: XXXIII, 98.

24, 12. art: XXXIII, 72.

25, 20. friendship: XXXIII, 375.

25, 24. versions: Voltaire's Sottisier, MS Rotograph in the Modern Language Association deposit, Library of Congress.

26, 14. rien: VIII, 512–13.

26, 27. philosophy: XXXIV, 348.

27, 15. Works: H. Celarié, *Monsieur de Voltaire, sa famille et ses amis*, Paris, 1928, p. 103.

28, 29. it: XXXIII, 438–39.

29, 10. youth: XXXVIII, 476.

29, 26. work: XXXVIII, 379–80.

30, 28. friends: XXXVIII, 477.

31, 6. souls: XXXVIII, 507.

31, 15. youth: XLIII, 233.

32, 28. appreciate it: XL, 192–93.

33, 14. Ariosto: XLIX, 356.

33, 19. expressions: XXV, 242–45.

33, 25. academy: P. Gesell, *Propos d'Anatole France*, Paris, 1921, pp. 47–51.

34, 8. annihilation: XLVI, 302–3.
34, 9. vicariously: XLV, 444.
34, 24. Ferney: XLV, 444, 205–7.
34, 29. children: Longchamp et Wagnière, *Mémoires sur Voltaire*, Paris, 1820, I, 63.
35, 1. mistress: XLV, 470.
35, 7. them: XLIV, 447.
35, 20. papist: XXXIX, 357.
35, 27. philosophy: XXXVIII, 310.
36, 3. stake: XXXVIII, 528; XLV, 524.
36, 10. Jerusalem: XLIX, 76–77.
36, 26. laughs: IX, 556–58.

CHAPTER III

38, 2. qualities: Longchamp et Wagnière, *Mémoires sur Voltaire*, Paris, 1820, II, 136.
38, 31. together: XXXVIII, 511.
39, 18. verse: *Mémoires sur Voltaire*, I, 92.
39, 21. line: XXV, 375.
39, 29. cue: *Mémoires sur Voltaire*, I, 49.
40, 2. produced: XXXIII, 282.
40, 15. director: See Philip Wheelwright in *Symposium* (July, 1933), p. 379.
40, 23. Fontenelle: XLVII, 170; XLVI, 45; XLI, 40.
40, 26. May: XLVI, 430. See also *Mémoires sur Voltaire*, I, 336.
41, 7. hero: XXV, 53.
41, 10. make: XXXV, 70.
41, 14. indignant: XXXVIII, 118.
41, 19. deceived: XXXVII, 256.
41, 30. one: XXXVII, 517.
42, 7. Sciences: XXXVII, 453.
42, 23. think: XXXVII, 506–7.
43, 10. air: XLIV, 343.
43, 24. one: XLIV, 359.
43, 29. yesterday: XLIV, 273.
44, 4. Barre: XLVII, 434; cf. XLVII, 436.
44, 9. horror: XLVII, 491.
45, 9. burning: XLIX, 93.

45, 17. assassinations: XLIX, 202.

46, 14. necessary: XXI, 88.

47, 24. man: XXXVIII, 147.

47, 28. affliction: XXXV, 456. Letter to Frederick the Great.

48, 9. shipwreck: XXXVII, 495; XXXVIII, 131, 160.

48, 16. proposed: P. Chaponnière, *Voltaire chez les Calvinistes*, Genève, 1932, p. 173.

49, 3. name: XXXVIII, 556.

50, 9. Providence: William R. Price, *The Symbolism of Voltaire's Novels*, Columbia University Press, 1911, and G. Ascoli (ed.) *Voltaire: Zadig*, Paris, 1929.

50, 31. made: "Voltaire's English Notebook," *Modern Philology*, XXVI (Feb., 1929), 320; cf. Voltaire, *Oeuvres*, IV, 156.

51, 9. things: XXXIII, 184.

51, 14. mud: XXXIV, 554; XXI, 54.

51, 23. Providence: XXXV, 481.

51, 29. it: XXXVI, 502.

52, 6. all: XXXVII, 161.

52, 12. lost: XXXVII, 304.

52, 16. motto: XXXVII, 548; XLV, 344, 359, 425.

52, 18. laugh: XXXVII, 548.

52, 22. *Joan: Mémoires sur Voltaire*, I, 25.

53, 8. epitaph: XXXVIII, 359.

53, 14. plaything: XXXVIII, 360.

53, 27. marionettes: XXXVIII, 360–61.

54, 10. notes: XXXVIII, 359.

54, 24. console: XLIII, 247.

55, 6. man: XLIII, 299.

55, 13. right: XLV, 400.

55, 22. devil: XLV, 425.

55, 25. vineyards: XLVI, 176.

56, 5. follow: XLVII, 531.

56, 16. life: XLVIII, 134.

56, 18. it: XLVIII, 397.

56, 22. left: XLVIII, 416.

56, 28. again: XLVIII, 534.

57, 9. before: XLIX, 438.

CHAPTER IV

58, 1. call: Pope, *Essay on Man*, II, 93.

59, 13. justice: *Symposium* (July, 1933), p. 380.

60, 30. felicity: XLVI, 547–48.

61, 3. concealed: XVII, 179; cf. XLIII, 309.

61, 11. angel: XXII, 53.

61, 28. fatal: IX, 409–11.

62, 15. ends: XLIV, 92.

64, 19. Majesty: XXV, 450, 457–58.

64, 31. change: I. O. Wade, "Voltaire's Name," PMLA, XLIV (June, 1929), 560–64.

65, 9. Villars: G. Desnoiresterres, *Voltaire et la société française au XVIIIe siècle*, Paris, 1871–76, I, 356.

65, 12. justice: F. Gebelin et A. Morize, *Correspondance de Montesquieu*, Paris, 1914, I, lettre 98.

65, 20. plausible: L. Foulet, *La Correspondance de Voltaire (1726–29)*, Paris, 1913, p. 60.

65, 25. freedom: XXXIII, 54, 120.

66, 16. gambades: XXXIII, 213.

66, 27. intolerable: XXXVII, 161.

67, 7. sleeve: XLII, 45.

68, 17. myself: XLIX, 527.

70, 19. honor: XLIX, 464.

70, 27. Capuchin: XXXVIII, 346; XXXIX, 335, 352; XLVI, 3, 563; XLIX, 381; L. 17; 164; *et passim.*

72, 23. poet: XXXIII, 213.

73, 12. criminelle: IX, 369.

73, 19. genius: IX, 370.

73, 32. Paris: XXXIII, 211–12.

74, 20. negro: Horace Walpole, *Reminiscences*, Paris, 1826, pp. 189–90.

75, 5. hatred: XXXIII, 293.

76, 10. writers: XXXIII, 294.

78, 20. bargain: XLIII, 335.

78, 23. argument: XXI, 219–21.

81, 24. *Lewis XIV:* XXXIII, 265.

81, 30. another: XXXIII, 271.

82, 11. experiments: XXXV, 212–13.

82, 19. replete: XXXV, 304.

82, 26. accomplished: XXXVII, 213, 242, 247.

82, 29. Sans-Souci: XXXVII, 273, 304.

83, 28. fare: XXXVI, 504.

84, 7. you: XXXVIII, 240.

85, 21. working: *Mémoires sur Voltaire*, I, 92-93.

86, 13. action: XLV, 237.

87, 31. about it: XXXVI, 319.

89, 6. fangs: XXXIX, 192.

90, 25. terms: For the best discussion of this affair see P. Chaponnière, *Voltaire chez les Calvinistes*, Genève, 1932, pp. 61 ff.

91, 12. impious man: *Ibid.*, pp. 177, 180.

91, 18. country: *Ibid.*, p. 103.

92, 3. desired: XL, 423.

93, 15. esteem: XXXVIII, 446-47, 450. A better text may be found in Théophile Dufour (ed.) *Correspondance générale de J.-J. Rousseau*, Genève, 1924-34, II, 203-5.

95, 31. Him: P.-M. Masson, critical edition of Rousseau's *Profession de foi du vicaire savoyard* (Paris, 1914), Introd., pp. x-xvii.

97, 18. repeated: E. H. Wright, *The Meaning of Rousseau*, London, 1929, p. 32. G. Valette, *Jean-Jacques Rousseau, genevois*, Paris, 1911, p. 396 n.

97, 23. brother: XLII, 192.

97, 26. own: XLIII, 263.

97, 29. brotherhood: XLIV, 83.

98, 18. Catholic: XLIV, 330.

98, 21. whore: XL, 457.

99, 25. cat: XX, 295.

100, 12. poem: XXXVIII, 556.

101, 1. forgotten: XXXIX, 99.

101, 10. worms: Desnoiresterres, *op. cit.*, V, 134-42.

102, 2. everything: *Ibid.*, V, 139-40.

102, 19. person: *Ibid.*, V. 142.

106, 1. well: Letter of June 14, 1759, à M. Vernes. Théophile Dufour (ed.), *op. cit.*, IV, 270.

106, 8. asylum: Letter of Jan. 20, 1760. *Ibid.*, V, 32.

106, 10. against him: XLI, 141.

106, 14. pity: XL, 438.

106, 28. background: XLI, 205.

107, 16. brother: XLI, 240.

107, 12. insult him: XLI, 262.

107, 21. Tournay: XLI, 271–72.

109, 1. religion: See A. R. Morehouse, *Voltaire and Jean Meslier*, Yale Univ. Press, 1936.

109, 27. of his: XLII, 122.

110, 12. priests: XLII, 136.

110, 25. paradoxes: XLII, 142.

111, 1. philosophy: XLII, 145–46.

111, 3. books: XLII, 150. For details, see G. R. Havens, *Voltaire's Marginalia on the Pages of Rousseau*, The Ohio State Univ., 1933.

111, 7. shame: XLII, 167–68.

111, 12. persevered: XLII, 238.

111, 18. year: XLII, 277.

111, 31. fullness: XLII, 310.

112, 4. propaganda: XLII, 446.

112, 24. aversions: XLII, 549, 446–47, 464–65.

113, 4. burghers: XLII, 520.

113, 25. martyr: XLII, 521.

114, 30. subject: XLIII, 256.

115, 12. him: XLIII, 268.

118, 6. atheist: Rousseau, *Oeuvres*, éd. Hachette, III, 196–97.

120, 6. punished: XXV, 310–14.

120, 11. letters: XLIII, 418.

120, 25. me: XLIII, 418.

120, 26. useful: XLIII, 318.

123, 12. bosom: XXXVI, 428–30.

123, 18. hypocrites: XXXVI, 221.

123, 20. hypocrisy: XXXVI, 297.

123, 26. Providence: Ed. G. Ascoli, Paris, 1929, I, xiii–xvii.

124, 7. Peru: See W. R. Price, *The Symbolism of Voltaire's Novels*, Columbia Univ. Press, 1911, pp. 238 ff.

124, 13. disciples: XLV, 331. (Matt. x. 16).

124, 28. vanity: XXXVIII, 199.

125, 5. France: *Mémoires sur Voltaire*, I, 45.

125, 25. religion: XLV, 513.

126, 2. book: XLV, 516–18.

126, 12. poisoned: XLV, 519.

126, 22. fools: XLV, 518–19.

129, 1. stairway: XLVI, 23–24.

129, 17. children: XLVI, 335.

129, 23. water: XLVI, 337.

130, 2. sleeve: XLVI, 335.

130, 15. impossible: XXXVI, 446, 558.

130, 18. aid: XXXVI, 134; XLVIII, 446.

131, 2. malice: *Grande revue*, CXXXV, 450. Cf. Voltaire, XXXIII, 29, 34.

131, 15. days: XLIV, 550.

131, 22. busier: XLIX, 537.

131, 26. happily: *Ibid.*

132, 13. views: XXXIX, 334.

132, 21. imbecility: F. Newman, *The Short Story's Mutations*, New York, 1926, pp. 41–42.

133, 29. suppressed: Kingsley Martin, *French Liberal Thought in the 18th Century*, London, 1929, pp. 137–38. Cf. Voltaire, XXXVI, 431–32; XLV, 363.

134, 13. me: XXXV, 192.

134, 20. court: XXXVI, 431–32, 531.

135, 6. Louis: XXXVI, 539.

135, 19. other: XLV, 362–63.

136, 29. bushel: XLIII, 127.

137, 30. your: L, 52.

138, 16. him: XXXIV, 18.

139, 6. responsible: Cf. P. Chaponnière, *op. cit.*, p. 127.

CHAPTER V

140, 5. critics: Cf. G. Desnoiresterres, *Iconographie de Voltaire*, Paris, 1879, p. 80.

141, 28. deity: XXXIII, 271.

142, 13. excommunicated: XLV, 193.

142, 25. friends: Cf. Paul Chaponnière, *Voltaire chez les Calvinistes*, Genève, 1932, p. 173.

143, 7. years: XXXV, 194.

143, 14. friends: See the letters to Thieriot published by F. Caussy: *Revue politique et littéraire*, Oct. 2, 9, 1909.

143, 22. belong: XXXV, 415.

144, 8. love me: XXXVI, 420–21.

144, 30. child: XXXVI, 544.

145, 27. Voltaire: XXXVI, 544-45.

146, 13. death bed: XXXIII, 126, 134.

146, 21. Denis: XXXVII, 522.

147, 18. present: XXXIX, 333.

147, 19. lovers: See also (G. Jean-Aubry ed.) Voltaire: *Lettres d'Alsace*, Paris, 1938, published too late to be utilized in my text. The Introduction contains the extraordinary hypothesis that Voltaire himself, at the age of sixty, hoped to have a child by Mme Denis.

148, 21. household: *The Alfred Morrison Collection of Autographs*, London, 1883-97, II, 15-28.

148, 29. old: H. Celarié, M. *de Voltaire, sa famille et ses amis*, Paris, 1928, p. 148.

149, 1. Fontaine: F. Caussy, in *Revue politique et littéraire* (Dec. 10, 17, 1910), 48(2), 737-41; 776-80.

149, 25. self-reproach: H. Celarié, op. cit., p. 163.

150, 6. correspondence: Cf. XXXIII, 239, 241, 242, 270; XXXV, 138, 188 *et passim*, 562. XXXVI, 115-16; XXXVII, 15, 378 n. 6; XXXVIII, 47; XXXIX, 214; XLVI, 532; XLVIII, 446.

150, 11. vicariously: XLIV, 241.

150, 27. nobleman: L, 323.

150, 31. philosopher: L, 323.

151, 19. ink-well: P. Chaponnière, op. cit., p. 169.

151, 28. details: *Mémoires sur Voltaire*, Paris, 1820, I, 95.

152, 8. it: P. Chaponnière, op. cit., p. 172.

153, 3. subject: F. Caussy, *Grande revue* (Feb. 1911), LXV, 547-63; 673-96.

153, 14. to me: XXXVI, 211 n.

153, 31. other: XXXVII, 138.

154, 3. Paris: XXXVII, 80.

154, 14. matter: Desnoiresterres, *Voltaire et la société française au XVIIIe siècle*, Paris, 1871-76, IV, 93.

154, 19. rind: XXXVII, 321, 349.

155, 2. it: XXXVII, 217-18.

155, 11. mockery: XXXVII, 201.

155, 29. illusions: XXXVII, 304.

156, 5. Algarotti: XXXVII, 438.

157, 11. North: XXXVII, 542.

157, 15. virtue: Desnoiresterres, op. cit., IV, 94.

158, 9. Rousseau: XLIX, 540.

158, 12. territory: XLV, 254.

158, 21. fine genius: XLVI, 561.

158, 24. Voltaire: XLVI, 547.

158, 30. Frederick: XLIX, 191.

159, 2. qualities: XLIX, 214.

159, 11. wise: XLIX, 337.

159, 13. humane: XLIX, 328.

159, 14. d'Alembert: XLIX, 331.

159, 20. *Mahomet:* XLIX, 331–32.

159, 27. *redintegratio:* XLIX, 574.

160, 9. destiny: XXXVII, 377.

161, 9. Tencin: See P. M. Masson, *Une Vie de femme au XVIIIe siècle: Mme de Tencin* (1682–1749), Paris, 1910.

161, 20. men: XXXIII, 419 n.

162, 25. to me: XXXIII, 139.

163, 15. to you: XLIX, 80–81.

163, 26. Hénault: F. Caussy, "Une correspondance inédite," in *Le Correspondant* (Feb. 10, 1909), pp. 590–602.

164, 9. attachment: XLVIII, 374, 567.

164, 25. terms: Cf. Diderot, *Oeuvres complètes*, Paris (Garnier), 1875-77, V, 381.

165, 12. mine: XXXV, 126.

167, 27. together: N. L. Torrey, "The First Edition of Candide," in *Modern Language Notes*, XLVIII (May, 1933), 307–10.

168, 14. hand: Besides the letters published in the Moland edition, see those published by F. Caussy in *Revue d'histoire littéraire* (1908, 1909) (Thieriot to Voltaire), and in *Revue politique et littéraire* (Oct. 2, 9, 1909) (Voltaire to Thieriot).

170, 16. *Man:* XXXIII, 303; XXXIV, 56.

171, 2. elect: XXXVII, 294, 283.

171, 31. hope: XXXVIII, 183.

174, 4. heart: XLIV, 116.

174, 18. points: XLVII, 548.

174, 22. it: XLIV, 354, 379.

174, 28. tolerable: Cf. L, 455.

175, 5. earth: XXVI, 107.

175, 14. cowardice: XLIV, 378.

175, 22. faithful: XLIV, 11.

175, 24. heart: XLI, 40.

175, 30. cause: XLIII, 383.
176, 4. elements: XLIV, 88.
176, 9. distance: L, 332.
177, 12. enlightened: XL, 411.
177, 24. *famille:* XLI, 215.
177, 27. fanaticism: XL, 453, *et sqq.*
177, 29. principles: XLII, 253.
178, 11. together: L, 150.
178, 14. friends: XLVIII, 96; XLVII, 220.
178, 16. humanity: XLVI, 300.
178, 21. gardens: XLIII, 183.
179, 7. antichrist: XLII, 252–53.
179, 24. dialogue: Desnoiresterres, *op. cit.,* VIII, 129.
180, 15. indulgence: Diderot, *Oeuvres,* Paris, 1875–79, III, 394.

CHAPTER VI

183, 4. *castrat:* L, 137, 157.
183, 22. maxims: XXIX, 496.
184, 2. rats: L, 236.
184, 8. disgust: L, 25, 44.
184, 10. reverses: L, 111.
184, 18. Racine: L, 145.
184, 22. Frederick: XLIX, 574.
185, 1. her: XLIX, 571; cf. L, 12.
185, 23. Condor: L, 116.
185, 27. mysticism: *Ibid.*
186, 13. fulfillment: L, 15.
189, 28. dead: L, 246.
190, 7. them: XLV, 231.
190, 19. nature: Caussy, *Voltaire, seigneur de village,* Paris, 1912, pp. 131–40.
190, 26. industry: See Webster's *New International Dictionary.*
191, 13. cuttings: Caussy, *op. cit.,* pp. 70–71.
192, 17. watches: *Ibid.,* pp. 211, 225–26, 258–60.
196, 3. neighborhood: *Ibid.,* pp. 325–31.
196, 27. misrepresentation: François Cornou, *Trente années de luttes contre Voltaire . . . Elie Fréron,* Paris, 1922. Cornou speaks of "the Prussian Voltaire."

197, 9. humanity: XLIX, 315.

198, 10. enough: XLIV, 256–57.

198, 24. enlightened: XLIV, 265.

198, 29. nation: XLIV, 275.

199, 1. intelligence: XLV, 123.

199, 12. horns: XLV, 164.

199, 25. done: Paul Chaponnière, *op. cit.*, p. 163.

200, 24. country: XLVI, 352.

201, 2. presence: XLIX, 27.

201, 8. chaos: XLIX, 77.

201, 19. beneficence: L, 43.

201, 26. leave: L, 363.

202, 3, wings: L, 389.

202, 13. boundaries: Caussy, *op. cit.*, p. 331.

203, 18. laughter: Longchamp et Wagnière, *Mémoires sur Voltaire*, Paris, 1820, I, 120–22.

203, 22. Deffand: L, 363.

206, 9. life: Longchamp et Wagnière, *op. cit.*, p. 145.

206, 24. house: *Ibid.*, p. 143.

207, 27. fanaticism: Cf. F. Lachèvre, *Voltaire mourant*, Paris, 1908.

CHAPTER VII

209, 30. Absolute: J. R. Carré, *Réflexions sur l'anti-Pascal de Voltaire*, Paris, 1935, pp. 83 ff.

212, 5. over them: C. Ferval, *Mme du Deffand*, Paris, 1933, p. 325.

212, 23. yours: XXII, 33; cf. XXII, 405.

214, 2. cowardice: J. R. Carré, *op. cit.*, pp. 119–20.

215, 5. thirty: XXXIII, 122.

215, 8. times: L, 457.

215, 27. ship: See the final chapter of *Candide*.

216, 4. system: XXXI, 19.

216, 16. reproach: P. Chaponnière, *Voltaire chez les Calvinistes*, Genève, 1932, pp. xv–xvi.

217, 9. Voltaire: C. Ferval, *Mme du Deffand*, Paris, 1933.

217, 16. soon: XXXIII, 101.

217, 26. fables: XXXVIII, 183; XIX, 65.

217, 30. man: Cf. XXVIII, 326.

218, 1. earth: XLVI, 232.

218, 10. heads: XXXVIII, 184.
218, 20. nothing: XL, 194.
218, 28. disease: XL, 204.
219, 13. age: XLI, 529.
220, 13. bothered: XLIII, 207–8.
221, 7. aid: XLIII, 223.
221, 19. expected: XLV, 523.
222, 6. marionettes: XLIII, 310.
222, 10. give it: L, 322.
222, 17. about it: XLVIII, 59.
222, 30. everything: XLVIII, 67.
223, 25. asininity: L, 212–13.
223, 30. beings: XLIX, 418.
224, 2. universe: L, 372.
224, 21. alive: XLIX, 178.
224, 26. theater: L, 307.
224, 28. occurred: See, for an interesting example, Diderot, *Le Neveu de Rameau, Oeuvres*, V, 417.
225, 11. impossible: XLVI, 10–11.
225, 24. premier: XLVI, 96.
226, 2. consideration: L, 388.
226, 10. cruel: XLIV, 189.
226, 14. death: Cf. Longchamp et Wagnière, *op. cit.*, I, 452.
226, 18. live: XLVIII, 58.

CHAPTER VIII

228, 20. ideal: See A. O. Lovejoy, "The Parallel between Deism and Classicism," *Modern Philology* (Feb., 1932), XXIX, 281–99.
230, 30. since: Kingsley Martin: *French Liberal Thought in the 18th Century*, London, 1929, p. 127.
231, 22. Voltaire: XVIII, 365. *Dict. phil.*, "Dieu, dieux."
231, 27. embarrassed: XXXVII, 25.
232, 1. vain: Morris R. Cohen: *Reason and Nature*, New York, 1931, p. 267.
232, 26. heart: XIX, 438–39. *Dict. phil.*, "Impie."
233, 26. mouth: XIX, 439.
234, 3. one: X, 403. *Epître sur le traité des trois imposteurs*.
234, 5. compliment: XXXII, 562.

234, 22. viole: IX, 390. *Discours en vers sur l'homme.*

234, 25. thereby: MS Sottisier, folio 18.

235, 13. just: XXVII, 55–56.

235, 27. conduct: In his *Émile* (Profession de foi du vicaire savoyard). Cf. G. R. Havens: "The Nature Doctrine of Voltaire," PMLA XL (Dec., 1925), 852–62.

236, 17. superstition: XXVII, 56.

237, 20. *Jean-Jacques:* XLVI, 258; cf. XLVI, 479.

237, 29. error: XXVII, 56.

238, 11. probability: *Dict. phil.*, "Ame," XVII, 132.

238, 14. *philosophiques:* XXII, 123.

238, 20. Sadduceans: N. L. Torrey, "Voltaire's Reaction to Diderot," PMLA, L (Dec., 1935), 1135.

238, 28. fellow: *The Private Papers of James Boswell.* Privately printed, 1928. IV, 29.

239, 9. atheist. See the recently published critical edition of Voltaire's *Poème sur la loi naturelle* by Francis J. Crowley, Univ. of California Press, 1938.

239, 16. sanction: Cf. XVII, 475–76; XLVI, 103–7; XXVI, 328–29; XVIII, 380.

239, 27. Barre: L, 454.

239, 29. mass: K. Martin, *op. cit.*, p. 145.

240, 1. mob: N. L. Torrey, *Voltaire and the English Deists*, Yale Univ. Press, 1930, p. 171.

240, 19. right: XXXVII, 468–69. Quoted by G. Pellissier, *Voltaire philosophe*, Paris, 1908, p. 175.

241, 28. source: Cf. *Dict. phil.*, "Religion." XX, 342 ff.

241, 31. Abraham: Cf. *Candide*, XXI, 163; *Dict. phil.*, "Abraham," XVII, 30, *et sqq.*

242, 9. condemned: Cf. *Le Philosophe ignorant*, XXVI, 82–85.

243, 4. nature: IX, 440.

243, 24. God: Voltaire, *Traité de métaphysique* (H. Temple Patterson, ed.), Manchester Univ. Press, 1937, p. 16.

243, 32. things: *Dict. phil.*, "Providence," XX, 295.

244, 5. functions: Voltaire, *Traité de métaphysique*, (H. Temple Patterson, ed.), Manchester Univ. Press, 1937, p. 62.

244, 7. evil: *Ibid.*, p. 16. Cf. G. Pellissier, *op. cit.*, pp. 186–7.

244, 20. people: J. A. C. Fagginer Auer, *Humanism States Its Case*, Boston, 1933, p. 53.

245, 3. idealism: G. Pellissier: *op. cit.*, 185–89.

245, 8. escaped: Cf. E. Bréhier, *Histoire de la philosophie*, Paris, 1934, I, 402–3.

245, 10. conception: A. O. Lovejoy, *The Great Chain of Being*, Harvard Univ. Press, 1936, pp. 183–84.

246, 12. imagination: La Mettrie, *L'Homme-machine* (ed., M. Solovine), Paris, 1921, p. 103–4.

248, 16. side: (Reference lost.)

249, 7. nature: Morris R. Cohen, *op. cit.*, p. 408.

249, 23. law: *Ibid.*, p. 99.

250, 5. claims: *Ibid.*, p. 13.

250, 13. wisdom: *Ibid.*, p. 28.

251, 22. abode: XXVI, 60. For earlier expressions of the same mood, see XXII, 405–6.

252, 2. infinite: Quoted from Andrew R. Morehouse, *Voltaire and Jean Meslier*, Yale Univ. Press, 1936, p. 142, where Voltaire's cosmic religion is defended. See also E. Sonet, *Voltaire et l'influence anglaise*, Rennes, 1926, pp. 86–89.

252, 12. universe: *Op. cit.*, p. 143.

253, 16. image: *New York Times Magazine*, Nov. 9, 1930.

253, 26. adoration: XXII, 405.

255, 3. Eternal: X, 299–302.

255, 8. majesty: A. Bastide, *Les Problèmes de la vie mystique*, Paris, 1931, p. 75.

256, 4. ice: Longchamp et Wagnière, *Mémoires sur Voltaire*, Paris, 1820, II, 166–68.

256, 26. universe: XXI, 54–55.

257, 3. knowledge: Cf. J.-R. Carré, *Réflexions sur l'anti-Pascal de Voltaire*, Paris, 1935, p. 49.

257, 20. Him: XX, 342.

257, 25. uniform: Cf. XXXIII, 311. *Les Adorateurs*.

257, 30. conscience: XX, 342–48.

258, 14. oak-trees: XLIV, 224.

258, 18. experiences: Cf. XIX, 79.

258, 30. heaven: L, 116.

259, 17. inhabitants: Cf. *Micromégas*, XXI, 122.

262, 14. evil: G. Pellissier, *op. cit.*, p. 176.

263, 8. humanism: Jean Thomas, *L'Humanisme de Diderot*, pp. 150–56. In other respects an excellent study.

264, 10. appeal: Cf. *Ibid.*, p. 153.

264, 20. to it: Cf. J. A. C. Fagginer Auer, *op. cit.*, p. 45.

265, 15. experience: Cf. *Ibid.*, p. 35.

266, 8. he: XIX, 580.

266, 16. position: Cf. J. A. C. Fagginer Auer, *op. cit.*, pp. 8–9.

267, 9. punishment: *Il faut prendre un parti*, XXVIII, 532–33.

268, 16. Christianity: H. N. Brailsford, *Voltaire*, London, 1935, pp. 102–12.

269, 14. it: J. A. C. Fagginer Auer, *op. cit.*, pp. 4–5.

270, 28. validity: Morris R. Cohen, *op. cit.*, p. 379–83.

271, 14. be: XIX, 64–68.

273, 14. decomposed: N. L. Torrey, "Voltaire's Reaction to Diderot," PMLA, L (Dec., 1935), 1136. Diderot, *Oeuvres*, Paris, 1875–79, (Garnier), II, 20.

273, 17. dogmatism: Cf. *Dict. phil.*, "Dieu, dieux," XVIII, 372–76.

274, 11. way: *Singularités de la nature*, XXVII, 145–46.

275, 7. situations: *Op. cit.*, p. 367.

276, 15. eradicated: *Dict. phil.*, "Méchant," XX, 53–54.

276, 32. sophisms: *Dieu et les hommes*, XXVIII, 221.

277, 18. well: J. A. C. Fagginer Auer, *op. cit.*, pp. 42–43.

278, 25. works: Cf. G. R. Havens and N. L. Torrey, "The Private Library of Voltaire at Leningrad," PMLA, XLIII (Dec., 1928), pp. 990–1009.

279, 17. men: XLI, 570.

281, 9. master: XX, 342–48.

Index

INDEX

INDEX

INDEX

INDEX

INDEX

Lanson, Gustave, 1, 251

La Tour, le père de, 10, 123

La Trimouille, Charles-René Armand de, 19

Lausanne, Voltaire acquires property near, 29, 52, 83

La Vallière, Duc de, 68

Lecouvreur, Adrienne: friendship with Voltaire, 24, 71–73, 166; poem on death of, 72

Lefebvre (young poet), 47, 77

Lefranc de Pompignan, Marquis, 84, 87, 105, 131

Le Gentil de la Galaisière, 182

Leibnitz, Gottfried Wilhelm von, 82; philosophical optimism, 9, 11, 48, 49, 99

Lekain, Henri Louis, 43, 54, 159

Lenclos, Ninon de, 16, 63, 98

Leningrad, Voltaire's library in, 102, 278, 300

Lespinasse, Julie de, 169, 171, 216

Le Tourneur, P., 182

Letters concerning the English Nation, see *Lettres Philosophiques*

Lettre à Christophe de Beaumont (Rousseau), 112

Lettre à d'Alembert sur les spectacles (Rousseau), 102

Lettres d'Alsace (ed. Jean-Aubry), 293

Lettres écrites de la campagne (Tronchin), 116

Lettres écrites de la montagne (Rousseau), 116

Lettres persanes (Montesquieu), 121, 240

Lettres philosophiques (*Letters concerning the English Nation*), 74, 81, 117, 122, 164, 166, 238

Levantine Company, 193

Levasseur, Thérèse, 118

Libertinism, 15–36

Life and Death of an Ideal, The (Guérard), 285

Linant, Abbé Michel de, 47

Linguet, Simon-Nicolas-Henri, 198

Lisbon earthquake: poem on, 11, 39, 93, 98–101, 167, 211, 212; effect of on Voltaire, 38, 50, 59

Locke, John: Voltaire's interest in, 4, 82, 231, 242, 273; influence on Voltaire's mysticism, 259

Longchamp, S. G., 37, 255, 287, 288, 290, 291, 293, 296, 297, 299

Louis IX (St. Louis), 135

Louis XIV, 264; classicism of age of, 12, 15, 16, 168, 172

Louis XV, 19, 70, 152, 163

Louis XVI, 223

Louis-le-Grand, collège, 16, 17

Lovejoy, A. O., 245, 285, 297, 299

Lower classes, 197

Lucretius, 13

Lusignan (character played by Voltaire), 39

Lutzelbourg, Comtesse de, 53, 54

Luxembourg, Duchesse de, 114

Lying, protective, 121, 127

Mably, Abbé de, 183

Mme du Deffand (Ferval), 296

Magnificent Council, 105

Mahomet, 50, 67, 80, 123, 159

Maine, Duchesse du, 170

Man: focus of Voltaire's philosophy, 6; a "fallen angel," 209–11; classical conception of, 272

Mandeville, Bernard de, *Fable of the Bees,* 82

Mariamne, 162, 217

Marie Leszczynski, wife of Louis XV, 130

Marivaux, Pierre Carlet de Chamblain de, 76

Marmontel, Jean-François, 182

Martin, Kingsley, 230, 292, 297, 298

Massacre of St. Bartholomew, 36, 40, 43

Masson, P.-M., 290, 294

Mathematics, Voltaire's attitude toward, 175

Maupertuis, Pierre-Louis Moreau de, 132, 155

Maupertuis-Koenig affair, 41, 52, 132, 156, 158

INDEX

INDEX

INDEX

INDEX

INDEX

INDEX

Voltaire ruler + under Europe's
most cosmopolitan & humane era -

Cp. Noyes' efforts to defend pious &
V^s V' views at Colmar + Tourney catalog
letters, & contrary!   (Cp. Noyes 417)

Tourny calls the _Diner du Comte de Boulainvilliers_
one of the most effective + witty of V^s anti-religious

V. Religion:
1736 - Remarques sur les Pensées de Pascal - 1728

From 68 to end of life - feverish work x l'Infame
18-20 hours a day

29ᵉ chapter on Vᵉ Religion -
Definition, Deism = p. 228
Deism was classic in pref.pres -
oneness of humanity - golden age -
Universal morals + Universal Reason

230/ Defense of Deism

230/ V believes, existence of an Intelligent Supreme Being
Newtonian empiricism + moral intuition +
mystical rapture -

32/ V ignorant; attributes of the Being same - justice -
God as Blictri - i.e. Incomprehensibly just + merciful

234/ Discours sur l'homme - Devil blames god for evil

235/ Vᵉ fullest expression of faith in the
Poème sur la loi naturelle   (cf God ...
Profession de foi des Théistes *

god no card to Chinese, Hindus, Tatars +
Mongols + to us - "Adore me + be just -"

All nations originally recognised but one God to whom
they rendered a simple + unadulterated cult ... p.squns ?
Juvenilia

236 claims that his Deism was "of Adam, Seth & Noah —
first ancient, universal & divine —

" We adore the Divinity, pre + eternal, the rewarder of
virtue, the avenger of crime — " ✦

238 But V sceptical as to soul's immortality +
reward + punishment after

238 Marginal note on Descartes' Pensées philosophiques.
X immortality. Soul —
" I know nothing. Soul..... (à Bisswll)

238 But V never says that the Prof. of Faith. Theist. is
what he believes —
was the poem written this ⅞ Lamettrie's atheism +
influence on the amoral F II ?

239 Skepticism as to God + Soul + pragmatic
value of those ideas —

240 F II refuted the Loi Naturelle & V. assumed g right ✦
+ since he wrote it ... Sanc of social order

240 Montesquieu wanted an established religion —
Esprit des Lois — ✦
Rousseau Diderot had an intolerant attitude +
wants a Civil religion —

243 To V. Conscience by. house] God but his ✦
voice of Humanity
all crimes are born of social ypanu...
V's God is beyond human good + evil —